ORGANIZATIONAL
DYNAMISM

ORGANIZATIONAL DYNAMISM
Unleashing Power in the Workforce

R. Wayne Pace

QUORUM BOOKS
Westport, Connecticut • London

Library of Congress Cataloging-in-Publication Data

Pace, R. Wayne.
  Organizational dynamism : unleashing power in the workforce / R. Wayne Pace.
    p.   cm.
  Includes bibliographical references and index.
  ISBN 1–56720–517–8 (alk. paper)
  1. Organizational effectiveness.   I. Title.
  HD58.9.P33   2002
  658.4′063—dc21   2001049182

British Library Cataloguing in Publication Data is available.

Library of Congress Catalog Card Number: 2001049182
ISBN 1–56720–517–8

First published in 2002

Quorum Books, 88 Post Road West, Westport, CT 06881
An imprint of Greenwood Publishing Group, Inc.
www.quorumbooks.com

Printed in the United States of America

The paper used in this book complies with the
Permanent Paper Standard issued by the National
Information Standards Organization (Z39.48–1984).

10 9 8 7 6 5 4 3 2 1

Copyright Acknowledgment

The author and publisher gratefully acknowledge permission for use of the following material:

Excerpts from Irving Stone's *The Passionate Journey* (New York: Doubleday), 1969.

Contents

Figures and Table

Preface

I was thumbing through Abraham Maslow's book called *Eupsychian Management* when I came across a brief account of a woman who worked as personnel manager in a chewing gum factory and simply couldn't get excited about chewing gum. Maslow referred to her as a person who had developed anhedonia.[1]

The term didn't appear in my *Merriam-Webster Dictionary*, but was defined in my unabridged *Random House Dictionary* as the "lack of pleasure or of the capacity to experience it."[2]

Later, when I was exploring the meaning of anhedonia in greater depth, I pursued the term through the twenty-volume set of the unabridged *Oxford Dictionary of the English Language*. There I found anhedonia in all of its splendor, with original attributions and technical uses in the psychological literature. The core of the concept was a passivity, joylessness, dreariness, a lack of zest.[3]

I recognized immediately that I had suffered for some years from borderline anhedonia, especially in the workplace. I had forced myself to create an office at home so that I could avoid the joylessness of my office at work. Thus began a period of reflection on the causes and effects of employee plateauing, unrest, disaffection, resentment, decline, and decay.

Some of my deeper feelings were triggered by a very small booklet released by the National Association of Manufacturers called *What's Wrong with Work?*[4] which consisted of a series of presentations and a question-and-answer session involving five distinguished academicians and practitioners in organization development: John Paul Jones, Vice President of

OD for Federated Department Stores; Richard Beckhard, Senior Lecturer at MIT's Sloan School of Management; George G. Raymond, Jr., President of the Raymond Corporation; James Richard, Vice President of Polaroid Corporation; and Warren G. Bennis, then of the Organization Studies Group at MIT.

Jones, who moderated the panel, provided a brief introduction that included the observation "What's wrong with work? My answer is: Nothing, if it has meaning and if it's fun. But much is wrong if it is without challenge, without warmth, and does not satisfy human needs that go way beyond the simple need of making a living." He observed further that people have struggled to adapt themselves to the organizations in which they are employed, and that these adaptations are often to their own detriment. An initial conclusion became apparent: we should be seeking to release the enormous human potential being stifled by pernicious work systems that bend workers and deter them from contributing fully to their own development and to the development of the organization.

The explorations into borderline anhedonia in the workplace began when a few of us, who were working in seemingly stifling bureaucracies, decided that a team of academicians and practitioners could efficiently conduct an ongoing discussion of work systems' effects. A "work systems study group" was formed, consisting primarily of faculty members in the school of management of the local university and some practitioners who had taken early "retirement" or were actively working in the area, but had migrated from the east and midwest to the intermountain west. The "study group" met regularly to examine factors in work systems that may stifle members of the workforce. This small volume seeks to present the discoveries made then and since.

If you have ever experienced borderline anhedonia in the workplace, this book is for you. If you have asked the question "What's wrong with where I work?" this book is for you. If you have ever watched colleagues wrestle with borderline anhedonia in their workplaces, or if you have employees to serve who may be living in a workplace that cultivates borderline anhedonia, this book is for you. This book will help you reinvent, reengineer, renew, rediscover, and revitalize your workplace.

NOTES

1. Maslow, Abraham H. 1965. *Eupsychian Management: A Journal.* Homewood, IL: Richard D. Irwin, Inc., p. 30.

2. Stein, Jess (Ed.). 1967. *The Random House Dictionary of the English Language.* New York: Random House, Inc., p. 58.

3. *Oxford Unabridged Dictionary.* 1992. London: Oxford University.

4. Jones, John Paul. 1967. *What's Wrong with Work?* New York: National Association of Manufacturers.

Acknowledgments

The genesis of every idea has its foundations in the receptivity of those who come in contact with the idea. The exploration of dynamism and its antithesis—borderline anhedonia—has been nurtured by my close colleagues Eric Stephan and Gordon Mills of the Marriott School of Management at Brigham Young University. Sean McDevitt and Heather Thompson, graduate students in organizational behavior, assisted in statistical analyses of data and served as confidants in a world of uncertainty.

Early discussions with John McMurray, Arnold Parrott, Steven Mitchell, Deona Lambert Walker, Pamela Hayes, Charlene Billingsley, and my most supportive spouse, Gae Tueller Pace, gave sustenance to the possibilities of pursuing these lines of thinking. Brent Peterson of the Franklin Covey Corporation, a colleague and coauthor, has been a model of dynamism for my emulation and for the edification of all those with whom he works.

Later contacts with colleagues at Southern Cross University, New South Wales, and the University of Adelaide, South Australia, Australia, and the opportunities to present the ideas in seminars and lectures in the Netherlands, Singapore, The People's Republic of China, Mexico, Egypt, New Zealand, and the United States have led to their refinement. Few of those venues would have materialized without the constant vigilance of Adela McMurray, Peter Miller, Leonie Jennings, John Barrie, Una Spiers, Max Zornada, and Malcolm MacIntosh.

The true refinement of the concepts and questions to be pursued was achieved in numerous meetings, workshops, and simulations with Douglas Ray McGregor of the Parker Hannifin Corporation, whom I have worked with these many years. We have published together and have conducted seminars with and without simulations. We have discussed and cussed, refined and re-refined, and elaborated and reconstructed thoughts endlessly, and all with one after another glorious outcome.

I cannot forget the enlightening sessions with Mel LeBaron, who had the vision of workable workplaces long before they were so sought after. The years working with Don F. Faules as a collaborator, editor, and author were not only enjoyable but also revealing of the inner strengths required to maintain a vital existence and not be consumed by anhedonia.

The historical roots for many of the concepts came from Edwin Locke and Gary Latham, Richard Hackman and Greg Oldham, Abraham Maslow, John Gardner, Charles Garfield, Russell Ackoff, Judith Bardwick, William G. Scott and Kirk Hart, Warren Bennis, Roger Harrison, Mathew Juechter, Mary Guy, Ralph Kilmann, Martin Seligman, Alfred Korzybski, W. Charles Redding, and, especially, Donald B. Miller, who wrote about personal vitality at least two decades before it became popular. May each of them forever have the uplifting spirit of the workplace.

Long-standing affiliations with and involvement in the International Communication Association, the Western States Communication Association, and the Academy of Human Resource Development have allowed me to be in touch with both scholars and practitioners who have enlightened and enriched my understanding of most of the underlying concepts and premises presented here.

I want to acknowledge the munificent contribution that my family has made to my life: my parents, Ralph W. and Elda F. Pace; my uncles and aunts; my brothers—Ronald Pace and Elden Pace—and my sisters—Leah Camp and Joye Williams; my children—Michael, Rebecca, Lucinda, Gregory, Angela, and Lavinia—and their spouses, and, again, my loyal and generous spouse, Gae Tueller Pace. As part of our extended family, Marva and Richard Heaton provided comfort and solace. Many thanks go to Ken and Delma Baldridge for their ever-attentive kindness. May they all have the joy of a vital dynamism and avoid the plague of listlessness and borderline anhedonia in their lives.

But, of all the people who have made such a rich and indelible impression on me, none have provoked me to be more productive than those administrators and colleagues (who shall remain nameless) who fostered those alienating, cursed environments that evoked feelings of anhedonia when I wanted them least, but whereby I was able to understand organizational anhedonia best. Though your practices and demeanor repulse me, I credit you with the spark that ignited a decade of exploration.

Introduction

The main purpose of this book is to help those responsible for the direction and effectiveness of organizations to understand, recognize, and enhance the dynamism of their organizations. Company executives, upper and middle managers, supervisors, and staff leaders should benefit from the ideas they pull out of this book. The content goes beyond hype and pep and looks at the fundamental factors that intensify feelings about the value of work and organizations. I recommend this book to professionals and managers working in organizations including corporations, government agencies, educational institutions, health care companies, religious groups, and social and service clubs. Human resource specialists in management and development should derive a great deal from the concepts and practices.

To achieve this purpose, the book contains some theoretical background, a cluster of instruments that identify features of dynamism in organizations, and a bevy of suggestions for developing and implementing a systematic strategy for enhancing dynamism in your organization.

This book is a guide. It will help you to identify and enhance individual and organizational dynamism. Dynamism, one of the three features of credibility, combines with competence and trustworthiness to inspire belief. Organizations without credibility cannot be effective; employees must perceive credibility in the organization if they are to be effectively managed. With credibility, individuals and organizations can have a powerful influence in the world of commerce, government, religion, and social relations. Without credibility—without competence, trustworthiness, dyna-

mism—both individuals and organizations take on an aura of unbeliev-
ability and can exercise only a meager influence in the world.

Incompetence, untrustworthiness, and lack of dynamism—listlessness
or borderline anhedonia—are at the core of both individual and organizational failure. This book focuses on dynamism and its opposite—listlessness, or borderline anhedonia. We will explore the phenomenally powerful
foundations of dynamism and examine some of the ways that dynamism
can be recognized and enhanced in organizations.

Whenever energy is released, dynamism is apparent; wherever peak
performances occur, great energy is revealed. When greatness is present in
almost any form, but especially in people, an intensity of energy is also
present. People who express an abundance of energy are thrilling to be
around. They radiate enthusiasm to others. Individuals and organizations
that have contact with such people become elevated in spirit, in purpose,
and in actions.

Harmon and Jacobs (1985) assert that "energy is the basis of all creativity.
... Energy spurs innovation. ... High achievers are set apart from the rest by
the way they use the energy available to them. ... With energy comes discipline." High-achieving individuals "are able to accomplish more than the
average because they channel all their available energies into activities designed to achieve the goals they have set for themselves."[1] From this, we
can draw an impelling connection between energy and goal achievement.
The dynamism of leaders is infectious and stirs other people to expend
more energy. The release of energy is recognized as dynamism.

The experience of dynamism in an organization may have been what
prompted C. William Pollard to say that "people provide the life, the vitality, the conscience, and, yes, even the soul of the firm."[2] The soul of something is its immaterial essence, the animating principle or actuating cause
of a life. The soul gives vitality and energy to individual lives and dynamism enhances the natural vitality and energy of individuals, giving soul,
life, and energy to organizations.

Dynamism must be translated into actions, services, and activities that
result in the achievement of goals that benefit someone or something. Although profit and return on investment are the ultimate measures of corpo-
ate success, organizations that meet the technical requirements for success
are also those in which the welfare of employees is most apparent. In fact,
those organizations that invest in the growth and development of their employees transform the personality and character of their organization.
Through the development of organizational character, companies can create a deeper, stronger, and more powerful sense of dynamism that draws all
members of the organization into full fellowship. An animated corporate
character converts energy into productive outputs.

Dynamism underlies the successful implementation of organizational
programs. It represents a philosophical and pragmatic position that cannot

be ignored by consultants, leaders, or teachers. Dynamism is equally efficacious in government agencies and military organizations, in corporations and other for-profit companies, in educational and social service organizations, in volunteer community service and religious organizations, and in the vast array of mutual-benefit associations. Fraternal associations, professional clubs, and philanthropic organizations are also affected by dynamism.

For more than ten years, the Work Vitality Research Group within the Department of Organizational Leadership and Strategy at Brigham Young University studied factors that enhance organizational functioning. The results of their studies identified dynamism as a critical variable differentiating organizations' viability.

Of course, this book is not the final answer to the continued maintenance of viable organizations, but it does address one issue critical to successful organizations.

Organizational Dynamism develops along a problem-solving continuum from the nature of the problem to its solution.

SYNOPSIS/OVERVIEW

Part I: The Elements of Dynamism

Chapter 1: Dynamism: To Be Endowed with Power. We examine a model of the elements of dynamism in individuals and organizations. The importance of dynamism in organization effectiveness is highlighted.

Chapter 2: Anhedonia: The Blues at Work. We look at the problem of anhedonia, a nonclinical form of depression characterized by listlessness, which may be the major hindrance to achieving the technical goals of the organization. This chapter includes an account of an organization member experiencing borderline anhedonia, who lost his soul and character as his dynamism disappeared.

Chapter 3: Work System: The Wind that Bends. We explore the work systems that lead to borderline anhedonia. This chapter also gives a simple five-element model that can be used to identify and analyze anhedonia and its effects. Climate, an effect of the system, is examined.

Chapter 4: Careers on Fire: The Four Basic Work Perceptions. This chapter examines the foundation of dynamism and establishes a simple theoretical explanation for why individuals and organizations express dynamism in their work lives. The Joe Metaphor is used to illuminate the application of positive work perceptions to worker careers, which results in a model of career development grounded in dynamism. The metaphor of a prescribed fire demonstrates the translation of work perceptions into tragic effects or exhilarating benefits in organizations.

Chapter 5: Natural Work Goals: The Release Valves. This chapter shows how dynamism can be enhanced through the use of natural work goals.

Chapter 6: Thinking Modes: Optimism in the Workplace. We examine the effect of people's negative perceptions on their vitality and dynamism in the organization. This chapter derives its format from the work of Seligman on optimism, but uses general semantics as the theoretical framework.

Chapter 7: Operating Styles: Sociability in the Workplace. We introduce a four-cell matrix of operating styles, and examine the power of a person's operating style to trash dynamism or revitalize people.

Part II: The Strategies of Dynamism

Chapter 8: Competitiveness and Learning Organizations: A Dynamic Duo. We examine how dynamism affects the competitiveness of organizations, and introduce the concept of the learning organization and of action learning.

Chapter 9: Organizational Learning: Paradigm Five. We extend the concept of the learning organization and look at the roles of organizational learning and action learning in enhancing vitality and dynamism.

Chapter 10: Techniques for Achieving Goals: Projects. We illustrate the power of projects to be change mechanisms.

Chapter 11: Altra Teams: Beyond the Usual. This chapter introduces self-directed work teams and an advanced form of teams.

Chapter 12: Pragmatics and Sociability: Enabling Style. We examine how people's operating styles affect their own dynamism and the dynamism of the organization.

Chapter 13: The Whole Nine Yards in Easy Steps: Meeting the Challenge. This chapter summarizes the key points of the book and extends the concept of action learning.

Chapter 14: Confirmation: Evidences of Dynamism. This chapter reports case studies that illustrate the conditions that produce dynamism in organizations. They demonstrate that dynamism comes from positive POFE perceptions.

Appendix: Notches on Your Stock: Nine Measures of Dynamism

We present instruments for measuring aspects of dynamism and explain how to administer the tests, score the results, and interpret the findings.

NOTES

1. Harmon, Frederick G. and Jacobs, Garry. 1985. *The Vital Difference.* New York: American Management Association, pp. 5–7.

2. Pollard, C. William. 1996. *The Soul of the Firm.* New York: HarperBusiness, p. 13.

PART I

THE ELEMENTS OF DYNAMISM

1

Dynamism: To Be Endowed with Power

Bob Greene of the *Chicago Tribune* Media Services averred that "work is a mysterious thing; many of us claim to hate it, but it takes a grip on us that is so fierce that it captures emotions and loyalties we never knew were there."[1] The enlivening mystery of work occurs, as most organization members understand, only when the workplace captivates or at least intrigues us. Workplaces that energize us, refresh us, and fortify us have that mysterious, secret ingredient called dynamism. Vitality and dynamism both involve the release of energy, so we frequently use the terms as synonyms. The release of energy is often captured in words such as invigorated, fortified, irresistible, indomitable, animated, impelling, and endowed with power. Dynamism encompasses each of these characteristics and implies having individuals, teams, and systems that are vigorous, robust, refreshed, efficacious, cogent, and potent. Dynamism both attracts and impels enthusiasm. Dynamism is that mysterious element that captures emotions and commitment and intrigues organization members.

Tom Peters writing in his handbook for a management revolution, *Thriving on Chaos*, explained that promotions should be based on a person's ability to "create excitement, zest, and enthusiasm among their colleagues (before they become a boss), subordinates (after they become a boss), and even their peers in other functions."[2] He enthusiastically broadened this requirement from production workers to those in accounting, personnel, and engineering. An enthusiastic and genuinely excited supervisor can turn a dull problem into an exciting adventure. Such people are fun to be around and they bring dynamism to the workplace.

With dynamism, organizations can exceed expectations and create marvelous outcomes and sustained enthusiasm. Without dynamism, organizations may do well, but they will never be outstanding. J. Paul Getty's formula for success sorts this idea out: "Rise early, work hard, strike oil." That's good advice, but most of us will not strike oil. In fact we may become irritated by the idea that something spectacular must occur for success to emerge. Robert Neville said it best: "Living with a Saint is more grueling than being one." Roger Harrison captured the essence of many failures to have outstanding organizations when he said, "The problem is that we cannot design work systems that compel outstanding performance."[3] We shall return to Harrison's idea in a later chapter, but it deserves mentioning here. Enhancing dynamism is the surest way to elicit outstanding individual, team, and organizational performance.

MODEL OF DYNAMISM

The process of enhancing dynamism or endowing organization members with power in a workplace is simple. The model of dynamism used in this book has six elements: (1) the work system, (2) work perceptions, (3) natural growth goals, (4) vitality, (5) outputs, and (6) feedback. Organization members are vitalized when they feel supported in working toward one or more natural work goals. Energy accumulates with the anticipation of reaching natural work goals. Energy is released with the achievement of natural work goals.

If revitalization can be accomplished in this relatively simple manner, why doesn't every worker feel vitalized every day? The reality of organization life is that floods of distractions drain vitality from people and organizations every day. Pep talks are not the answer. Just thinking that things will be better tomorrow is not the answer. It takes more than having a vision. An attack must be made on each element of the work system that undermines dynamism.

WORK SYSTEM

Work systems seldom rage at their members; they just blow ill winds that bend and shake vulnerable branches. Sometimes insecure roots give way, and the once-steady trunk lies broken on the path, as solitary figures get downsized. Rather than attracting people, working can be just a troublesome mess with little to recommend it. Too often the system wins in this battle of winds and branches. Work systems have mechanisms that stifle the natural energy of their members. Stage One in the process of releasing dynamism, therefore, is to create positive changes in the work system.

Elements of the work system have an impact on workers that result in either positive or negative work perceptions. The effect of positive work per-

Figure 1.1
A Model of Organizational Dynamism

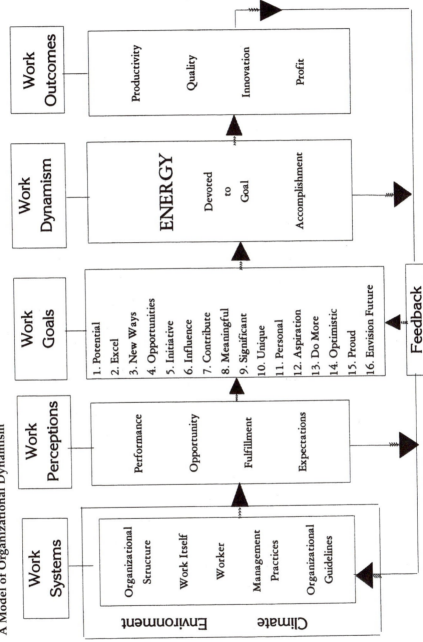

ceptions is *con anima*, to act in a spirited manner or with spirit. We normally associate positive work perceptions with enthusiasm and energy. Positive work perceptions energize workers. Negative work perceptions result in anhedonia.

WORK PERCEPTIONS

Recent research indicates that a worker's feelings of "psychological empowerment," or enthusiasm and vitality, are a function of four work perceptions: performance, opportunity, fulfillment, and expectations. The evidence is contained in the research reports of Thomas and Velthouse, Pace and Jaw, Spreitzer, and Pace and McGregor.[4] Work perceptions consist of the sense people make of their workplaces.

Stage Two in the vitalization process consists therefore of creating positive work perceptions. Workers' perceptions evolve over time as they experience the workplace and attempt to make sense of it in terms of their own personalities and attitudes. Different workers can experience the same work conditions, yet have quite different work perceptions. We've created an acronym for the four critical work perceptions. The acronym is POFE (pronounced "pofay"). A brief definition of each perception may begin to focus your thinking on these ideas. A later chapter discusses the work perceptions in greater detail.

Performance. The perceptions employees have of their ability to work at high levels of competence in the organization. Performance perceptions encompass self-efficacy and self-confidence. Positive performance perceptions represent optimism about a worker's ability to do his or her work better.

Opportunity. The perceptions employees have of the extent of their influence and impact in the organization. Positive opportunity perceptions represent optimism about a workers' role in the organization and his or her ability to move up in the organization.

Fulfillment. The perceptions employees have of the extent of their autonomy and self-determination in the organization, as well as how free they are to work as they please.

Expectations. The perceptions employees have of whether their aspirations are being attained, and how meaningful their own work is.

In sum, vitality is a psychological construct manifest by four positive perceptions: performance, opportunity, fulfillment, and expectations that reflect an orientation of enthusiasm toward work roles.

NATURAL WORK GOALS

The third element in the revitalization process concerns how positive work perceptions are triggered to release their vitalizing power. This part of the model was derived from research on the effect of goals on human behavior. The importance of goals has been explained in this way: "Once the individual has a goal and once he or she chooses to act on it, the three direct mechanisms—effort, persistence, and direction—are brought into play more or less automatically."[5] This means that once you begin to pursue a goal, your behavior takes on a direction, you devote energy toward achieving the goal, and you persist until you achieve the goal.

Sometimes, however, the automatic dimensions are not adequate to achieve the goal. To achieve these goals, workers must creatively discover ways to reach the goals. These goals require an action plan and some strategies. As we shall point out in a later chapter, natural work goals are more impelling than regular technical goals; they make it easier to do your work.

Stage Three in the dynamism process consists of setting natural work goals. Natural work goals are the ideas, the aims, and the purposes innate to human beings that enable them to work effectively. Natural work goals give intensity, persistence, and direction to actions more naturally than do technical goals. Anything that deters natural work goals blocks vitality and corrupts dynamism.

Past research affirms the necessity of deliberately setting meaningful work goals. Setting goals is a natural human process that facilitates human survival, happiness, and well-being.

The enhancement of dynamism in an organization depends on the achievement of natural work goals. Natural work goals are derived directly from work perceptions. Thus, the dynamism of organization members is revealed by their responses to natural work goals. The Natural Work Goals Profile is an instrument that secures a measure of natural work goal achievement in an organization.

Factor analyses indicate that the Natural Work Goals Profile has three fairly strong factors—enabling, enthusiasm, and individuality. High scores on the Natural Work Goals Profile indicate that workers feel enabled, enthusiastic, and are able to express individualism in the workplace, all of which are triggers for vitality and dynamism. In terms of work perceptions, the enabling factor represents perceptions of performance and opportunity; the enthusiasm factor represents perceptions of fulfillment and expectations; and the individuality factor represents a general sense of being able to do things your way, which may be a feeling that is part of each of the work perceptions' categories.

PROACTIVE ENERGY

Stage Four in the revitalization process simply indicates that proactive energy is being released as a consequence of positive work perceptions and achieved natural work goals. If large numbers of personnel have high scores, we may infer that the organization is vitalized. Vitalized organizations possess many of the following features:

1. The organization involves the whole person.
2. Altruism abounds because work transcends personal advantage.
3. People willingly labor long hours.
4. People anticipate what needs to be done without direction from superiors.
5. High morale, teamwork, and a sense of camaraderie exist.[6]

OUTCOMES

Stage Five, outcomes, results from having consistently vitalized organization members. At this stage, productivity and quality increase, responses to problems are immediate and direct, organization members are solving problems on their own, everyone experiences high morale and feels that the organization is a better place in which to work.

FEEDBACK

The Sixth and final stage, feedback, confirms goal accomplishment and tells workers that their efforts are appreciated and on target. Feedback that overlooks achievements leads workers to feel discouraged. In many organizations, feedback takes the form of "on the spot" corrections and informal counseling sessions that are usually focused on technical procedures and actions rather than on natural work goals. Such an emphasis can lead to satisfied or dissatisfied workers, but it certainly does not lead to vitalized workers who bring dynamism to the organization. It is important to realize, of course, that feedback may be misinterpreted and result in distortions of meaning. Hopefully, all feedback will be understood and result in positive reactions.

The dynamism model describes the process by which proactive energy is influenced by elements in the work system, as revealed in a worker's positive or negative work perceptions and each individual's ability to achieve natural work goals in the work environment. Theoretically, the organization is responsible for assisting or at least allowing organization members to set natural work goals and for doing anything reasonable to encourage the achievement of those goals.

PROLEGOMENON

In her penetrating book *The Drama of the Gifted Child*, Alice Miller speaks to the issue of vitality and observes that "the true opposite of depression is not gaiety or absence of pain, but vitality; the freedom to experience spontaneous feelings." She also comments on an important part of vitality: "It is only after the self becomes liberated from repression that it begins to grow, express itself, and develop its true spirit and creativity."[7]

In her novel *The Women's Room*, Marilyn French comments about the coast of Maine. She writes, "One reason I like the Maine coast so much is that . . . the sea pounds in and no matter how many times I see it, it excites me. . . . The sheer naked power of those great waves constantly rolling up with such an ominous rumble, hitting against the rocks and sending up skyfulls of white froth. It is so powerful and so beautiful and so terrifying at the same time that for me it is a symbol of what life is all about."[8]

Waves come at the beach like they want to make a difference. If you check on the development of a beach over six months, you will see extraordinary changes wrought by the steady, deliberate waves. Sections of an entire beach can be thrust up and dragged down. This powerful metaphor for change may have impelled the thinking of David McClelland when he devised the theory of achievement motivation. He explains that achievement motivation is represented by a person who "spends his [her] time thinking about doing things better." He said that "we measure this need for achievement by the frequency a person thinks about doing things better."[9]

I find an amazing similarity in the aims and strategies of the total quality movement and achievement motivation. Philip Crosby, for example, writes that "making quality certain means 'getting people to do better all the worthwhile things they ought to be doing anyway.' "[10] Critics of lack of quality in business and industry, such as Jim Windle of Purdue University, lay the blame for faltering productivity and lowered quality on what he called the NGAD Syndrome, or the *"nobody gives a damn"* feeling that inhabits nearly everyone nowadays.[11] Phrases such as "This place is a prison" and "I'm lost in the system" lament the widespread existence of the NGAD Syndrome. Macleod comments, "It is sad that millions of people live their lives with little of the work-life satisfaction that should be achievable for almost everyone in our affluent country. This situation also has disturbing implications to employers who are saddled with the low productivity, effectiveness, and efficiency of work forces characterized by such attitudes."[12]

W. Edwards Deming, best known for his work in reversing the bad-quality image in Japanese industry, argues that in business "the only survivors at the end of two decades will be companies with constancy of purpose for quality, productivity, and service." By constancy of purpose he means the persistent pursuit to do things better. Deming argues that "everyone in the company must attack improvement of quality, not just the problems that walk in, but as a plan of knowledge by which to find problems and the causes thereof. . . . Efforts toward improvement of quality must be total."[13] Every employee, every manager, every executive must "give a damn," and must want to do better.

McClelland and Winter demonstrated that it is possible to help adults acquire a strong need to achieve, giving us the theoretical justification for enhancing a constancy of purpose.[14] Miller referred to this enthusiasm for doing quality work as *vitality*.[15] He outlined both an organizational strategy and a national strategy for making the cultivation of vitality a critical issue in creating productive employees.

But, as they say, no one gave a damn, partly because work vitality was difficult to define and more difficult to measure. Nevertheless, Yankelovich found that "the symptoms of worker frustration were visible everywhere: in absenteeism, tardiness, carelessness, indifference, high turnover, numbers of union grievances, slowdowns in the periods preceding collective bargaining and even sabotage. Mostly, worker frustration showed in poor product quality."[16]

On the other hand, by 1987 INC Magazine reported that employees in the 500 fastest-growing small and midsize private companies in America were "more satisfied with their jobs, and had more respect for their companies, than the employees of Corporate America." Those employees found themselves in jobs that "offer challenges and a sense of accomplishment. They experience a company culture that values initiative and ideas. And they are confident that they work for companies that put out quality products, treat their employees with respect, and compete effectively in the marketplace."[17]

Yankelovich predicted that small changes may make a large difference in how employees respond to their work. He said:

If employers will give a little, [employees] will give a little. Employers should not assume in advance that they couldn't, in fact, give people what they truly want. Perhaps we have been misled by the job enrichment movement, which has overstated and to some extent misinterpreted the work requirements of the majority. It is true that for a large minority (about 35 percent of the work force), particularly the better educated, the substance of the work itself must be inherently interesting and challenging. The majority, however, are not demanding "meaningful work" in this sense. What most people mean by "interesting work" and "challenge on the job" is not what an artist or a research scientist means. It is astonishing how little it takes for most people to feel wanted, needed, challenged, useful in their work. To overstate somewhat, it is possible that there are very few *inherently* undesirable jobs. But in millions of jobs today people are treated shabbily and paid poorly besides. And this combination makes their jobs undesirable.[18]

Recently, we have had an upsurge in writings that describe ways to "bring spirit to the workplace," to achieve "empowerment in bureaucratic organizations," and to find fulfilling employment that allows you to "work from the heart." The answer for overcoming sagging productivity and drooping quality is "spirit" or "vitality." Employees who exude dynamism produce more at a higher quality. Employees with dynamism bring constancy of purpose to their work.

Galagan explains, "more and more companies are realizing that you can't do good business without that indefinable extra that people bring to a job."[19] We lag behind today because we have not focused our energies on defining, measuring, and developing dynamism in the workplace.

Dynamism is more than having happy employees. Every organization has financial resources, physical resources, and human resources. The manner in which these resources are used determines the success of an organization. Although money and the overall strategy for its use is important, and new equipment, technologies, and processes can increase output and quality, the keys to success are the employees who must design, implement, and use the other resources.

Dynamism says that employees who find their work interesting and fulfilling can also find ways to make their work more efficient and productive. Employees who experience the spirit of dynamism in the workplace are more resourceful and confident.

What comes first, interesting work or employees who feel dynamism at work? Can dynamic employees make their work more interesting and fulfilling? Rosabeth Moss Kanter argues that some people who seek to "remedy what they see as less than optimal" become activists for reform but also remain loyal to the organization.[20] Such people "empower themselves in the midst of bureaucratic limitations."[21] Employees who want to increase dynamism at a workplace where there is no conscious effort to help them must empower themselves.

Because certain activists can take hold of their own bootstraps and make the fundamental shift from stifled, uncommitted employees to confident, fully contributing employees, it is clear that it is possible to make this transition. The key rests in realizing and understanding the conditions that facilitate and encourage dynamism. Individual employees produce high-quality goods and services when seven conditions exist in the organization:

1. Employees have a sense of ownership and are responsible for whole tasks or process.
2. Employees possess multiple skills and can perform a variety of tasks well.
3. Employees have a feeling of autonomy in making work choices.
4. Employees work cooperatively.
5. Employees are well enough informed to recognize problems in their work.
6. Employees can influence what happens in the organization.
7. Employees are recognized and rewarded for their contributions to the organization.

Employees who lack the sense, feelings, and abilities identified in these seven conditions in workplaces that fail to meet these fundamental conditions constrain workers from investing themselves fully in their work. Meeting just one of the seven conditions may trigger a sense of empowerment not felt before. Rather than feeling stifled, employees will be exhilarated. This infectious drive will be transmitted to other employees. For a brief moment, some employees will experience vigorous involvement at work. But, in the end, without more widespread demonstrations of dynamism, the spirit is lost, employees run out of steam, vitality oozes from the system, and dehumanization of the workforce continues unabated.

A growing malaise drains the human resources of the organization, and eventually the financial and physical resources. When a person appears to need medical attention, the first act of a physician is to check the person's vital signs. Similarly, when employees appear to be waning in productivity and quality, the sources of dynamism at work should be the focus of diagnosis and analysis. The signs of lost dynamism are manifest in the way in which workers respond to their jobs.

You might say that dynamism is the "soul of the firm." As C. William Pollard said in his simple but impelling analysis of why people work, "People want to work for a cause, not just for a living."[22] Harvey A. Hornstein refers to business leaders who seek to instill dynamism in their companies as managers with "courage," committed to revitalizing their companies without sacrificing their jobs. He asserts that "no organizational regeneration, no national industrial renaissance can take place without individual acts of courage."[23]

Harmon and Jacobs refer to dynamism as "disciplined energy."[24] Great companies focus the disciplined energy of employees and achieve a sustained output that makes a vital difference between them and others in the corporate world.

Employees in thousands of organizations experience dynamism every day. Chapter 14 contains cases of a wide variety of organizations in which dynamism has surged to prominence. You may recognize some of the organizations and their stories while others have not been profiled before. These cases provide evidence of the salutary effects of dynamism. These are the accounts of people and the organizations in which they have been endowed with power.

SUMMARY

In this chapter we showed the close connection between outstanding performance and dynamism in the workplace. Six stages in the dynamism model—the work system, work perceptions, work goals, dynamism, outcomes, and feedback—were explained. The importance of dynamism in organizations was argued. Organizational conditions conducive to the release of dynamism were examined.

NOTES

1. Greene, Bob. Revitalization: The Number One Priority. *Chicago Tribune,* January 19, 1995, Business Section, p. 1.

2. Peters, Tom. 1987. *Thriving on Chaos.* New York: Harper & Row, Publishers, pp. 540–541.

3. Harrison, R. 1987. Harnessing Personal Energy: How Companies Can Inspire Employees. *Organizational Dynamics*, Fall, pp. 5–20.

4. Thomas, K.W. and Velthouse, B.A. 1990. Cognitive Elements of Empowerment. *Academy of Management Review*, 15, pp. 666–681; Pace, R.W. and Jaw, D. 1993. Organizational Vitality: The Key to Production and Quality Improvement. *The Journal of National Chengchi University*, 66, pp. 385–395; Spreitzer, Gretchen. 1995. Psychological Empowerment in the Workplace: Dimensions, Measurement, and Validation. *Academy of Management Journal*, 38 (5), pp. 1442–1465; Pace, R.W. and McGregor, D.R. 1996. Should Your Team Be Revitalized? In M. Silberman and C. Auerbach (Eds.), *1996 McGraw-Hill Team and Organization Development Sourcebook*, New York: McGraw-Hill, pp. 98–106.

5. Locke, E.A. and Latham, G.P. 1990. *A Theory of Goal Setting and Task Performance*. Upper Saddle River, NJ: Prentice-Hall, pp. 1–26.

6. Harrison. Harnessing Personal Energy.

7. Miller, Alice. 1981. *The Drama of the Gifted Child*. New York: Basic Books, pp. 22, 55.

8. French, Marilyn. 1977. *The Women's Room*. New York: Jove Publications, p. 12.

9. McClelland, David C. 1969. Achievement Motivation. *Sales Meetings*, September, p. 27.

10. Crosby, Philip B. 1979. *Quality Is Free*. New York: New American Library, p. 3.

11. Windle, Jim. 1981. And Still Nobody Gives a Damn. *Purdue University Perspective*, p. 3.

12. Macleod, J.S. 1985. The Work Place as Prison. *Employment Relations Today*, Autumn, pp. 215–218.

13. Deming, W. Edwards. 1982. *Fourteen Steps to Total Quality*. Cambridge, MA: MIT Center for Advanced Engineering Study, pp. 91–103.

14. McClelland, David C. and Winter, David G. 1969. *Motivating Economic Achievement*. New York: The Free Press.

15. Miller, Donald B. 1977. *Personal Vitality*. Reading, MA: Addison-Wesley Publishing Company.

16. Yankelovich, Daniel. 1981. *New Rules: Searching for Self-Fulfillment in a World Turned Upside Down*. New York: Bantam New Age Book, pp. 16, 39, 41.

17. Hartman, Curtis and Pearlstein, Steven. 1987. The Joy of Working. *INC Magazine*, November, p. 61.

18. Yankelovich. *New Rules*.

19. Galagan, P. 1988. Bringing Spirit Back to the Workplace. *Training and Development Journal*, September, p. 37.

20. Kanter, R.M. 1976. The Job Makes the Person. *Psychology Today*, May, pp. 28–30.

21. Macher, K. 1988. Empowerment and the Bureaucracy. *Training and Development Journal*, September, pp. 41–45.

22. Pollard, C. William. 1996. *The Soul of the Firm*. New York: HarperBusiness, p. 45.

23. Hornstein, Harvey A. 1986. *Managerial Courage: Revitalizing Your Company without Sacrificing Your Job*. New York: John Wiley & Sons, p. 3.

24. Harmon, Frederick G. and Jacobs, Garry. 1985. *The Vital Difference*. New York: AMACOM.

Anhedonia: The Blues at Work

The cover story in *USA Today* for May 10, 2001, literally blared its message: Firms spend billions to fire up workers—with little luck. The Gallup pollsters analyzed data on large numbers of organizations and concluded that "55% of employees have no enthusiasm for their work," that "one in five (19%) are so uninterested or negative about their jobs that they poison the workplace to the point that companies might be better off if they called in sick." Quoting David Whyte, a motivational speaker, the article concludes that "it's only a very small proportion of humanity who tap-dance into the office every day."

In the article, Spencer Johnson is quoted as saying that "only long-lasting motivation will come from employees who bring it to work with them in the form of God, spirituality, or something else that causes them to rise to a higher purpose." The most common form of so-called "motivation" is rewards, but the research is full of data that shows that money is a full-fledged satisfier, not a motivator, and doesn't inspire energetic work habits. In fact, the *USA Today* article explained that "to some workers, almost any prize smacks of paying children to do chores around the house. And when some employees are rewarded for performance, others may feel that they also worked hard and were slighted."

Both the idea of rewards and motivation implies that you're having something done to you, resulting in feelings that you are being manipulated. That is a serious downside to contemporary ways of vitalizing employees. Gallup speculates that an increase in work output equivalent to eighteen more minutes of work during each eight-hour day would increase the gross domestic product of the United States by $355 billion. The problem is serious and calls for a new conceptual foundation. Motivational speakers, cash awards, trinkets, skydiving, hot coal walking, and rock climbing are not the answer. The workplace itself must be revitalized and anhedonia struck down.

THE ELIMINATION OF ANHEDONIA

Some illnesses fall in the gap between the fatal and the annoying. The space between the annoying and the fatal might be called borderline. That is, the ailment, malady, or problem is more than just annoying to the afflicted people, but to others it is not viewed as particularly fatal. Those who feel burdened with a borderline ailment are often not taken very seriously. In a world of calamity, tragedy, and catastrophe, borderline ailments are usually ignored. However, to those who experience the gnawing pressure of persistent borderline irritations, the pain and discomfort may be more damaging than a local cataclysm. Borderline adversity imposes gradually intensifying and damaging repercussions on the burdened individual.

Borderline ailments and afflictions are those like loneliness and shyness.[1] So you're shy or lonely? They may be irritating and annoying, but they aren't necessarily fatal. Borderline problems are generally associated with nonspecific effects such as low anxiety tolerance, poor impulse control, and an inability to engage in work or hobbies in a meaningful way. Borderline problems lack the signs associated with psychoses and neuroticisms and other serious mental difficulties, but they do involve many common semantic disorders such as projection, seeing our own unpleasant characteristics in others, and identification, indiscriminately carrying responses in one situation over to other situations with the assumption that the two situations are identical when they are in fact different.[2]

BORDERLINE ANHEDONIA

Anhedonia fits the pattern of borderline problems and refers to a passive joylessness, discouragement, and lack of zest in a person's demeanor.[3] Borderline anhedonia is the experience people have when their potential is stifled by work systems and organizations.

Borderline anhedonia is not a clinical state like pathological depression, but it may lead to the more serious nervous distresses and emotional and semantic disorders of personality such as neuroses, psychoses, and schizophrenia. Even disorders such as paranoia, manic-depression, involutional melancholia, and the constitutionally psychopathic personality may evolve from borderline anhedonia, depending on the severity of work conditions. Borderline anhedonia is reflected in the frequent alienation, disillusionment, and lack of respect when referring to what is happening to co-workers. It triggers both depression and violence in organizational relationships.

The daily news is replete with examples of regular outbursts that result in mayhem and death, of postal workers and schoolchildren firing on colleagues and classmates in both spontaneous and calculated designs to rid them of the sources of creeping anhedonia. Executives crawl home to hide from the oppressions and obsessions of the workplace, custodians work in silent indignity, teachers and social workers clutch their chairs in white-knuckle anxiety as they prepare to confront students and clients.

I have had the opportunity to serve for most of my adult life as a professor in several universities around the world. Some would consider this to be the least likely occupation to be subject to anhedonia. But, both rage and indolence run rampant in the cells of academia, playing out the consequences of anhedonia. Caplow and McGee, in their analysis of the problems of individual scholars, conclude that "the violent opposition between the academic man's image of himself as a kind of oligarch, independent of lay authority, and the galling subjection which he actually experiences is presumably responsible for the combination of private resentment and public submissiveness that so often characterizes the faculty attitude toward administrators."[4] There can be little doubt among members of the academic community that resentment, submissiveness, and a long catalog of related anhedonic reactions occur in colleges and universities.

Outside academic circles, however, anhedonic patterns are sufficiently widespread to constitute a plague. Janice Castro caught the trend when she reported that "the back-to-work season has begun, but for millions of Americans, the gung-ho is gone."[5] Scott and Hart note that new employees in the supermarket industry are trained in the operation of computer-based checkout stands, "but within a week the graduate of that program will find the job dull, routine, and personally unrewarding. . . . In organizational America, more people tend boring machines than sophisticated electronic gunnery systems. Thus, if the employees of organizational America were ever to comprehend the life-destroying implications of their jobs, there would be a frightful turmoil."[6]

Judith M. Bardwick asserts that "plateauing" in organizations, or the dwindling potential for promotions, leads to circumstances in which "those who are no longer rising but remain dependable and competent, who make no trouble but do not shine, are easy to ignore. They are passively punished by neglect. Being ignored is in some way more eviscerating than being criticized. At its worst extreme, being ignored makes people feel insignificant. At the deepest psychological level, they can feel so insignificant they don't exist. Of all the messages that can be communicated, that is the cruelest."[7] Incredibly, organizations around the world are deliberately creating insignificant employees, which in turn exacerbates feelings of anhedonia.

When employees feel insignificant, they feel that they are unable to cope. They become frustrated and experience confusion in their lives. You can be pretty certain that anhedonia has set in when others notice a decline in your enthusiasm, creativity, innovativeness, confidence, commitment, and general productivity at work. The tragedy of anhedonia at work is expressed in impelling paradoxes such as "I'm getting a salary from an organization, but I couldn't care less if it goes broke or fails," or "the very organization to which I am committed is killing me."

One of *Time*'s September 1989 cover stories reported the results of a survey of 12,000 workers in which 11 percent of middle managers and 24 percent of nonmanagement employees described their offices or factories as "a prison," a sentiment heard in back rooms and in quiet conversations in and outside the office.[8]

Anhedonia—listlessness and lack of zest—is brought on by a number of different experiences; seasickness, for example, may produce a temporary form of anhedonia, but in the workplace, anhedonia occurs when employees have a negative perception of the workplace.

Anhedonia in the workplace is not new to organizations. Three decades ago, Bennis called our attention to five human problems confronting contemporary organizations: integration, social influence, collaboration, adaptation, and decay. "Decay"[9] in human terms leads to anhedonia. In organizations, decay may occur both in the technical processes involving the work itself and in the social processes involving the people.

Harrison explained that "both white-collar and blue-collar workers respond to boring, repetitive tasks and close supervision by withdrawing effort and attention from the work; quality and productivity suffer accordingly. Management responds by managing more closely and by automating the work to as great an extent as possible. Because the workers feel more closely controlled and have even less responsibility than before, they feel less committed, and they withdraw their commitment and attention even more from the work. And so the cycle continues."[10]

SYMPTOMS OF ANHEDONIA

Bardwick prepared a list of symptoms of disillusionment at work—all features of anhedonia in the workplace.[11] They include

An "I don't care" attitude about work.

Noninvolvement.

Withdrawal from people.

Lack of initiative.

Lack of energy.

Having no specific goals and no time frame.

Passive forms of aggression, such as overt agreement, but basic noncompliance.

Inability to make decisions.

An increase in the number of hours worked with no increase in output.

Due dates being missed.

Incomplete work and work that needs to be redone.

Routine tasks taking much longer.

Work being put off.

Doing only what is required.

Lack of new ideas.

Increase in the number of errors.

Insisting on doing things the old way.

Coming in late and leaving early.

Never being in a hurry.

No follow-through.

Being hung up on details.

Prolonging decisions.

Being obsessed with rules.

Just not getting things done.

Increase in illness.

Inappropriate dress or rigidly adhering to irrelevant dress codes.

Being critical of others.

Insisting on being the leader/refusing the leadership role.

Not volunteering for special appointments.

Not helping others.

Insisting that things be done your way.

Refusing to give an opinion.

Chronic fatigue.

Marked gain or loss in weight for no obvious reason.

Using drugs or heavy use of alcohol or tobacco.

Tendency to fly off the handle.

Tension or irritability.

Loss of sense of humor.

Excessive amounts of putdown humor.

Minor problems being very upsetting.

Fears about work surfacing that were not experienced before.

Mistrust of others.

Feeling of urgency about time lines.

Constantly seeking reassurances that one is liked.

Forgetfulness.

Living in the past.

No sense of what's really important.

Feeling of being excluded.

No long-range perspective.

Quality of busyness at work.

Complaining of being too busy at home.

Complaining of being too busy at work to have time for self.

Feeling that life is repetitive.

Feeling weighed down by responsibilities.

Feeling of being trapped by habits.

Anhedonia can be understood best as constant blue days in the workplace. If you have continuing blue days where you work, at home, at the company, around town, at the club, and with family members, you may be experiencing anhedonia. Things may not be good and you need to do something about them. Don't attack someone. Don't leave or run away. Don't lie down and die. Read on and discover where the gung-ho feeling went; then get it back.

THE PERSONAL WORLD OF AN ANHEDONIC: A CASE

This is the story of a person who woke up one day to discover that he was anhedonic. This is much akin to the awakening of a person who imbibes regularly and one day realizes that he's an alcoholic. The narrative is written in the first person, with "I" pronouns reflecting the turning inward and accounting of a life turned listless. The story is about a university professor, but it is not restricted to "the best job that beats working for a living."[12] It may be about your job and company, or your position in the government, or your life at home.

The Account

I was born and raised in a rural community, graduating from a high school of more than a thousand students, however, as a result of the consolidation of small districts into one of moderate size. I was a good student and was accepted at a fairly well-known private university. Although I was shy and never particularly outgoing, I had a strong interest in music and sang in musicals both in high school and in college. I never dated much and actually married later in life.

Along with my musical talents, I also demonstrated an interest and skill in radio and television production, but my primary goal was to obtain a teaching position in a college or university. I completed a master's degree in the field of broadcasting and was asked to take a position as Instructor in the department where I received my master's degree. I was assigned to teach basic courses in the area, handle production laboratories, and assist with the university radio and television station operations.

It would not be an understatement to say that I was literally ecstatic about my role and its possibilities. I came to work early, worked late, and devoted a great deal of energy to completing every assignment that came my way. I was able to invest in some small parcels of land and to begin to build a small investment portfolio. The university regularly provided opportunities to take advantage of tax-deferred and retirement investments. I often wondered what could be better than this. Nevertheless, it became clear after a couple of years that my classroom and laboratory duties would not change. I was not improving my skills or taking on additional responsibilities. After my second-year review, it became obvious that at the university, the completion of a doctoral degree was absolutely essential if I were to receive tenure and be promoted beyond the rank of Instructor.

With the enthusiastic support of other faculty, I decided to secure a leave of absence from the university to complete doctoral course work, but to return to the university to complete the dissertation, a strategy that several other faculty had followed. It was revealed to me by the Chair of the department, however, that the university had been criticized for providing leaves of absence for advanced studies for some faculty when others completed the work on their own and applied for a position with a doctoral degree in hand.

The necessity of completing doctoral work weighed so heavily on my mind that during the next academic year I corresponded with and was eventually accepted into a doctoral program at a state university in another part of the country. I left my position with some regrets, but with the assurance that with a doctoral degree I would be a prime candidate for a permanent position later on. With renewed enthusiasm, I approached graduate studies with fervor and actually swept through the courses and research to finish in two years rather than three. I notified the department of my success, but they indicated that there was no opening as yet; so, I applied for a position at a university in the Midwest. I was hired as an Assistant Professor to teach introductory courses, handle laboratories, and work with the university television station. This was almost exactly the same assignments that I had in my former position prior to completing doctoral work.

My determination and enthusiasm had actually been accelerated by the additional theory and skills I had acquired during doctoral studies. I became more interested in doing research and advising both master's and doctoral candidates. The next two years passed quickly. I published an article or two and learned what it meant to be a full-fledged faculty member in a university. Just as I was being considered for my third-year review, I received a call from the Chair of my former department, inquiring whether I would be available to accept a position. I was again ecstatic. I said I was. Shortly thereafter, I received a formal invitation to accept a position as Assistant Professor, teaching introductory courses, supervising laboratory activities of students, and doing other things that faculty do, such as developing my own research program, advising students, and serving on thesis committees for graduate students pursuing a master's degree. This was exactly what I wanted. I departed from the state university around midsummer, as soon as my formal responsibilities could be terminated, and arrived on a quiet campus. I moved into an office in the basement of the building where the university radio and television stations were located, which was also close to the broadcasting laboratories.

I have never been more excited about anything than returning to my "home" university to work with former teachers as colleagues and equals. I literally ran to the office and to class. I loved faculty meetings and visiting with students and other faculty in the halls and after classes had ended. This was truly the good life. In the midst of this euphoria, I had a woman in a basic course who was a bit older than most, but who was gentle, beautiful, and kind. We fell in love immediately. It took the urging of my closest colleagues to get me to propose, but I did and we were married. We were both a bit older and started a family immediately.

Soon we had two children and were concerned about making ends meet. I had not had a change in teaching and laboratory supervision assignments for about four years, and I had spent two years as an Instructor and two years as an Assistant Professor before joining the current faculty, and four years as an Assistant Professor in the present assignment. I thought it was time for a promotion. I had published an occasional article, but publishing was not the highest priority in the department. We were a "professional" faculty, with individuals who had quite a bit of work experience in the real world.

I argued my case in the department and was eventually submitted for promotion to Associate Professor. I received promotion to Associate Professor when I was 38 years of age. I was promoted to Full Professor when I reached 55. During the 17 intervening years, I discovered what it meant to develop anhedonia.

After receiving confirmation that I had in fact received promotion to Associate Professor, I began reflecting on what I wanted to contribute to the department, college, and university, and what kinds of changes I would like to have made in my teaching assignments. I felt that it was time to move into upper-division courses, to work more with graduate students, even teach some graduate seminars and direct graduate theses. Several senior faculty members were beginning to look toward retirement and I should look forward to taking their responsibilities.

A few new faculty members were hired at the rank of full professor and others were promoted to full professor. The new faculty and newly promoted faculty were given the kinds of assignments that I anticipated for myself. I began to wonder what was happening. My immediate colleagues said they liked what I was doing and wanted me to continue doing the things I was good at. The routine of meeting the same classes and coordinating laboratories wasn't as challenging as it had been earlier.

With a little more free time on my hands, I began to cultivate the property I had purchased earlier and actually developed a small farm with some animals and alfalfa and wheat on some acres. I found myself dragging into the university, and rushing home as soon as possible to take care of the farm. I took less interest in faculty meetings, although I still attended when they didn't conflict with farm plans. I heard some occasional grumbling from colleagues, but I completed all of my assignments. I just didn't stay around for visits. I was able to do some additional volunteer work in my church, which was very satisfying and seemed to contribute to the well-being of community members.

Some small things occurred during this time. I was in need of a better typewriter—these were the days when electric typewriters were just coming on the scene—and a few were becoming available. I had my eye on a good one and spoke with the Chair of the department about having it assigned to my office. A day or so later, I saw one of the full professors carrying the typewriter down the hallway toward his office. I ran down and grabbed him by the arm and said that he was taking my typewriter. He set the typewriter down in the middle of the hallway and explained to me at the top of his voice that this was his typewriter. I decided to pick up the typewriter, but as I bent over he gave me a shove. I stumbled, but grasped the carriage of the typewriter, and regained my balance just in time to give him a big shove away from the typewriter. He screamed and fell backwards. I picked up the typewriter and started for my office. He clutched the typewriter, and we had a tug of war. At that moment, the Chair of the department intervened, and took the typewriter back to the department office. The other faculty member and I didn't speak for months. Neither of us got a good typewriter until the next year, long after everyone in the department had theirs upgraded.

I sat and stewed in my office, then left for the farm. During the next few months, I only came to the office when I had specific assignments to complete. I discovered that I was being given more trivial, petty tasks to complete, like preparing a proposal for the reorganization of the broadcasting area. I drafted what I thought was a set of good suggestions and presented them at a faculty meeting. They were summarily voted down.

I was given the task of organizing commencement exercises, but I now had a full-blown farm, a family, and quite a few volunteer church activities, and I couldn't get anyone else to help on the committee. A colleague finally came to my rescue and put together a commencement program. I didn't go to commencement because I had a sick calf.

For three years I worked the farm and did my other assignments, and only went to the university for classes and laboratory exercises. I stopped going to faculty meetings and didn't even talk with other faculty in the hall-ways. I heard rumors that the department was going to reorganize again, and that the broadcasting faculty was looking to move me into another part of the department, out of broadcasting. I asked for and received a sabbatical leave to do some research for a mining company. I spent the year commut-ing from the farm to the mine, where I assisted the personnel director in re-fining his job and improving the operations of the mine. I wrote more than fifty proprietary research reports on personnel issues. None were pub-lished, but they were all circulated to corporate executives who expressed very positive remarks about the value of the reports. In fact, two of the sons of the President of the company eventually enrolled in the department to complete their university studies, probably as a direct consequence of the good work that I was doing.

When I returned, no one even asked about what I had been doing during the past year. I filed copies of the reports and went back to managing labo-ratories and teaching basic courses in broadcasting. The department was still reorganizing; some additional new faculty had been hired and new se-quences of studies were being considered. I realized one day that scuttle-butt around the department had me leaving the university and devoting full time to the farm. I couldn't do that—the farm wasn't large enough to re-place my university salary, and my university salary wasn't large enough to support our family without income from the farm.

I struggled to the university each day, with the dreaded alternatives get-ting bolder and bolder—leave the university, move to some other area, do something to justify my position. I would never get promoted to Full Pro-fessor. I had lost the support of my colleagues. I couldn't leave for another job. I was stuck in a swamp of desolation. I had a hard time going to class. I didn't want to face my colleagues. I resisted going home to meet my wife and children. I knew people were talking about me in the community. I was going nowhere, and I couldn't help it. I became restless and listless. I couldn't sit still and I couldn't move. Despair became a glut in my life. I was overcome with alienation, emotional distress, and lost faith in my col-leagues and the university system. I had no respect for myself. I was dis-couraged and dejected. Full-scale anhedonia had set in.

SUMMARY

In this chapter, anhedonia was defined and its devastating effects on workplace productivity described. The case of a professional was recounted to reveal the insidious consequences of anhedonia on a person's work life.

NOTES

1. Riesman, David, Glazer, Nathan, and Denny, Reuel. 1953. *The Lonely Crowd*. New York: Doubleday Anchor Books; Zimbardo, Philip G. 1977. *Shyness:*

What It Is, What to Do about It. Reading, MA: Addison-Wesley Publishing Company; Slater, Philip. 1970. *The Pursuit of Loneliness: American Culture at the Breaking Point.* Boston, MA: Beacon Press.

2. Johnson, Wendell. 1946. *People in Quandries.* New York: Harper & Row, Publishers.

3. Stein, Jess (Ed.). 1966. *The Random House Dictionary of the English Language.* New York: Random House, Inc.

4. Caplow, Theodore and McGee, Reece J. 1958. *The Academic Marketplace.* New York: Basic Books.

5. Castro, Janice. 1989. Where Did the Gung-ho Go? *Time*, September 11, pp. 52–56.

6. Scott, William G. and Hart, David K. 1989. *Organizational Values in America.* New Brunswick, NJ: Transaction Publishers, p. 79.

7. Bardwick, Judith M. 1986. *The Plateauing Trap.* New York: Bantam Books, pp. 78–79.

8. Castro. Where Did the Gung-ho Go?

9. Bennis, Warren. 1966. Organizational Revitalization. *California Management Review*, Fall, pp. 51–60.

10. Harrison, Roger. 1987. Harnessing Personal Energy: How Companies Can Inspire Employees. *Organizational Dynamics*, Fall, pp. 5–20.

11. Bardwick. 1986. *The Plateauing Trap.*

12. Professor X. 1973. *This Beats Working for a Living: The Dark Secrets of a College Professor.* New Rochelle, NY: Arlington House.

3

Work System: The Wind that Bends

Models of systems are often abstract, complex, and cumbersome. Current models have not provided a simple but comprehensive set of categories for understanding the essential elements of a work system. Another need in models of work systems is to have a model that places the worker at the center of the system in order to underline the importance of the individual human being in the work system.

This chapter describes a work system model that serves the purposes described above and may be useful in representing the essential elements of a work system. The goal of this chapter is to define and briefly discuss the five elements that comprise a work system. The elements are mutually exclusive and collectively exhaustive in identifying what constitutes a work system.

LOOSELY COUPLED SYSTEMS

This model does not, however, attempt to identify or comment upon internal processes within and between the elements. This model of a work system acknowledges that some contemporary theories argue that organizational systems may be tightly or loosely coupled.[1] To be loosely coupled means that a change in one element may affect other elements, as implied by the idea of interdependence, though the effect may not be evident right away. The change may be absorbed by one element and passed on to others at a later date. One element of a system may adapt with relative ease without immediately affecting the rest of the system. If part of the system fails, for example, that failure may be confined to a limited part of the system for a period of time.

Work or organizational systems tend to be loosely coupled. Loosely coupled systems are better able to cope with unexpected challenges and disruptions and also tend to be more responsive to changes in their environments, making them more open and adaptable.[2]

ELEMENTS OF A WORK SYSTEM

Work systems come into existence through the identification of work goals that can be achieved more effectively through collective effort. Work is the term we use when we talk about expending effort to achieve or complete a particular task. Work is the physical and mental effort put into doing or making something.

As soon as more than one person is needed to make or do something—to work—we find the beginnings of a work system. When one person finds it necessary to recruit others to help accomplish work, the organizer must define the work to be completed, how the worker fits into the system, and how the flow of activities is to be regulated for greatest efficiency. From the acts of organizing, five essential elements of a work system can be identified: (1) the worker, (2) the work itself (what needs to be done and how it is to be done), (3) the structure of the organization (the way in which individuals and roles relate), (4) the organization guidelines (the statements, agreements, plans, rules, and policies that govern the ways work ought to be done), and (5) the leadership practices (the directions and controls used to maintain the collectivity and move toward goal accomplishment).

Systems, in general, are a set of elements or parts that are interdependent and interact with one another so as to function as an operating whole. A work system may be recognized and distinguished by boundaries that separate it from its environment. The environment of a work system is composed of all the factors that impinge upon the work system. Although we acknowledge the critical influence that the institutions embedded in a society have on work systems, the primary focus of this chapter is on the five essential elements of a work system.

The culture or cultures operating in the environment of a work system, and often in the work system itself, may have a facilitating or hindering influence on the system's functioning. The explicit and implicit guidelines for thinking, doing, and possessing things of a culture may be carried over into the work system to help create an internal culture or climate. The intent of this chapter is not to deny the environment and its impact on a work system, but to set the issues of environment aside while the elements of the system itself are identified and described.

THE CLOVERLEAF SYMBOL

A work system can be symbolized by a four-leaf clover, with the worker at the center and the other elements on the periphery (see Figure 3.1). This model emphasizes the fundamental assumptions that workers have a great

Figure 3.1
The Work System Model

creative capacity for being ingenious, that energy exists naturally within the individual, and that energy is transported into the work system through the workers. This means that the vigor in all elements of the system is a function of the energy released by the workers.

The cloverleaf model implies that the work system, like a garden, must be cultivated and nourished so that it grows and develops to reflect the life and energy of its human members. In fact, it may be assumed that the other elements of the work system are designed to foster and encourage workers to achieve the goals of the work system. This model of a work system places the worker in the central position and represents the desirable relationship between workers and other elements of the system.

THE WORK SYSTEM MODEL

The cloverleaf model focuses attention on what Scott and Hart call the Individual Imperative,[3] which argues that individuals have the natural right to actualize their potentials throughout their lives and that the primary justification of work systems is to promote the actualization of individual potentials. We shall now describe the five essential elements of a work system.

The Worker

The work system is developed through the efforts of the individuals of which it is comprised. The manner in which human efforts are applied to the system depends on the other elements of the work system—work, structure, guidelines, and leadership.

Individual Preferences

Human beings resemble one another in many ways, but each one is uniquely different. Their internal biological mechanisms are quite similar, as is their general appearance. On the other hand, they differ from one another on the basis of psychological and behavioral traits and characteristics that combine to create individual preferences. Four factors (personality, attitudes, perceptions, and attributions) are most useful in understanding why people have different preferences.

Personality. An individual's personality in the workplace is composed of beliefs about: (1) sociability; (2) power and status differences; and (3) self-esteem and reputation. A person's internal dialogue in one instance might record him or her saying, "I am a sociable person with quite a bit of power and status, and with a great deal of self-regard; my reputation is unblemished." You might expect a different reaction from such a personality than from a person who said to himself or herself, "I am unsociable and powerless with no status at all, and have no regard for myself, leaving me with no reputation."

Attitudes. Attitudes represent a complex interplay between a person's thoughts, feelings, and intentions.[4] A positive attitude toward something means that a person has good intentions toward, feels good about, and has optimistic thoughts about something. A negative attitude means that a person has bad intentions toward, feels bad about, and has pessimistic thoughts about something. Again, you would expect different reactions from people who have negative attitudes about things in contrast to those who have positive attitudes. An adage offered by many is "change your attitudes, change your lives." This is sound philosophy.

Perceptions. Perceptions are the processes by which individuals focus on some aspects of their world and ignore other aspects of it, thereby making sense of what is happening to them. Perceptual processes involve searching for, getting, and processing information about the people, objects, and events in a person's environment, and then organizing that information to make sense out of it. The result is called a *mindset.*[5] Mindsets often become fixed and rigid, allowing us to have a more stable world; actually, the world isn't stable, only the mindset is. Stereotypes and closed-mindedness come from fixed mindsets, and vacillation and indecision usually come from mindsets that are too flexible. We interpret other people, things, and events in terms of our mindsets.

Attributions. Attributions are the explanations people give for why they and others do what they do.[6] Attributions attempt to explain what causes behavior. Causes of behavior are usually internal (personality, attitudes, genetics) or external (unreasonable workloads, chance occurrences, and circumstances). When people say that they lose things because they're just awkward, you can recognize that they are pessimistic and attribute unhappy things to internal causes. Attributions provide powerful explanations for why unhappy things occur, why bad things happen to good people. People tend to underestimate the strength of external causes of behavior and overestimate the strength of internal causes of behavior when seeking to understand why people behave the way they do.

The Work Itself

Work consists of (1) the formal tasks workers engage in, and (2) the ways in which the tasks assigned to them by the organization should be done in order to achieve the goals.[7] Work consists of what workers do to create goods and services.

The work itself usually has three characteristics: (1) range, (2) depth, and (3) relationships.[8] Range refers to the number of different tasks a worker performs to complete a given job. The greater the number of tasks a worker performs, usually, the longer it takes to do a job. Depth refers to the amount of discretion a person has to determine specific job activities and outcomes. Highly specialized jobs are those having few tasks to accomplish and precisely defined means by which to accomplish them. Relationships involve the number of interpersonal contacts required to perform a particular job. Workers with similar background, skills, and interests have a basis for more interpersonal contacts than do heterogeneous workers, and similar backgrounds help workers to arrive at satisfying social relationships with less stress and effort.[9] The kind of work a person does has a powerful influence on other aspects of his or her life. Routine, highly controlled work done with a machine often provides less satisfaction than work that allows discretion and uses personal skills.

Work Technology. Although we have alluded to the idea of technology as part of the discussion of the work itself, we have not as yet provided a direct definition. Although technology has many different definitions, it is becoming generally understood to refer to the ways in which work is done. Said another way, technology represents the actions an individual performs upon an object, with or without the aid of tools or mechanical devices, in order to make some change in the object.[10] Bulldozers and laptop computers are both technology; they can bring about changes in the objects to which they are applied.

Technologies are involved at different levels in the performance of work. The way in which individual workers perform a task has a technology associated with it. Each group or work team has a technology, or way of doing work. The overall flow of materials and the actions performed on each item or part of a product comprise a technology. The way in which clients are handled in a social service agency represents a different technology.

A sociotechnical systems approach to work seeks to define the "unit operations," the main steps in the process of transforming raw materials into a finished product, then to redefine work-unit boundaries around unit operations and discover or create technologies that facilitate the transformational process. Unit operations define the work process of the organization and help people control the technology instead of being controlled by the technology.[11]

The critical goal of a technical analysis of an organization's operations is to identify "key variances," or places in the technical process where deviations from normal or usual procedures might occur. Variances are not problems, but technical requirements to be met in the normal process of creating the product. Breakdowns in the technology or human errors are not variances, since variances represent differences in the usual or best way in which the work is done.[12]

The identification of variances and how they are controlled during the work process allows workers to discover ways that the variances might be better brought under control by improving the technology or changing the design of the work system.

Leadership

The primary goal of leaders is to get the work done through other people, so they fulfill an essential control function. Leaders make decisions about the resources subordinates need to do their work and how they should use them. Some leaders work directly with workers, others work with other leaders at different levels in the organizational structure.

Practices. Two fairly basic approaches describe the range and depth of leadership practices in most organizations or work systems: First, some consensus has been achieved around the idea that leaders engage in approximately five main functions: planning, organizing, staffing, directing, and controlling,[13] usually called the operational school of management; second, some sound evidence suggests that leaders perform about ten generic roles, divided into three basic groups: (a) interpersonal roles—figurehead, leader, liaison, (b) informational roles—monitor, disseminator, spokesperson, and (c) decision roles—entrepreneur, disturbance handler, resource allocator, and negotiator.[14]

Processes. Leaders are at the center of much of what happens in a work system. Included among the central leadership processes are problem solving and decision making, innovation and creativity, leadership and influence, power and conflict management, team building and group functioning, performance evaluation and control, communication and information accessibility, culture development, socialization and career planning, human resource development, and organization change. The work system cannot be understood clearly without understanding the function of leadership in the system. Leadership may be the most widely studied element of the work system. Some people think that the complete system can be understood by looking only at leadership practices and how leadership affects the human processes in a work system. Unfortunately, such is not the case. All elements of the system are interdependent and affect one another.

Organization Structure

Organization structure refers to relationships among the tasks, roles, and members of the work system.[15] Organization structure appears to be defined by two key variables: complexity and centralization.[16]

Complexity. Organization complexity is a function of three factors: (1) The degree to which differences exist between units (horizontal differentiation). Universities have a large number of specialties and tend to be horizontally differentiated. (2) The levels of authority between workers and top executives (vertical differentiation). Whether an organization's structure is taller or flatter depends on the span of control or number of subordinates a person can supervise effectively. A workforce of 4,096 employees, for example, would require 1,365 supervisors using a span of control of four, but only 585 supervisors with a span of control of eight.[17] The sheer size of the organization may dictate having a narrower span of control, although the type of jobs and the abilities of workers to make independent decisions may allow for a wider span of control. (3) The degree to which the location of any organization's facilities and workforce are dispersed geographically (spatial differentiation). An organization with branch offices in twenty different locations tends to be more complex than an organization with its entire operation in one place.

Centralization. Centralization is the degree to which decision making is concentrated at a single point in the organization. Decentralization, in contrast, is the extent to which decision-making authority is dispersed throughout the organization. The amount of formal authority given to workers to make decisions about their work activities is a measure of centralization. Policies and leadership styles that limit decision making move organizations toward centralization. Situations in which workers are prohibited from participating in decisions about their work represent centralization. If some form of discretion is provided at low levels in the organization, but the decisions are closely monitored, the organization is still functioning with high degrees of centralization. The use of autonomous work groups is an effort to decentralize decision making in organizations.

Organizational Guidelines

Guidelines are the vast array of statements that control and formalize decisions and actions of organization members. Formalization, the process by which jobs and tasks become standardized, is achieved by specifying the extent to which job procedures and activities must be done. Perceptions of workers concerning the extent to which job procedures and activities are specified and enforced give a fair measure of formalization in an organization. Professionalization also produces standardized or formal behaviors through the socialization of workers before they enter employment. Professionalization is achieved by the selection process, by specifying role expectations, by training in job skills, and by having workers perform rituals to demonstrate competence in the organization.

Organizational guidelines are statements that direct decisions in an organization. They include such statements as goals, missions, purposes, standards, deadlines, targets, quotas, policies, strategies, procedures, rules, and regulations.[18]

EFFECTS OF WORK SYSTEMS

The Work System is comprised of five elements. They are interrelated and interdependent in operation, but they can be discussed in discrete units: the worker, the work itself, leadership practices and processes, organization structure, and organizational guidelines.

Work systems are created and maintained by the people in the system. Thus, four of the elements of the work system are directly affected by the fifth element, the worker. The impact of workers on the way in which the system functions has been greatly misunderstood and grossly neglected.

We have learned from both research and experience that work systems cannot be designed to elicit top performances from workers; top performance must be given voluntarily; it cannot be purchased or designed into a system. The only way to unleash the power of workers is to remove the constraints and restrictions of the work system from the workers. What are some of those restraints? We shall discuss the other basic elements of the work system, then examine the worker and the restraints more closely.

Effects of the Work Itself

The work itself has both positive and negative effects on workers. Certain characteristics lead to psychological states that actually cultivate highly motivated work performance. For example, the variety of skills involved in the work, the extent to which workers identify with what they are doing, and the significance of the work being done all contribute to the meaningfulness of work. Meaningful work has positive effects on workers, and can help to unleash the power of employees in the workplace.

Although meaningful work tends to encourage employees, the most powerful influence on workers is the degree of autonomy they have in the workplace. Autonomy frees employees to decide for themselves how they will do the meaningful work. Freedom, in turn, gives workers responsibility for the results of their work efforts. Absolutely nothing fires up workers as much as autonomy does.

If workers have meaningful tasks to accomplish and the freedom to decide how to complete and improve the way they do the work, what they need most after that is feedback from the job. Feedback should give employees knowledge about the actual results of their work activities. Feedback doesn't have to do with rewards; rather, it has to do with information that confirms the efforts of the workers, and shows what kind of impact they have been having in the organization.

When meaningfulness, autonomy, and feedback are part of the work itself, they combine to create invigorating and vitalizing work. Nevertheless, there is one hitch in the system. The ability of these factors to release workers to contribute strongly to the organization rests on the strength of a person's "growth needs." According to Hackman and Oldham, "people with high growth need strength will experience the psychological states more strongly when their objective job is high in MPS [motivating potential score] than will their low growth need strength counterparts. And ... individuals with high growth need strength will respond more positively to the psychological states, when they are present, than will low growth need individuals."[19]

Growth Need Strength. Growth need strength is clarified by translating growth needs, which are part of a person's fundamental needs system, into goals to be achieved. We use the term *natural work goals* to refer to the growth needs that are the critical releases of vitality and dynamism in workers.

Natural Work Goals. Natural work goals unleash the energy of workers to regulate the intensity and duration of the effort workers give to their work and to direct the attention of workers toward relevant actions, thus giving a clearer picture of what is to be achieved.[20]

Work goals further workers' own happiness while achieving the goals of the organization. Through the achievement of natural work goals, workers become more competent, autonomous, influential, emotionally stable, adaptive, and dependable.

Locke and Latham have specified the way goals function. They explain that "goal directedness is a cardinal attribute of the behavior of all living organisms"[21] and may be observed at all levels in the lives of human beings. Three common features characterize goal-directed action:

Self-Generation. The actions of living organisms are fueled by energy sources integral to the organism as a whole; energy is not put into human beings, it is part of their system.

Value Significance. The survival of living organisms is conditional; that is, living organisms can go out of existence. To maintain their existence, living organisms must take specific actions; if they do not take such actions, they die. Thus, all goal-directed action has value for the organism.

Goal Causation. In purposeful action, the individual's *idea* of and desire to achieve the goal is what causes action. The idea serves as the efficient cause, but the action is aimed toward some state. Purposeful, goal-directed action is caused by the individual's aspiration to achieve the goal.

Together, these features mean that accomplishing the work itself, even if it is meaningful, with autonomy, and provides feedback, is simply a means to achieving one or more natural work goals. What makes work goals "natural" is that they are derived from the capacity of human beings to project images of what might be and what ought to be, to imagine things being different from what they are, and to infer and deduce explanations for how things function. These are natural, inherent, and instinctive features of all human beings.

Once natural work goals are understood and accepted, they serve as reference points for guiding subsequent actions leading to the goal. If the work itself is designed to allow workers to achieve natural work goals, the workers routinely, spontaneously, and regularly complete the technical aspects of their work with enthusiasm and commitment. The work goals themselves will be discussed in greater detail in a later chapter.

In the context of natural work goals, the effects of the work itself on employees' work performance may be summarized in a few statements:

1. People whose work allows them to achieve natural work goals tend to be more motivated and to work with more energy than those who perform work without achieving natural work goals.
2. People whose work allows them to achieve natural work goals tend to experience meaningfulness, autonomy, and feedback more frequently than those who perform work without achieving natural work goals.
3. People whose work allows them to achieve natural work goals tend to respond more positively to enriched work.
4. Thus an organization that wants to have a high-performance workforce must assist its workers in achieving natural work goals.

Employees whose work does not accomplish and encompass natural work goals may reject work with motivating psychological characteristics (meaningfulness, autonomy, feedback), thus defeating efforts to unleash the power of workers in the organization through the work itself.

Effects of Organization Structure

Organization structure represents reporting relationships and other connections among organization members. Workers experience several general effects as a result of the structural aspects of organizations:

1. Individual initiative is limited by the centralization of authority.
2. Information selectivity is encouraged by a controlling, centralized hierarchy.
3. Message flow is curtailed by the centralization needed to coordinate actions.
4. Sharing frames of reference is limited by specialization and status differences.
5. Hierarchical authority structure leads to fear of punishment.
6. Feeling power over others is encouraged by the centralization of authority.
7. Distance between units often leads to the ineffective utilization of resources.
8. Centralization can lead to goal distortion and the failure to accomplish objectives.
9. Complexity can lead to low interest and reduced energy input.

Inefficient relationships can have devastating consequences on workers. Just look at the list of effects: loss of interest, distortion of goals, ineffective use of resources, abuse of power, curtailed information flow, and the erosion of innovations.

Is it any wonder that contemporary solutions to structural problems are teams, decentralization, quality circles, reengineering, open-book management, collective individualism, multidimensional organizations, and virtual organizations, and that the main topics are empowerment, chaos theory, structural holes, searching for order in an orderly world, empowerment, organizational learning, and, of course, revitalization of the workforce? This situation cries out to every manager and executive to reduce the structure and allow workers more freedom.

Effects of Organizational Guidelines

Guidelines provide information for organization members about where the organization is going, what they should be doing, how they should think about organization problems and solutions, and what actions they should take to make the organization successful. Nevertheless, guidelines limit decision making and seriously undermine innovative thinking. Postmodern analysts suggest that today guidelines control the dialogue in work systems. Because management determines the guidelines, management controls the discourse about what is important in the system.[22]

Individuals are alienated by organization impersonalization resulting from formalization. Lack of participation in making decisions leads to feelings of resistance to carrying out policies. Formalization reduces trust among individuals at different levels in the organization, which leads to hostility and opposition to programs and the deterioration of human relationships because of deference to policy statements rather than to human problems.

Most work systems have more guidelines than are good for the worker and the organization. One of the first goals in reducing the impact of the work system on workers is to eliminate as many guidelines as you can. Be bold to begin with and let a little chaos reign, pulling in and restricting workers only as a last resort. This may take some courage, but it will be worth it.

Effects of Leadership Practices

Leadership practices consist of what a person does and says to get others to carry out their work. Leadership practices are the primary means by which employees discover that the organization (a) trusts them and allows them the freedom to take risks, (b) supports them and gives them responsibility in doing their jobs, (c) openly provides accurate and adequate information about the organization, (d) attentively listens to and gets reliable and candid information from them, (e) actively consults them so that they see that their involvement is influential in decisions in the organization, and (f) has a concern for high standards and challenging work.

Leadership practices contribute positively or negatively to the work environment. Leadership practices create a climate by the way in which (1) work is assigned, (2) suggestions for improving efficiency are given, (3) instructions are given for developing work skills and technical aspects of the job, and (4) selection and placement interviews are conducted.

When leaders say and do things that others interpret as not trusting, unsupportive, hiding information, providing inaccurate and inadequate information, not being attentive to and not listening to them, failing to consult them and empower them, and encouraging low standards and inefficiency, then climates of apathy, hostility, defensiveness, and apathy tend to develop.

Organization leaders, almost without fail, should review their management styles to see to what extent they meet seven basic criteria. Does your leadership style do the following?

1. Create an atmosphere in which the people whom you supervise feel free to experiment, try out new things, and talk-back to you.
2. Encourage the people you supervise to think creatively and have fun in the workplace.
3. Foster a climate in which employees at all levels treat one another as friends.
4. Support your employees by creating an attractive picture of the future and confirming their decisions and behaviors.
5. Uplift your people by applauding, rather than criticizing, their thinking and actions.
6. Communicate a culture of integrity, reliability, honesty, and trust.
7. Reveal you to be a person who enjoys tranquility and confidence in life.

The leader who meets these seven requirements need not worry about whether the leadership functions have been performed adequately. A leader who reflects these seven standards will be supported by those with whom he or she works. These are the new standards for new-age leaders. If you do these things, you will free your people from restraints of the work system, and they will love you for it.

Effects of Individual Worker Preferences

As Pogo, a somewhat famous comic strip character, observed at one time, "We have met the enemy and it is us." On occasion, workers may be their own worst enemies. Workers' preferences often place a stranglehold on their thinking, decisions, feelings, and actions—keeping them in boxes. They build their own prisons out of brick and cannot blow them down.

Beliefs, feelings, dispositions, and attributions create sets through which workers see the world and their work systems. There seem to be four sets of perceptions that have a critical effect on how employees respond to their work.

The first are employees' perceptions of how well they are performing or doing their work; these perceptions come from our beliefs about what we are doing, how we feel about it, what we are disposed to achieve, and what we think are the causes of both our successes and failures in the way we do our work. All employees would like to do better. Their performance perceptions tell them how well they are doing, and encourage or discourage them from doing better.

The second are employees' perceptions of the opportunities they have in the organization; those perceptions come from their beliefs about what they are able to do, the rewards they get, the advancements they think they ought to have, and how they feel about them, what they are disposed to try to achieve, and what they think are the causes of their successes and failures in getting opportunities. All employees want to move ahead in the organization, and opportunity perceptions are the ones that facilitate and deter them from moving ahead.

The third are employees' perceptions of the fulfillment they experience; these perceptions come from their beliefs about what the organization is doing to allow them to work uniquely, and what they think are the causes of their successes and failures in being innovative. Fulfillment perceptions give employees their views about how freely they are able to work.

The fourth are employees' perceptions of how high their aspirations are and how well those expectations have been met; those perceptions come from their beliefs about what they should get from the organization, how they are being treated, what they aspire to accomplish, and how they feel about those aspirations and expectations, and what they think are the causes of their successes and failures in achieving their expectations. Employees want more. Expectations perceptions give them their views about what they want more of and what they anticipate getting from the organization.

Effects of Negative Work Perceptions. Almost without exception, negative biases on all four sets of worker perceptions measurably impact worker productivity.

1. Negative perceptions of performance tell workers that they are incapable of doing their work at a satisfactory level, and communicate the silent message that the worker is a failure. Discontent and antagonism build to create a sullen atmosphere.

2. Negative perceptions of opportunity tell workers that they are plateaued and will not share in the benefits of being a member of the organization. Those who do not share lose; thus, workers view themselves as losers. Negative perceptions of opportunity result in losses of self-esteem, reduced commitment to the organization, passivity, and grumbling. Negative perceptions of opportunity create a mindset in others that the worker is in fact a loser.

3. Negative perceptions of fulfillment tell workers that they lack talent, have little creativity, and are slaves to the organization. This leads to doubts about the necessity to sacrifice for the organization, to work hard, and to obey the rules. Ultimately, negative perceptions of fulfillment sap all creative energies and result in a dull, lifeless person who is a prisoner of the organization.

4. Negative perceptions of expectations tell workers that they live useless, uninspired, meaningless existences. This leads to serious dissatisfactions with the organization, potentially aggressive interaction, and low morale. If other perceptions are also negative, perceptions of unmet expectations cast a dark shadow over work in the organization, resulting in a strong distaste for living and working. The organization may become abhorrent to the worker. Failed expectations are often the cause of "burnout," and can be a noxious source of virulent denunciations of the organization and the workplace.

ORGANIZATIONAL CLIMATE

Perceptions of work conditions, supervision, compensation, advancement, relationships with colleagues, organization rules, decision-making practices, and available resources comprise the organizational climate or what some call "the feel of the workplace."[23]

Organization elements do not directly create an organization's climate. For example, an organization may have many rules and regulations, but their effect on the climate depends on the workers' *perceptions* of (1) the value of the rules and (2) the activities regulated: regulations about the use of a telephone may be inhibiting whereas a rule about when work starts may be facilitating.[24]

Ultimately, a positive climate is a function of the workers' feelings that the organization trusts them and allows them the freedom to take risks; supports them and gives them responsibility in doing their jobs; openly provides accurate and adequate information about the organization; attentively listens to and gets reliable and candid information from organization members; actively consults organization members who influence decisions in the organization; and has a concern for high standards and challenging work.[25]

The climate affects both *physical exertion of the body* and *mental exertion of the mind*. A willingness to exert considerable effort on behalf of the organization is one aspect of organizational commitment,[26] along with a strong belief in the organization's values and a desire to maintain membership in the organization. In Guzley's research, participation emerged as a predictor of commitment for employees with five or more years' tenure in the organization. She reasoned that participation was of greater importance to employees who had established a sense of control over their job situation, which occurred only after they had some degree of tenure in the organization. "Once a sense of control and acceptance has been established, employees' need to feel that their communication has influence may gain importance. In fact, without a sense of such influence employees may become dissatisfied and leave the organization; that is, their organizational commitment is likely to decrease."[27] Thus, we may conclude that organizational climate affects employee turnover. A positive communication climate encourages commitment to the organization.

Changes in the work system may, conversely, have negative effects on workers' perceptions. For example, the introduction of training programs, self-directed work teams, and organization symbols may influence workers' perceptions of the organization's trust, supportiveness, or consultativeness. Self-directed work teams appear to have a variety of good effects, including the enhancement of work effort and productivity, but the best long-term effect may be the creation and maintenance of positive perceptions of the organization.

A General Strategy for Enhancing the Climate of a Workplace

Although making changes in workplaces and in organization policies are good ways to begin the process of revitalizing an organization and its workers, it is equally important to come to grips with interpersonal relationships. First, get a handle on the current communication climate. The Communication Climate Inventory (CCI), included in the Appendix, may be used for a fee to determine the general status of your organization's communication climate. With only twelve items, it doesn't take long for employees to complete. After it has been scored and analyzed, interview as many employees as possible about what needs to be done in the six areas of the CCI to enhance their workplace climate.[28]

Examine the climate from the point of view of workers. Look closely at possible constraints. That is, what keeps employees from doing what they'd like to do? What's preventing them from changing things? Do they think that management is untrustworthy or not supportive? Why do they think they are not consulted, or asked to be involved in decisions that affect them?

Second, you must be prepared to act on the information that you get from the CCI. If top management doesn't respond to the workers' concerns, they will feel that management levels are less trustworthy. Prepare a plan to tackle factors that lead to an unhealthy climate.

SUMMARY

In this chapter we described a model that classifies the major elements of an organization's work system. Five central elements were identified: the worker, the work itself, leadership practices, organization structure, and organization guidelines. In addition, we analyzed the primary consequences and effects of these five elements on organizational climate and effectiveness. This analysis lays the foundation for finding ways to avert the most serious of the negative consequences. You might consider this a catalog of the possible lethal effects of living and working in organizations.

ROUTINE, THE ILLUSION OF DYNAMISM: A CASE

Notwithstanding the negative repercussions formal organizations tend to have on workers, there are situations in which organization work can seem exhilarating. A routine can be both comforting and stimulating. Irving Stone, in his novel *The Passionate Journey*,[29] recounts just such an experience involving a young man living on the Kansas frontier, who has ambitions of becoming an artist, but at the urging of his father accepts an appointment as a fledgling photographer. He goes to the studio and learns some basic photographic processes.

Stone explains that

After a few days John became enchanted with the anesthetic of routine. The more rigidly disciplined he kept that routine, the more duties and obligations he piled into it, the more completely did it serve the purpose of absorption. Since his graduation from grammar school he had lived according to inclination: when he was hungry he ate, whether it was mealtime or cold-kitchen time; when he was tired, he slept, whether it was midday or midnight; when he was able to work, he worked for as long as he was able; when he wanted company he sought out company, regardless of whom it might contain. He had been as wide open as the Kansas prairie for every wind that might arise; winds of doubt, skepticism, despair, and that worst of all enemies, the sense of meaninglessness.

But, ah, the difference when you had to be up at six, put a tub of water on the stove for a bath, sit down with the family for breakfast at seven and walk briskly into town in order to be at the studio before eight so that you were actually working when the church chimes announced the workday; to have so many little duties on hand that it was impossible to think about yourself, the world, its spirit or its meaning because the first thing you knew it was twelve o'clock and time for lunch because there were a series of appointments starting at one. In the late afternoon there were the hours of retouching, crouched over pictures of odd-looking strangers, trying to make them look beautiful or charming so that they would order a quantity of the reproductions. The day's work over, one walked home quickly in order to sit down to supper, and the family fun of argument and debate that went on during the meal. The evening was short and fairly easy to get over with: a visit, a game of chess, an hour of music with Frances, and it was time to go to bed: for one had to be up at six in order to bathe, breakfast, walk to town and stand before Ed Vail's jewelry window, gold watch in hand, making time co-ordinate itself.

Ah, blessed anodyne! How wonderful to be free! Those who claimed that rigid routine chained a man were foolish: routine was not a chain, it was a velvet tieback.

Ah, blessed structure, blessed rules, blessed anesthetic of routine, blessed soothing comfort of the organizational anodyne.

But probe beneath that nonoffending organizational routine and you may find layers of disillusionment, frustration, confusion, fear, and meaninglessness. Comfort with the organization may be fraudulent, making us hypocrites, when we pretend to bless the organization in innocence, presenting a mask to the world that conceals our true discontent. Ah, blessed illusion. Blessed anhedonia that must be curbed to release the power of the individual, in spite of the cruel, petty, narrow consequences of the organization on each of us.

NOTES

1. Weick, Karl E. 1976. Educational Organizations as Loosely Coupled Systems. *Administrative Science Quarterly*, 21, pp. 1–19.

2. Pace, R. Wayne and Faules, Don F. 1994. *Organizational Communication*, Third Edition. Englewood Cliffs, NJ: Prentice-Hall.

3. Scott, William G. and Hart, David K.1990. *Organizational Values in America*. New Brunswick, NJ: Transaction Publishers.

4. Rosenberg, Milton J., et al. 1960. *Attitude Organization and Change*. New Haven, CT: Yale University Press.

5. Fisher, Glen. 1988. *Mindsets*. Yarmouth, ME: Intercultural Press, Inc.

6. Seligman, Martin E.P. and Schulman, Peter. 1986. Explanatory Style as a Predictor of Productivity and Quitting among Life Insurance Sales Agents. *Journal of Personality and Social Psychology*, 50, pp. 832–838.

7. Griffin, Ricky W. 1982. *Task Design: An Integrative Approach*. Glenview, IL: Scott, Foresman & Company.

8. Gibson, James L., Ivancevich, John M., and Donnelly, James H., Jr. 1991. *Organizations*. Plano, TX: Business Publications.

9. Moorhead, Gregory and Griffin, Ricky W. 1989. *Organizational Behavior*, Second Edition. Boston: Houghton Mifflin Company, p. 214.

10. Perrow, Charles B. 1967. A Framework for the Comparative Analysis of Organizations. *American Sociological Review*, April, pp. 194–208.

11. Taylor, James C. and Felten, David F. 1967. *Performance by Design*. Englewood Cliffs, NJ: Prentice-Hall.

12. Taylor, James C. 1975. The Human Side of Work: The Socio-technical Approach to Work System Design. *Personnel Review*, 4, pp. 17–22.

13. MacKenzie, R. Alex. 1969. The Management Process in 3–D. *Harvard Business Review*, November–December, pp. 80–87; Wadia, Maneck S. 1967. The Operational School of Management: An Analysis. *Advanced Management Journal*, July, pp. 26–33.

14. Mintzberg, Henry. 1973. *The Nature of Managerial Work*. New York: Harper & Row.

15. Ansoff, Igor and McDonnell, Edward. 1990. *Implanting Strategic Management*, Second Edition. Englewood Cliffs, NJ: Prentice-Hall; Tosi, Henry L., Rizzo, John R., and Carroll, Stephen J. 1990. *Managing Organizational Behavior*, Second Edition. New York: Harper & Row.

16. Robbins, Stephen P. 1989. *Organizational Behavior*, Fourth Edition. Englewood Cliffs, NJ: Prentice-Hall.

17. Robbins, Stephen P. 1987. *Organization Theory*. Second Edition. Englewood Cliffs, NJ: Prentice-Hall.

18. Stoner, James A.F. 1978. *Management*. Englewood Cliffs, NJ: Prentice-Hall.

19. Hackman, J. Richard and Oldham, Greg R. 1980. *Work Redesign*. Reading, MA: Addison-Wesley Publishing Company, p. 85.

20. Locke, Edwin A. and Latham, Gary P. 1990. *A Theory of Goal Setting and Task Performance*. Englewood Cliffs, NJ: Prentice-Hall.

21. Ibid.

22. Townley, Barbara. 1994. *Reframing Human Resource Management: Power, Ethics and the Subject at Work*. London: Sage Publications.

23. James, L.R., and Jones, A.P. 1974. Organizational Climate: A Review of Theory and Research. *Psychological Bulletin*, 81, pp. 1096–1112; Steele, Fritz and Jenks, R.S. 1977. *The Feel of the Work Place*. Reading, MA: Addison-Wesley Publishing Company.

24. Poole, Marshall Scott. 1985. Communication and Organizational Climates: Review, Critique, and a New Perspective, in Robert D. McPhee and Phillip K. Tompkins (Eds.), *Organizational Communication: Traditional Themes and New Directions*. Beverly Hills, CA: Sage Publications, pp. 79–108.

25. Redding, W. Charles. 1972. *Communication within the Organization: An Interpretive Review of Theory and Research*. New York: Industrial Communication Council, Inc.

26. McMurray, Adela J., Scott, Don, and Pace, R. Wayne. 2000. The Relationship between Organizational Commitment and Organizational Climate. *Proceedings of the Academy of Human Resource Development*. Baton Rouge, LA: Academy of Human Resource Development, March 11.

27. Guzley, Ruth M. 1992. Organizational Climate and Communication Climate. *Management Communication Quarterly*, May, pp. 379–402.

28. Mills, Gordon E., Peterson, Brent D., and Pace, R. Wayne. 1989. Comprehensive Approach to Analyzing Organizational Communication. *Analysis in Human Resource and Organization Development*. Reading, MA: Addison-Wesley, pp. 183–192, and Appendix.

29. Stone, Irving. 1969. *The Passionate Journey*. New York: Doubleday & Company, pp. 63–64.

4

Careers on Fire: The Four Basic Work Perceptions

One of the most insightful observations that has been made about human beings is that their behavior is consistent with their perceptions of a situation. Perceptions, or the sense that people make out of their lives, have a powerful impact on people. For example, research shows that people who rate themselves as being in good health tend to live longer than those with comparable actual health who rate themselves as in poor health.

It has been argued that workers' positive perceptions of the system in which they work empowers them to work more energetically than workers with negative perceptions of the system. As Kinlaw said, "If managers and supervisors are going to get the best performance from their work groups, they must consider not only the actual work environment but employees' perceptions of the workplace. Successful management requires supervisors to look beyond the real work world and adopt a perceptual model for influencing performance as well, focusing on the perceptions that have an impact on performance."[1]

FOUR WORK PERCEPTIONS

Research and experience have taught us that four basic perceptions head the critical factors that impact the decisions and actions of workers:

1. Employees' perceptions of how well their expectations are met by the organization.
2. Employees' perceptions about what kinds of opportunities are available for them in the organization.

3. Employees' perceptions of the degree of fulfillment they derive from work in the organization.

4. Employees' perceptions of their performance in the organization.

These four perceptions are shaped by key elements of the work system—other workers, the leaders, the work itself, the organizational structure, and organizational guidelines. The perceptions are specific to the work system in which individuals are located. Thus, workers may be more or less affected by different perceptions and may react differently in another work system.

When the four work perceptions are positive, they combine to create dynamism. If any one of the perceptions turns out to be negative or disappears for some reason, the overall sense of enthusiasm diminishes. But when the four work perceptions are positive, workers complete their tasks with disciplined energy. Four empowering perceptions described in the research of Thomas and Velthouse appear to share components similar to the ones we have discussed, leading to the conclusion that empowerment, as they talk about it, and dynamism stem from the same perceptual bases.[2]

The way these perceptions vitalize individuals in the workplace follows this general line of analysis. At the beginning of our careers, we have a set of expectations rooted in a series of perceived promises. These promises are assurances—real or imagined—that someone or something (often the organization) will give us or help us accomplish something in the future. Employment itself is a form of promise. When we get a job, the assumption is tentatively established that the future may turn out the way we imagined it. Continued employment reinforces the promise. Advancement on the job enables us to confirm that the promises underlying the agreement of employment are being fulfilled. If things go well, we become confident that the promises were sincere. Although some occasional setbacks may occur, a career that progresses systematically appears to be based on sincere promises.

Expectations

Most of us start working with the anticipation that our work will lead to continued advances. Reid and Evans have observed, for example, that "people begin their careers hopeful that they will be continually promoted."[3] As we spend time in organizations, kept and unkept promises lead to met and upset expectations. One major factor that reveals work vitality is a person's reactions to how well his or her expectations have been met by the organization.

Hellriegel, Slocum, and Woodman suggest that "burnout" among professional employees is associated with having "unrealistic expectations concerning their work and their ability to accomplish desired goals, given the nature of the situation in which they find themselves."[4]

Expectations create aspirations for what should happen to a person at work. They develop from real or imagined promises imputed to the organization about what will happen in the future as part of their association with the organization. For example, if the workforce is composed of highly trained individuals who have devoted many years to preparing for work in the organization, they may bring with them anticipations about the work they are to do, how they are to be treated, what the organization will provide, and what the proper role of the organization in society is.

Anhedonia in an employee's work life is, in part, a failure to match expectations with realities. Niniger found that the satisfaction levels of employees whose expectations had been met were significantly higher than the satisfaction levels of those whose expectations were not met.[5]

Employees who perceive that their expectations are based on failed promises tend to became disillusioned. Eventually, an organization where expectations are viewed as not being met may experience seething unrest, potentially aggressive interaction, and low morale.

Fulfillment

One of the reasons why unmet expectations lead to such negative consequences on employees is the keen sense that failed expectations are a sign of an unfulfilled life. Fulfilled lives are those in which people do things their way. Fulfilled employees feel successful in doing what they want to in ways that they choose.

Peter Drucker wrote that "work appears as something unnatural, a disagreeable, meaningless and stultifying condition of getting the pay check, devoid of dignity as well as of importance. No wonder that this puts a premium on slovenly work, on slowdowns, and on other tricks to get the same pay check with less work. No wonder that results in an unhappy and discontented worker—because a pay check is not enough to base one's self-respect on."[6]

Fulfillment at work since 1946 does not appear to have changed much. Macleod, for example, reported that many employees

think of the work place in ways that are remarkably analogous to the way one might describe a prison. It is a place that they tolerate only because they feel they are compelled to. They "escape" at quitting time, on weekends, for vacations—and ultimately, when they retire. Many, including some in highly paid professional and executive positions, would ruefully admit that the term "wage slave" describes them all too accurately.

Macleod empathetically suggests that "prison inmates surely tend to think that their only chance for happiness and satisfaction is 'on the outside.' ... Many employees (including professionals and executives) seem to look upon their time on the job in much the same way. They watch the clock, they daydream, they expect little satisfaction on the job."

Macleod raises some relevant questions: "Is it any wonder that full job involvement and satisfaction is the exception instead of the rule? And is it any wonder that productivity, effectiveness, and efficiency are so much less than they could be?" She articulates our argument when she says that organizations and employees must find ways to achieve fulfillment, "not only for their own sake but also for the sake of better working effectiveness, productivity, and corporate success."[7]

So far two key indicators of work dynamism have been discussed: expectations and fulfillment. Two other indicators of work dynamism are equally important: opportunity and performance.

Opportunity

Opportunity represents a situation or condition favorable for the attainment of a goal. If you are employed in an organization where few conditions are favorable for you to achieve a goal, you will no doubt say that you lack opportunity. But, if you think, for example, that conditions are favorable for you to receive a promotion or a salary increase, you will tend to feel that you have opportunity in the organization. Employees feel enthusiastic about their work if they perceive themselves eligible for and able to advance themselves and their status in the organization.

For opportunities to exist, employees must be able to achieve their goals. Abel found, for example, that to fill a position successfully in the organization that he was studying, it was necessary for prospective applicants to meet certain norms and exhibit particular stylistic tendencies. Employees who understood and displayed the styles and met the norms were more likely to be promoted. Individuals promoted to top positions in the organization had styles that showed self-confidence, cheerfulness, boldness, and independence. Employees unable to display appropriate styles were not likely to be promoted.[8]

Employees appear to be able to discern when they have opportunities in an organization and when they do not. Managers also tend to recognize when an employee meets critical conditions and has opportunity in the organization. In our research, one of the most consistent predictors of promotion and salary increases was the manager's evaluation of the employee's opportunities in the organization, not how well the employee was actually performing. Employees nearly always reported having opportunity to the same degree perceived by their managers.

Opportunity may be the most powerful of the four perceptions, since it has such potentially devastating consequences when not present. To demonstrate how critical perceived opportunity is in the life of an employee, let us highlight five opportunity-affected categories of behavior identified by other researchers.[9]

Self-Esteem. Everyone is susceptible to the reflected image gained from others. Those who receive positive comments and rewards come to value themselves more highly. Those who feel locked into repetitious tasks or seem invisible to others gradually lose self-esteem. For example, employees in their mid-forties who have been passed over for promotion often become highly self-critical and lose confidence in the skills they once proudly displayed. What has changed, usually, is not their skillfulness, but their perceptions of opportunity.

Aspirations. Opportunity also affects an employee's aspirations. If the organization rewards actions that support certain types of goals, employees tend to develop aspirations to reach those goals. Employees who have been stuck in one position for a long time tend to curtail any initial aspirations. In the absence of such aspirations, they fail to see themselves in any other position. If a new position is eventually offered to them, they respond negatively because they have lost the internal vision of themselves that matches the new opportunity. Employees who consistently experience little or no opportunity gradually suppress any larger vision of their potential and represent themselves to others as tentative, self-doubting, and content to stay where they are.

Commitment. Opportunity also affects employees' commitment to the organization. Those who experience opportunity through personal growth and recognition tend to feed their positive feelings back to the organization. They become motivated to do more. Those who receive negative feedback gradually withdraw from the organization. The withdrawal may be subtle in that they continue to do what is asked but at minimally acceptable levels, or they may transfer their energy to some other organization or activity where the response is more positive.

Energy. Employees with blocked opportunity tend to turn to their peers for comfort and recognition. The recognition obtained from friends may have less to do with how well they perform their jobs at work and more to do with how skilled they are in sports, recipes, or gardening. They may devote more energy to contacts and information exchange on tangential activities and less energy to the work itself. Employees who see high opportunity respond to recognition focusing on the task and wasting less time in interactions not related to their work.

Problem Solving. Employees with high opportunity tend to proactively address problems in the organization. If they recognize or identify a potential problem, they act on their own initiative to solve it. For the person without opportunity, organizational problems reflect a personal discontent. Instead of acting to resolve problems, they tend to wait passively and grumble. If someone suggests a solution, they are the first to criticize it. Since their own life in the organization has been primarily negative, they may even derive some satisfaction from seeing the organization in trouble.

Performance

The fourth set of work perceptions has to with an employee's performance. Employees' perceptions of their performance focus on how well they think they are doing their work. Others have called these perceptions "self-efficacy" or just plain "self-confidence."[10] Two types of work tasks encompass the critical elements of job performance: functional tasks and behavioral tasks. The first has to do with how well an employee completes technical aspects of the job The second has to do with how well the employee handles interpersonal activities, including resolving conflicts, managing time, motivating others, working with a group, and working independently.

Gilbert has framed the issue of worker performance perceptions: "When we set about to engineer performance, we should view it in a context of value. We should not train someone to do something differently unless we place a value on the consequence—unless we see that consequence as a valuable accomplishment." He concludes with this aphorism: "Roughly speaking, competent people are those who can create valuable results without using excessively costly behavior."[11]

When workers feel unable to perform their work competently, that is, when they perceive themselves doing work that does not create valuable results but consumes time, energy, and resources, they feel frustrated. They diminish the vigor with which they approach their work.

Maintaining positive work perceptions require continuous acts of courage. As Herman observed, "a thoughtful examination of the day-to-day workings of organizations will quickly reveal that at all levels, an important determinant of organization performance is the thoughts and actions of individual people. Whether it is a chief executive assuming the risk and responsibility for pursuing a new acquisition, a middle manager making a full commitment to adopting employee-involvement groups in her division, an individual contributor doggedly following through on a technological inspiration, or an hourly employee sacrificing his free time in order to train and qualify for a new job, acts of individual courage count."[12]

We have often summarized the four key work perceptions in two different ways: as the acronym POFE (pronounced *pofay*) and as goals to be achieved in an organization. Performance is translated as the goal Do Better; opportunity represents the goal Move Ahead; fulfillment concerns the goal Work Free; and expectations lead to the goal Want More.

P = Do Better

O = Move Ahead

F = Work Free

E = Want More

Those are the code words of work perceptions. They are important in understanding why anhedonia sets in and why dynamism occurs.

CAREERS ON FIRE: THE JOE METAPHOR

In Lerner and Loew's famous musical *Paint Your Wagon*, the haunting song "They Call the Wind Maria" begins with a reference to the elements' names in the plains: "Away out here they got a name for wind and rain and fire. The rain is Tess, the fire is Joe, and they call the wind Maria."

Light Your Fire!

Joe, the fire, is often used as a metaphor to describe how people work in organizations: "If that person only had a spark," we say, or "He or she should get burning." When an employee makes a sudden move forward in the organization, we say that "there is a person who has flared up." Employees who are consistently good performers are often called "people who burn brightly." In Kaye's analysis of types of employees, she explains that productively plateaued employees are those who are recognized and appreciated, but "their fires need to be kept lit."[13]

The fire metaphor is accurate for both the virility of disciplined energy and the violence of unrestrained devastation. Each year, wildfires, leaving black and barren hillsides, ravage areas of the Western United States. Although most major fires are usually in remote locations, the summer of 1993 witnessed several relatively small fires consume grass and trees on the foothills and mountains of Central Utah's Wasatch range. Some wayward fireworks ignited a blaze in a small canyon east of our residence. Through a pair of binoculars we watched the smoke and flames as the fire lurched up embankments, poised on the end of a precipice, then leaped ravines to consume grass and trees.

In the evening, the fire glowed across the entire mountain. We were entranced by the flickering streams of light poised on the farthest peaks of the rocky terrain. The still, majestic mountain held the flames high in the sky with a dynamic salute.

Prescribed Fire Metaphor

People's work lives are something like *prescribed fires*. They are planned to achieve particular goals, but they are also affected by factors over which they have little control; however, if handled well, workers, like the prescribed fire, contribute to the health of the environment. People acquire a brightness that makes their lives more exciting when they too burn brightly.

To apply fire to a forest in a skillful manner requires an understanding of fire behavior. To skillfully maximize employee excitement requires an understanding of the factors of dynamism. A conceptual model of the fire metaphor yields eight general types of workers (see Figures 4.1 and 4.2).

Types of workers are defined by their positions on three of the work perceptions: expectations, fulfillment, and performance. Career levels are defined by perceptions of opportunity; the lowest career levels represent workers who lack opportunity in the workplace. The highest career levels include workers who have opportunity. Workers with either low or high levels of opportunity may have similar perceptions regarding expectations, fulfillment, and performance. For example, smoldering careers are characterized by low performance perceptions, low fulfillment perceptions, low expectations perceptions, and low perceptions of opportunity. Blazing careers are characterized by low performance perceptions, low fulfillment perceptions, and low expectations perceptions, but high opportunity perceptions.

Workers at flaming and raging career levels share similar perceptions of performance, fulfillment, and expectations, but differ on perceptions of opportunity. Workers with flickering and billowing careers differ only in terms of low and high perceptions of opportunity. Finally, workers at flaring and flashing levels differ primarily in terms of high and low perceptions of opportunity.

As useful as prescribed fire is in accomplishing forest management objectives, it can also contribute to air pollution. Perceptions are much the same in organizations; worker perceptions contribute to the accomplishment of personal and organizational objectives, but they may also have some occasional undesirable consequences. When differences in perceptions occur among workers, some workers do more, some workers move out, and some workers move down.

Negative effects are handled best when POFE perceptions are understood, when colleagues and managers are informed and supportive, and when plans to counteract the negative effects are available. Appropriately cultivated work perceptions equal positive dynamism that makes good workers and organizations. Managers often dump retardant on workers whose careers are blazing. Other workers whose careers are flickering have buckets of water thrown on them, while still other workers whose careers are just smoldering tinder are fanned until a full flame appears. Great supervisors set workers on fire, but a few great employees run the risk of burning out too soon.

Prescribed fires are affected by several elements: wind, moisture, air mass stability, and firing techniques.[14]

A worker's expectations and aspirations are represented by the wind, which blows and activates workers. As the wind fans a fire, so expectations fan a person's aspirations.

A worker's fulfillment and freedom are represented by moisture; moisture controls the rate of burn or the strength of one's dynamism. When

Figure 4.1
Lowest Level: Smoldering, Flickering, Flaring, and Flaming

Flaring

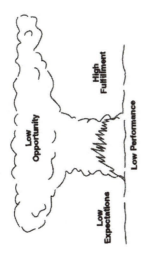

High Expectations — Low Opportunity — Low Fulfillment

High Performance

Flickering

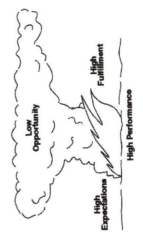

Low Expectations — Low Opportunity — High Fulfillment

Low Performance

Smoldering

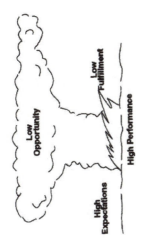

Low Expectations — Low Opportunity — Low Fulfillment

Low Performance

Flaming

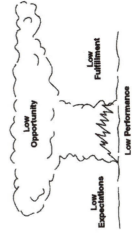

High Expectations — Low Opportunity — High Fulfillment

High Performance

Figure 4.2
Highest Level: Blazing, Billowing, Flashing, and Raging

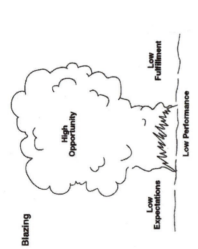

Blazing

High
Opportunity

Low
Expectations

Low
Fulfillment

Low Performance

Billowing

High
Opportunity

Low
Expectations

Low
Fulfillment

High Performance

Flashing

High
Opportunity

High
Expectations

Low
Fulfillment

High Performance

Raging

High
Opportunity

High
Expectations

High
Fulfillment

High Performance

moisture is too high, fires tend to burn slowly and irregularly, resulting in incomplete burns that don't meet the desired objectives. Too little moisture may allow a fire to burn out of control. In like manner, the right amount of fulfillment keeps an employee enthusiastic, whereas too little moisture may lead to burnout and too much moisture may dampen the fire.

A worker's opportunity and sense of moving ahead are represented by air mass stability, which affects the strength of convective activity or upward movement. Strong convective activity increases indrafts and results in erratic fire behavior. Stable air mass tends to control convective activity and produce more uniform burning conditions. Heavy air mass smothers convection, causing poor burning conditions. Lack of opportunity, like an excessively stable air mass, results in little upward activity and some discomfort; when the right amount of instability is present, enthusiasm builds, prospects become brighter, but upward movement may occur too rapidly, resulting in erratic behaviors and instability in the worker's life.

Firing techniques, or how fires are started and the actions that nurture the fire to keep it alive and burning, represent a worker's performance and desire to do well. Firing techniques are important. Fires move either in the same direction as the wind (head fire), in the opposite direction to the wind (back fire), or at a right angle to the wind (flank fire). When fires are started against the wind (back fire), different methods are used to get the fire started and to keep it active than when fires are started with the wind (head fire).

A worker's performance must likewise be fired up. Some workers have head fires that impel them to move in fast, intensive, wide areas of influence. They seem driven by powerful winds. Those workers may not need to be fired up very often. Their actions may depend upon and be affected by the wind (how expectations are met), by the moisture (how fulfilling work circumstances are), and by the air mass stability (whether conditions are appropriate for rapid upward advancement).

Other workers may need to have their careers fired up in different ways. Remember that firing techniques can only be as effective as the conditions allow, and may be aided or deterred by the effectiveness of those who are seeking to enhance and sustain dynamism in the organization.

CAREER PLATEAUING: A DYNAMISM EXPLANATION

For more than fifteen years, a more than casual interest has been exhibited in the phenomenon known as plateauing.[15] Epithets such as managerial malaise, topping out, burned out, stomped on and passed over, and peaked have been used to characterize workers who no longer have much opportunity (promotions, bonuses, additional responsibility, and increased recognition that lead to prestige and expanded reputations) at work. In other words, the air mass has become too stable for them and they are restricted, limited, and polluted.

Three causes of plateauing have been described in the literature: (1) the structure of the organization, (2) weak desires for mobility, and (3) substandard performance. Most models of plateauing, however, use only two variables: performance and potential for advancement (promotion). This results in a 2×2 matrix with four cells showing four types of employees: Stars, who are high on both performance and potential for advancement; Deadwoods, who are low on both performance and potential for advancement; Comers or Learners, who are low on performance but high on potential for advancement; and Solid Citizens, who are high on performance and low on potential for advancement (Figure 4.3). Solid Citizens and Deadwood are types of plateaued employees, one effective and the other ineffective; Stars and Learners are nonplateaued employees who differ in levels of performance.

In an effort to determine the extent to which plateaued and nonplateaued employees differed regarding performance ratings, we divided a sample of employees into two groups, based on promotion data—those who had received one or more promotions, whom we called nonplateaued, and those who had not received a promotion while with the company, whom we called plateaued. The bosses of the employees rated their levels of performance on a seven-point scale, with seven being high performance. We attempted to determine whether the employees who had high performance ratings had been promoted and whether the employees who had low performance ratings had not been promoted. Amazingly, the results were not statistically significant. In other words, it was just about as likely that a plateaued employee had a high performance rating as a nonplateaued employee. Poor performers were promoted about as often as high performers.

We also secured ratings from the bosses on what they thought the employees' opportunities were for advancement in the organization. In this division, we *were* able to distinguish between the plateaued and the nonplateaued employees. That is, workers rated high on opportunity received promotions regardless of their performance. More interestingly, we could also tell the difference between the two groups of employees on the basis of self-perceptions of opportunity. High-opportunity workers seem aware of

Figure 4.3
Model of Plateauing

		Performance	
		High	**Low**
Potential for Advancement	**High**	Stars	Learners
	Low	Solid Citizens	Dead Wood

their image and rate themselves as having high opportunity; low-opportunity workers rate themselves as such.

A Work Perceptions Profile (Appendix) was created to get a measure of the four work perceptions. Scores on the WPP were combined to arrive at a single index score for the four variables. We were able to distinguish between plateaued and nonplateaued employees, at a level of statistical significance beyond the 0.01 level of confidence, using the index score. Thus, high index scores were associated with nonplateaued employees and low index scores were associated with plateaued employees. Even though the scores differentiated between plateaued and nonplateaued employees at a statistically significant level, several other categories of employees began to emerge. The result was the creation of a new model of workers in organizations that we call POFE.

The POFE Career Model suggests that the traditional categories of employees (Stars, Deadwoods, Solid Citizens, and Learners) actually occupy different levels of opportunity that affect their work differently. A matrix developed from the four variables results in a two-level model of four categories each or a total of eight types of employees (Figure 4.4).

Performance, fulfillment, and expectations tend to determine the size of the blocks that represent a worker's life in the organization. High expectations, fulfillment, and performance create blocks of dynamism that are high, wide, and deep. Opportunity, a critical variable, drives a worker's movement upward in the organization. If perceptions of high opportunity are added to perceptions of high expectations, high fulfillment, and high performance, the result is an organizational Star, a high performer who is not plateaued. A worker is plateaued only when he or she has low opportunity.

Plateaued employees lack opportunity in the organization. For some, opportunity is lost gradually. Others are struck suddenly and forcefully with the awareness that something is not happening on the job. The new assignment does not come through. The promotion is delayed and eventually shelved. The excitement of going to meetings wears off. Pay raises seem to be leveling off. The feeling develops that nothing of significance is happening in the work unit. The worker is in the same job for a much longer time than he or she ever thought possible. The worker gets anxious, concerned, defensive, and bored at irregular intervals. The worker realizes that his or her work life has hit an excruciatingly low level of inactivity.

The scenario goes something like this: Although you work hard at what you are doing, the results you get are not the same as in the past; they are too routine. You say to yourself that you have been "passed over." Before long, you catch yourself thinking that the better assignments are going to other people, which verifies the feeling that you are *actually* passed over. Then, you are criticized for some small irregularity. Soon, you think, "I'm being stomped on," and every comment or slight supports those thoughts. Gradually, you find yourself thinking, "Well, if that's what's happening, I'm not

Figure 4.4
POFE Career Model

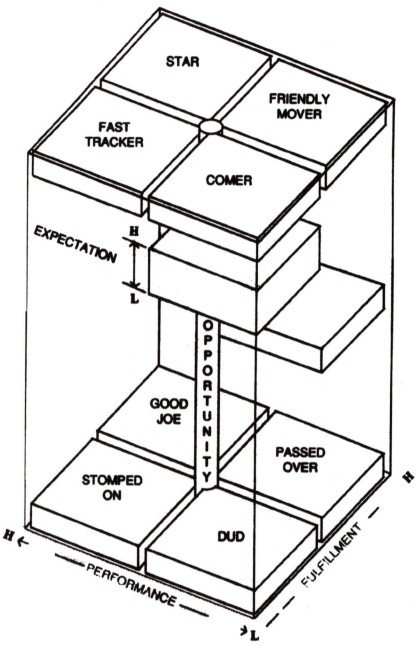

going to do anything." At that point, you withdraw and find that you are in fact a dud—with little opportunity, little fulfillment, unmet expectations, and low performance.

The story of employees dropping from comer to dud, from friendly mover to passed over, from fast tracker to stomped on, and from star to good Joe is all too common. On occasion, we see a spurt from someone who has been passed over but who receives some small opportunity and becomes a friendly mover. The good Joe is given an opening and shows some of the signs of greatness associated with the star, but then drifts back down the opportunity power line. The fast tracker who gets stomped on for trying to move toward star too soon is also another tale of sadness and sorrow.

Some support for this dual-level model of employee work life is found in Kaye's model of plateaued employees.[16] Four types of plateaued employees are identified: productively plateaued (Good Joe), passively plateaued (Dud), pleasantly plateaued (Stomped On), and partially plateaued (Passed Over). Because Kaye's model deals only with plateaued employees and not with the full range of employees, the model does not provide an analysis of so-called nonplateaued employees. Nevertheless, Kaye's description of productively plateaued employees says that they are doers who see possibilities for themselves, whose contributions are recognized and appreciated, and who feel strong loyalties to the organization, but "their fires need to be kept lit." This seems to imply that the difference between plateaued and nonplateaued employees is their level of dynamism and vitality.

The Work Perceptions Profile (Appendix) provides a reliable and valid measure of an employee's patterns of plateauing, one symptom of lack of dynamism. Plateauing may be both a consequence and a cause of dynamism problems. It is through solving the dynamism problem that employees become empowered to contribute more successfully to the organization.

SUMMARY

In this chapter, we elaborated on the four work perceptions—performance, opportunity, fulfillment, and opportunity—that contribute "fire" to an employee's career. The "fire" metaphor, Joe, was described and applied to understanding career "plateauing." Models of eight types of careers were analyzed. The Work Perceptions Profile was introduced as a measure of dynamism in the career of an employee.

NOTES

1. Kinlaw, D.C. 1988. What Employees "See" Is What Organizations "Get." *Management Solutions*. 41, pp. 38–42.

2. Thomas, K.W. and Velthouse, B.A. 1990. Cognitive Elements of Empowerment. *Academy of Management Review*. 15, pp. 666–681.

3. Reid, R.D. and Evans, M.R. 1983. The Career Plateau: What to Do When a Career Bogs Down. *Cornell Hotel and Restaurant Administration Quarterly.* 24 (August), pp. 83–91.

4. Hellriegel, Don, Slocum, John C., and Woodman, Richard W. 1986. *Organizational Behavior*, Fourth Edition. St. Paul, MN: West Publishing Company.

5. Niniger, James R. 1970. College Graduate Turnover in Industry: A Study of the Role of Expectations in Decisions to Terminate or Continue Participation in One Organization. Unpublished doctoral dissertation, University of Michigan.

6. Drucker, P.F. 1946. *Concept of the Corporation.* New York: The John Day Company.

7. Macleod, J.S. 1985. The Work Place as Prison. *Employment Relations Today*, Autumn, pp. 215–218.

8. Abel, K.R. 1971. Sensitivity to Workrole-Related Expectations and Perceived Promotability. Unpublished doctoral dissertation, University of California, Los Angeles.

9. Kanter, R.M. 1976. The Job Makes the Person. *Psychology Today*, May; Wheatley, M. 1981. The Impact of Organizational Structure on Issues of Sex Equity in Educational Policy and Management, in P.A. Schumck and W.W. Charters, Jr. (Eds.), *The Sex Dimension in Educational Policy and Management.* San Francisco: Academic Press.

10. Bandura, A. 1977. Self-Efficacy: Toward a Unifying Theory of Behavioral Change. *Psychological Review*, 84, pp. 191–215; Druckman, D. and Bjork, R.A. (Eds.). 1994. *Learning, Remembering, Believing: Enhancing Human Performance.* Washington, DC: National Academy of Sciences.

11. Gilbert, T.F. 1978. *Human Competence.* New York: McGraw-Hill Book Company.

12. Herman, S.M. 1990. Lost in the System. *Organization Development Journal*, Spring, pp. 3–19.

13. Kaye, Beverly. 1990. Categories of Plateaued Employees. *Training and Development Journal*, pp. 30–31.

14. Mobley, Hugh E., Jackson, Robert S., Balmer, William E., Ruziska, Wayne E., and Hough, Walter A. 1973. *A Guide for Prescribed Fire in Southern Forests.* Atlanta, GA: U.S. Department of Agriculture, Forest Service.

15. Warren, E.K., Ferrence, T.P., and Stoner, J.A. 1975. The Case of the Plateaued Performer. *Harvard Business Review*, 53 (1), pp. 30–38, 146–148.

16. Kaye. Categories of Plateaued Employees.

5

Natural Work Goals: The Release Valves

Most people familiar with motivation practices grimly admit that our strategies for motivating employees are often not particularly effective in the short run, and are even more ineffective in the long run. Efforts to sustain motivation have been equally ineffective. No system has been designed that compels workers to perform in outstanding ways. The literature on motivation is so extensive that it is almost intimidating. Nevertheless, there is agreement on some basic assumptions about motivation.

MOTIVATION

One assumption on which most people agree is that motivation has to do with the reasons why people take action. The question "What motivated that action?" asks about the causes of a person's actions. Something that causes action is called a *motive*. In the criminal justice system, prosecutors look for motives to explain why someone committed a crime. The term *motivation* has to do with what "causes" people to take action.

The term *cause* has been adopted to describe the way in which a phenomenon influences action that follows it. The concept of cause has, at its core, the idea of some form of force. Gravitation is associated with cause. What causes things to stay on the earth when the earth is rotating at a tremendous speed? Why do things that are thrown away from the earth come back down? They are caused or pulled by gravitational force to come down.

The connection between gravity as a force and motive as a force is as irrevocable as the sunrise. Brownowski asserts that the whole tradition of causality derives from the triumph of the law of gravitation. He explains that "when Newton brought in force as a cause, he was giving matter the human property of effort."[1] For a boulder to move, for example, some form of force must be applied to it. The essence of cause and effect is their sequence; cause must come before and effect must come after.

Cause or motive, in the Newtonian sense, is absolute and deterministic. That is, to be a cause, something must always precede that which is the effect. In motivation theory, the motive must exercise a definite and constant force on the human being. At least two quite different views of why people behave have been developed by experts.

Needs or Deficiency Causes of Behavior

The needs theory of motivation is one explanation for why people behave. It postulates that people have needs inside of them that cause behaviors. Needs are part of a person's genetic structure. People are born with needs. Thus, needs theory is a fundamental way of explaining why people behave. A need is "something" that must be responded to. Needs theorists hypothesize that "needs" come from our genetic structure, but tend to decay, leaving so-called "unfilled needs." All behaviors are responses to empty or unsatisfied needs. In fact, it has been said that satisfied needs are not motivating. The process of satisfying deficient needs leads to action. Your behavior can be explained by identifying the deficient needs that caused your actions.

Goals and Choices as Influences on Behavior

Another explanation for why people behave is called a goals or expectations and choices theory of motivation, which postulates that people believe that if they behave in a particular way, they will achieve certain goals. Choice theory argues that people make choices in seeking to achieve goals. Thus, a person chooses to act when he or she believes that a particular behavior will lead to some reachable, desired outcome. Outcomes must have a positive value to the person and it must be achievable by the effort the person is willing to exert.

The choices theory of motivation embraces the concept of perception, since the key questions people must answer when making choices are (1) whether they have the talent to achieve the goal, (2) whether the goal is valuable enough to justify expending adequate energy to achieve it, and (3) whether the goal can actually be achieved.

In choosing whether to adopt a needs approach or a choices approach to the concept of motivation and the enhancement of dynamism, you may be influenced by other beliefs, such as whether you believe people's lives are determined in advance by genetics, or whether you believe that people have the agency to make their own choices and decisions. In this book, a choices approach to human behavior has been adopted.

Satisfaction, Motivation, Vitalization

We must resolve one additional issue before directly examining the main topic of this chapter. We must draw distinctions among three key concepts that affect human behavior: satisfaction, motivation, and vitalization.

From Coercion to Satisfaction

Herzberg argued that a distinction ought to be drawn between factors that "satisfy" workers (create a sense of equitableness or fairness in a situation) and factors that "dissatisfy" workers (create a sense of injustice). He proposed two scales that rate employee reactions to the workplace. The "motivators scale" reports the extent to which employees are satisfied or not dissatisfied and the "hygiene" scale reports the extent to which employees are dissatisfied or not satisfied.[2]

Not Dissatisfied   Satisfied   [motivators scale]

1   2   3   4   5   6   7

Not Satisfied   Dissatisfied   [hygiene scale]

1   2   3   4   5   6   7

The theory suggests that satisfaction and dissatisfaction are on separate continuua. This means that a worker can be both satisfied and dissatisfied at the same time, or a worker may also be not satisfied and not dissatisfied at the same time, or dissatisfied and not dissatisfied at the same time.

Since Herzberg's motivator-hygiene theory is a needs-based theory, it relies on the concept of need deficiencies in formulating a definition of satisfaction and dissatisfaction. Satisfaction means that a person's needs are not deficient; hence the needs are not active as stimulators of action. In other words, satisfied needs are not motivators. We assume that needs not satisfied would be the closest to what we traditionally consider motivators in a needs theory of motivation.

Although the not dissatisfied–satisfied continuum is referred to as the motivators scale, it becomes clear that neither scale leads to motivated workers. In fact, the clearer conclusion is that the not dissatisfied–satisfied scale has to do with being placated and gratified, states that lead to *lethargy* rather than motivation. The term *motivation* clearly does not apply to situations in which workers are satisfied. A wide range of researchers have attempted without success to demonstrate that employee feelings of job satisfaction are motivating and result in higher levels of performance.

On the other hand, the not satisfied–dissatisfied scale is about being discouraged, disappointed, and aggravated, conditions not conducive to motivated behavior. In fact, it is much more likely that dissatisfied or even not satisfied workers are more likely to leave the organization or to be a bit disruptive than they are to be motivated.

Thus, we interpret Herzberg's scales to mean that workers who are satisfied are more likely to experience happiness and apathy than motivated behavior. Satisfaction and motivation are expressed in very different behaviors. *Satisfaction does NOT lead employees to increase physical effort or mental energy!*

Workers who are dissatisfied are more likely to feel unhappy and distressed. Such states do not characterize motivated workers. Thus, neither of Herzberg's concepts seems totally compatible with the idea of motivation. It is important that we not think of satisfaction factors as those that motivate worker behaviors. Motivation should be talked about in terms of factors that serve to "force" people to behave in certain, specific ways.

From Satisfaction to Motivation

The concept of motivation is closely associated with behavioral theories of organization that emerged in response to the more coercive bureaucratic form of organizing. Chester Barnard articulated a human systems theory of organizations, suggesting that organizations are people systems and not mechanically engineered structures. Barnard maintained that authority (a causative force) was a function of the willingness of subordinates to "go along."[3] Thus, we might say that motivated workers are those who can find no reason to resist the suggestions of their managers and co-workers.

Barnard felt that many persuasive messages were actually designed to widen a worker's "zone of indifference," or willingness to go along. Indifference in this setting meant a lack of resistance to following orders. Thus, if workers willingly go along with a manager's requests, they would be considered motivated. Under those conditions, motivation is portrayed on a scale indicating the extent to which employees willingly follow the directions of their managers. On the "willingness" or motivation scale, low scores (toward "1") indicate that employees are unwilling to achieve organizational goals (unmotivated), and high scores (toward "7") indicate that employees are willing to achieve organizational goals (are motivated).

```
Unwilling          Willing      [Motivation Scale]
     1  2  3  4  5  6  7
```

Highly motivated workers are those most willing to complete their work as instructed. Motivation, or the willingness to work harder, may come from striving to satisfy needs, such as respect and well-being. If employees have unsatisfied needs, the argument goes, they are willing to work harder if they can see ways in which their work assignments allow them to satisfy their needs. But, once the needs are satisfied, they no longer serve as motivators.

So, to motivate employees, find their unsatisfied needs and then provide opportunities for them to strive to satisfy them. Or, if employees have too many satisfied needs, the only alternative is to create situations in which their needs are not satisfied. This seems like an unnecessarily negative approach to enticing employees to go along with you.

From Motivation to Vitalization

If you wanted workers to move beyond being motivated, to being enthusiastic and highly animated about working and doing things, you would have to approach the entire work system differently. If you wanted workers who take the initiative to find and solve problems and to have the urge to do what's right and needed rather than to do only what they are assigned, you would be looking for workers who are more than motivated; they must be vitalized.

The shift from thinking about how to motivate workers to thinking about how to vitalize workers requires the adoption of a new paradigm or mindset. The difference between "motivation" and "vitalization" is, on the surface, one of degree; vitalized workers are workers who are highly motivated. However, the shift from motivation to vitalization requires a different way of thinking about people.

Motivation has to do with directing people's efforts, but vitalization has to do with releasing people's energy. The difference between motivation and vitalization is like the difference between a photograph and a hologram. A photograph is a one-dimensional representation of a dynamic person, object, or event, whereas a hologram is a three-dimensional representation. A hologram is even more than a three-dimensional picture; holograms contain all the elements of the picture in each of the smallest parts of the hologram. That means that you can take the hologram apart and still see the entire picture in one of the small parts. Holograms allow one to see all sides of an object on what is ostensibly a flat surface. Holograms and vitalization are concepts for the next generation of managers. Vitalization, like a hologram, represents dynamic people in three-dimensional space and contains all of the elements that release people to work with dynamism by marshaling their resources and using them with freely given energy.

A dynamism mindset requires us to think of people in terms of that which is quintessentially human about human beings—the ability of people to imagine things being different from what they are, to project thoughts backward and forward in time, and to further their own happiness and well-being. People can study themselves and regulate their own consciousness. Korzybski called this the "time-binding" capacity of human beings.[4]

Bois extended the concept of time binding when he wrote:

Progress is not an additive affair; it goes by cycles that increase their outputs in geometrical progression. The shorter the interval between cycles, the faster the total advance within a definite period of years. We don't know how fast the new nations will reach a level of development that is comparable to ours. Complete dedication to creating a new order of things may advance them far ahead of us. Instead of the algebraic formula of time-binding . . . , we could use an alternative formulation and say *that the capacity to invent is the characteristic of Homo sapiens*. This means that a fully functioning human being sees tradition not as something to preserve in a static form but as something to exploit, something like the humus formed by fallen leaves, which facilitates the growth of new crops.[5]

Korzybski, commenting on this natural human capacity to invent and progress, articulates these fundamental concepts with enthusiasm: "Humans are, unlike animals, naturally qualified not only to progress, but to progress more and more rapidly, with an always accelerating acceleration, as the generations pass. Whatever squares with that law of time-binding is right and makes for human weal; whatever contravenes it is wrong and makes for human woe."[6]

Keyser reinforces the claim that human beings are naturally time binders: "Though we humans are not a species of animal, we are natural beings: it is as natural for humans to bind time as it is for fish to swim, for birds to fly, for plants to live after the manner of plants. It is as natural for human beings to make things as it is natural for animals *not* to do so. This fact is fundamental. Another one, also fundamental, is this: the time-binding faculty—the characteristic of humanity—is not an effect of civilization but its cause; it is not civilized energy, it is the energy that *civilizes*; it is not a product of wealth, whether material or spiritual wealth, but . . . the creator of wealth, both material and spiritual."[7]

Dynamism is a manifestation of the natural endowment of human beings as time binders. Dynamism and vitalization assume a more dignified and elevated role than motivation in understanding the choices that people make and what it is that frees them for greatness. Human beings are the creators of their own existence. They are creators of both material and spiritual wealth. As such, they must be understood not as pawns to be manipulated and motivated, but as the vessels of civilizing energy.

Differences among Satisfiers, Motivators, and Vitalizers

Can people actually distinguish among the work conditions leading to satisfaction, motivation, and vitalization? Our experience is that they can. We developed an instrument to determine to what extent workers can differentiate among things that satisfy them, motivate them, and vitalize them.

The survey, called Distinguishing among Satisfiers, Motivators, and Vitalizers, can determine the extent to which your distinctions are consistent with the Key. Give it a try to see for yourself.

Distinguishing among Satisfiers, Motivators, and Vitalizers

A factors *satisfy*. These factors tend to make you contented and pleased. To be satisfied means that you are comfortable and contented with where you are working and what you are doing.

B factors *motivate*. These factors tend to stimulate you to take some action. To be motivated means that you are provoked.

C factors *vitalize*. These factors tend to release your enthusiasm and invigorate you. To be vitalized means that you are excited, thrilled, and highly animated about working.

Instructions: Each of the items listed below results in one of the factors described above. Assign each of the statements to one of the three factors by placing an X in one of the columns. If you feel, for example, that Item 1, Steady Employment, makes you feel invigorated, then you should place an X in Column C.

Factors that	A Satisfy Me	B Motivate Me	C Vitalize Me
1. to have steady employment.			
2. to feel my job is important.			
3. to work at one's highest potential in a specific area of expertise.			
4. to have adequate rest periods.			
5. to do interesting work.			
6. to use all of one's capacities to develop excellence in several areas of knowledge and skill.			
7. to receive sympathetic help with personal problems.			
8. to have an opportunity for self-improvement.			
9. to explore new opportunities and new ways of doing things.			
10. to turn out quality products and services.			
11. to have good pay.			
12. to initiate new ideas, influence others, and serve as a prime mover.			
13. to get along well with others on the job.			
14. to be respected as a person.			
15. to be totally involved in a project and reluctant to let others down.			
16. to have a local employee paper.			
17. to know what is going on in the organization.			
18. to contribute to the well-being of others.			
19. to have a retirement program and other benefits.			

Factors that	A Satisfy Me	B Motivate Me	C Vitalize Me
20. to have one's efforts add up to some thing meaningful.			
21. to be loyal to the company.			
22. to not have to work too hard.			
23. to be free to make responsible and independent decisions.			
24. to have a written job description.			
25. to have an employee council.			
26. to do challenging work.			
27. to do things in my own unique, personal, and individual way.			
28. to be complimented by my boss when I do a good job.			
29. to get a good performance rating.			
30. to aspire to accomplish more than what seems possible.			
31. to be paid more than others for doing the same job.			
32. to work without direct or close supervision.			
33. to have superior physical working conditions.			
34. to respond optimistically and with pleasure and pride in what others accomplish.			
35. to have tactful discipline when I do a bad job.			
36. to have an efficient supervisor.			
37. to have fair vacation arrangements.			
38. to agree with the organizations' objectives.			
39. to attend staff meetings.			
40. to envision the possibilities of future accomplishments.			

Analyzing Distinctions between Satisfiers, Motivators, and Vitalizers: Go back over the columns marked A, B, C, and check the items on this answer sheet where your choices correspond with key.

THE KEY

Satisfies		Motivates		Vitalizes	
❑	1	❑	2	❑	3
❑	4	❑	5	❑	6
❑	7	❑	8	❑	9
❑	11	❑	10	❑	12
❑	13	❑	14	❑	15
❑	16	❑	17	❑	18
❑	19	❑	21	❑	20
❑	22	❑	26	❑	23
❑	24	❑	28	❑	27
❑	25	❑	31	❑	30
❑	29	❑	32	❑	34
❑	33	❑	36	❑	40
❑	35				
❑	37	**12 TOTAL**		**12 TOTAL**	
❑	38				
❑	39				

16 TOTAL

NATURAL WORK GOALS: THE WAY TO ACCESS VITALITY AND ENHANCE DYNAMISM

In Chapter 1, we addressed the concept of "natural work goals" somewhat briefly and indicated that they appeared to be the means by which we access a person's vitality and enhance the dynamism of organizations. We shall explore the role of natural work goals in the enhancement of dynamism now.

Needs versus Goals

Hackman and Oldham explain that "some people have strong needs for personal accomplishment, for learning, and for developing themselves beyond where they are now. These people are said to have strong growth needs."[8] They raise the issue discussed earlier in this chapter about the difference between a needs approach to human behavior and a choice approach. We have chosen to adopt the choice paradigm to explain the actions of human beings. The concept of goals is much more compatible with choice than is the idea of inherent needs. Thus, we attempt to consistently recognize goals as the vehicle by which human energy is released and directed.

Goals

A goal is the aim or the end of an effort. A goal is an idea, not an object. Goals can affect behavior before any behavior has been performed or reinforced. Goals encompass intentions, plans, purposes, tasks, and objectives.

Goal directedness is a cardinal attribute of the behavior of all living organisms. It may be observed at all levels of life. Three common features characterize goal-directed action:

1. Self-generation. The actions of individuals are fueled by energy generated by the organism as a whole. The energy source is *not* put into it.
2. Value significance. An individual can go out of existence; survival is conditional. To maintain its existence, every living thing must take specific actions; if it does not take such actions, it dies. Thus, all goal-directed action has value significance for the organism.
3. Goal causation. In purposeful action, the individual's idea of and desire to achieve the goal is what causes action. The idea serves as the efficient cause, but the action is aimed toward a future state. Purposeful goal-directed action is released as a result of the individual's desire.[9]

Once a goal is understood and accepted, although it may remain in the background or periphery of consciousness, it serves as a reference point for guiding and giving meaning to subsequent mental and physical actions leading to the goal.

Three mechanisms explain the effect of goals on actions. Goals regulate the intensity of efforts expended on tasks; high-demand goals may require greater intensity to achieve. Goals affect the duration of efforts expended on tasks; challenging goals may lead individuals to work longer at a task. Goals lead individuals to direct attention toward and take action on relevant activities; specific goals may lead to less variability in their achievement by giving a clearer picture of what is to be achieved.

Everyone has noted the astonishing sources of energy that seem available to those who enjoy what they are doing or find meaning in what they are doing.[10]

Growth is the human process of expanding and developing; growth results from continuous learning and maturation. The interrelated concepts of developing, learning, and maturing encompass the sense of growth.

Natural work goals are those conscious intentions to achieve some purposeful action that allows people to grow and expand their lives at work. Natural work goals direct actions and result in more authentic interest in the organization. The achievement of natural work goals results in better employees and better relationships among members at all levels in the organization. The inability to achieve natural work goals leads to uncommitted, lethargic, and apathetic employees.

In sum, the term *goal* refers to statements that people make concerning what they want to achieve. Goals and the purposeful action needed to achieve the goals are quintessentially human. Locke and Latham point out the power of natural work goals when they explain that "people need and desire to attain goals. Such actions are required for their survival, happiness, and well-being."[11] Bois confirmed the deep-seated nature of natural work goals when he wrote, "Altruism is not a matter of choice; it belongs to the nature of man."[12] Altruism is one of the primary work goals.

Work goals have to do with what people want to achieve at work. Natural goals allow people to express their humanness and enhance their lives.

Natural goals are derived from the nature of human consciousness; they are derived from the capacity of human beings to think backward and forward in time, to imagine things, to visualize different configurations, to create images of what might be and what ought to be, to infer and deduce conclusions, and to further their own happiness and well-being. Employees who work in organizations that encourage them to achieve natural work goals as part of their everyday work assignments become energized and bring dynamism to the organization.[13]

People would be refreshed and renewed if they could wipe the slate clean and do one little thing that they really cared about deeply, one little thing that they could do with burning conviction.[14]

The term "Eupsychian" refers to the kind of culture that would be generated by a thousand self-actualizing people. Abraham Maslow, in his book *Eupsychian Management*, gives numerous examples of what we call "natural goals."[15] Other philosophers have implied that this concept of natural goals underlies enthusiasm for work and other forms of accomplishment.[16]

A List of Natural Work Goals

We shall illustrate some potential work goals with sixteen that have emerged out of research on this concept.[17]

To work to my highest potential in a specific area of expertise.

To develop excellence in several areas of knowledge and skill.

To explore new ways of doing things.

To discover new opportunities in my work.

To initiate new ideas to improve my work.

To influence others in order to improve my work.

To contribute to the well-being of others.

To do work that is meaningful.

To do work that is significant.

To do things in my own unique way.

To do things in my own personal way.

To have high aspirations.

To do more than what seems possible.

To feel optimistic.

To feel proud of what others accomplish.

To envision the possibilities of future accomplishments.

These sixteen goals have been translated into a Natural Work Goals Profile (NWGP), which is administered to organization members to measure the extent of dynamism preparedness in the organization (Appendix). The Profile appears to have two dominant factors distributed along two continua: enable/constrain and enthusiasm/apathy, with a third less dominant factor that has to do with individuality.

Restoring Dynamism by Achieving Natural Work Goals

At this point, we would like to illustrate how natural work goals may be used to revitalize workers in an organization. The six-step process we are describing was elaborated in greater detail in Silberman.[18]

First, select several moderately difficult goals that are challenging to achieve, but that when accomplished will give success experiences early.

Look over the list of sixteen natural work goals and select one that is relevant to the employees in your organization. For example, consider NWG Number One, to work at one's highest potential in a specific area of expertise. Brainstorm some tentative ideas for how employees in the organization could achieve this goal. Make a tentative decision about how difficult and challenging the goal will be to accomplish, and another tentative decision about the likelihood of having early successes in achieving the goal.

Idea

Very easy to achieve 1 2 3 4 5 Very difficult to achieve

Unlikely to get early success 1 2 3 4 5 Very likely to get early success

Study the list of natural work goals and select another one, such as NWG Number Eight, to do work that is meaningful. Now, brainstorm again some tentative ideas for what could be done to change organization processes so that employees could achieve this goal. After looking over the list of things that might need to be done, make a tentative decision about how difficult it will be for employees to accomplish the goal, and another tentative decision about the likelihood of having early successes in achieving the goal.

Idea

Very easy to achieve 1 2 3 4 5 Very difficult to achieve

Unlikely to get early success 1 2 3 4 5 Very likely to get early success

Continue to select natural work goals and to brainstorm ways organization members could achieve the goals. Evaluate the difficulty of achieving the goals and the likelihood of getting early successes. As soon as you feel that all of the relevant natural work goals have been evaluated, select three to six goals to be implemented. For each goal selected, place the goal at the top of a new page and list the tentative ideas resulting from the brainstorming.

Second, identify programs and activities that could be used to achieve each goal. Take the page for the first goal and study the tentative ideas for similarities. Mark the goals that fit together. Add new ideas as they occur to you. Continue through the list of tentative ideas until all ideas listed have been grouped.

Third, give each group of ideas a programmatic name. For example, ideas associated with the goal to work at one's highest potential might have a cluster of ideas that all involve acquiring additional skills. These might be called a program for "starting a training program." The program and activities should be related but somewhat independent of each other. To be successful it is important that the programs and activities do not overlap, yet they must complement one another. For example, a plant beautification program would be independent of a series of open houses, but they would complement one another.

Fourth, make certain that the programs and activities are consistent with the culture of the organization.

To this point in the process, we have been concerned primarily with the identification of individual natural work goals and the creation of programs and activities to achieve those goals to enhance individual vigor and enthusiasm. To sustain the energy and vitality generated by the potential achievement of these goals, we must make certain that the programs and activities are consistent with and supportive of the culture of the organization. This step in the process requires everyone involved to reflect on what is important and acceptable to the employees and the organization as a whole.

The culture consists of things shared by members of the organization. The objects, talk, behavior, and emotions shared by organization members determine what is acceptable to do in an organization. For example, in a high-tech manufacturing business the culture may make it difficult to implement an after-hours fine arts program to allow employees to express themselves in painting, sculpting, and classical music, or to sponsor a company golf team. Although such activities and programs might find acceptance in another context, in this organization, they would just conflict with the culture.

Conflicts with the culture of an organization are part of almost all change projects. In some cases, the achievement of some natural work goals are in and of themselves culture change interventions. However, in this example, to be successful, programs and activities would need to be compatible with the ongoing culture of the organization.

Fifth, prepare specific action plans to implement the programs and activities that will lead to achieving the natural work goals. This step in the process of implementing natural work goals involves stating the actions in relatively concrete sets of behavioral sequences that can be carried out to achieve each of the goals.

A concrete behavioral sequence simply specifies what is to be done, one action after another. For example, to implement a leadership training program that uses distance learning, you might include the following steps:

1. The manager of human resource development appoints a coordinator of distance learning.
2. The coordinator contacts a local college or university that offers closed-circuit courses and has distance-learning facilities, and asks about the possibility of teaching a leadership course over closed-circuit television.
3. The coordinator works with engineering to install closed-circuit television facilities.
4. The coordinator assists in the selection of a trainer.
5. The coordinator helps design the training program and how it will be facilitated.

The coordinator and the human resource development manager decide how the course will be offered.

Sixth, provide confirmation of success in achieving the natural work goals. Confirmation is a better term to use in this context than reward, since the term *reward* connotes an act of "force" to cause behavior. Here, we are concerned about communicating to the organization members that their work has been confirmed, and that they have been successful in achieving the natural work goals and carrying out the plans and programs. Achievement of the goals is the reward. Organization members, however, seek confirmation that what they are doing is acceptable.

Most reward programs are in fact simply confirmations. Traditional awards, such as letters of commendation, plaques, certificates, coupons, or cash payments, are, literally, not rewards; they are more accurately thought of as confirmations. That is, plaques indicate to employees that what they have been doing is acceptable, is consistent with the culture of the organization, and is valued by the organization. It is important to provide confirmation. One of the vitalizing programs that organizations should consider is that of confirming on a regular basis the accomplishments of organization members.

SUMMARY

Growth is the human process of expanding and developing; growth results from continuous learning and maturing. Developing, learning, and maturing are interrelated concepts that encompass the sense of growth. Through growth, individuals become stronger, more dependable, more accomplished, more competent, happier, more autonomous, more influential, more emotionally stable, and more adaptive.

There is good evidence that goals energize and direct behavior. In fact, we assume that all of life's aspirations are shaped by a series of goals that lead us to progressively higher levels of achievement. Natural work goals are strengthened through their regular achievement. Vitality and dynamism in the workplace depend, to a great extent, on achieving natural work goals. This emphasis on growth and learning in the workplace may be unique in our time, or it may be that it has just become more important to us at this time. In any case, we must seriously seek to achieve natural work goals to enhance the learning, growth, and vitality of the workforce and to enhance the dynamism of the organization. Any individual or team achievement must also be confirmed by the organization.

NOTES

1. Brownowski, J. 1978. *The Common Sense of Science*. Cambridge, MA: Harvard University Press, pp. 64–65.

2. Herzberg, F., Mausner, B., and Snyderman, B. 1959. *The Motivation to Work.* New York: Wiley & Sons; Herzberg, F. 1968. One More Time: How Do You Motivate Employees? *Harvard Business Review*, 46 (1), pp. 53–62.

3. Barnard, Chester I. 1938. *The Functions of the Executive.* Cambridge, MA: Harvard University Press.

4. Keyser, C.J. Korzybski's Concept of Man, in Korzybski, A. 1950. *Manhood of Humanity*, Second Edition. Lakeville, CT: International Non-Aristotelian Library, 90–91.

5. Bois, J. Samuel. 1978. *The Art of Awareness.* Dubuque, IA: Wm. C. Brown Company Publishers, pp. 121–128, 195.

6. Korzybski. *Manhood of Humanity.*

7. Keyser, p. 315.

8. Hackman, J. Richard and Oldham, Greg H. 1980. *Work Redesign.* Reading, MA: Addison-Wesley Company, p. 85.

9. Locke, Edwin A. and Latham, Gary P. 1990. *A Theory of Goal Setting and Task Performance.* Englewood Cliffs, NJ: Prentice-Hall, pp. 1–6, 20.

10. Gardner, John. 1963. *Self-Renewal: The Individual and the Innovative Society.* New York: Harper & Row.

11. Locke and Latham. *Theory of Goal Setting.*

12. Bois. *Art of Awareness.*

13. Locke and Latham. *Theory of Goal Setting.*

14. Gardner. *Self-Renewal.*

15. Maslow, Abraham H. 1965. *Eupsychian Management.* Homewood, IL: Richard D. Irwin, Inc.

16. Gardner. *Self-Renewal*; Hackman and Oldham. *Work Redesign*; Cox, Allan. 1984. *The Making of the Achiever.* New York: Dodd, Mead & Company; Garfield, Charles. 1986. *Peak Performers.* New York: Avon Books, pp. 57–58; Robbins, Anthony. 1986. *Unlimited Power.* New York: Fawcett Columbine; Tracy, Brian. 1993. *Maximum Achievement.* New York: Simon & Schuster.

17. Pace, R. Wayne, Regan, Les, Miller, Peter, and Dunn, Lee. 1998. Natural Growth Goals and Short-Term Training: A Boomerang Effect. *International Journal of Training and Development*, 2 (2), pp. 128–140; Colby, C. Layden and Pace, R. Wayne. 2000. An Assessment of the Validity of the Natural Work Goals Profile. *Proceedings of the Academy of Human Resource Development.* Baton Rouge, LA: Academy of Human Resource Development, pp. 547–554.

18. Silberman, Mel (Ed.). 1996. *The 1996 McGraw-Hill Training and Performance Sourcebook.* New York: McGraw-Hill, article 33, pp. 181–186.

6

Thinking Modes: Optimism in the Workplace

Just getting up in the morning and going to work make some truisms real, such as success makes people more optimistic about what they are doing. Optimistic people are successful because they see themselves as problem solvers; they have a quiver of alternatives for pursuing a problem. When one alternative misses the point, optimistic people simply move on to another approach.

OPTIMISTS KEEP TRYING

According to Seligman, "the individual optimist perseveres. In the face of routine setbacks, and even of major failures, [the optimist] persists."[1] Optimists are highly adaptable, like really good basketball players such as John Stockton, guard for the Utah Jazz professional basketball team in the 1990s. Stockton brings the ball down the floor, weaving among both offensive and defensive players and constantly looking for any open player, but mostly for Karl Malone cutting for the basket. He makes dozens of split-second adjustments, constantly seeking alternative routes and passing lanes. Optimistic people are like Stockton; they make the most of their talents and encourage others to do the same. That's why we like optimistic people. They exude energy. They work in an atmosphere of dynamism.

On the other hand, we all have our points of discouragement that can lead to a bit of pessimism. Losses are some of the most common sources of discouragement. Losses may be the best test of whether we are optimistic or pessimistic thinkers. Consider the different kinds of losses that bring on unhappy times. You can lose people through death, divorce, prison, or moving away; you can lose relationships when you fail to perform as others expect and get fired, or break up with a friend; you can lose your self-respect by being rejected or by associating with someone who is down and out; you can lose your skills through accidents, growing older, and through disuse and neglect; and you can lose opportunities through your failure to act. Losses are truly unhappy events that can lead to anger, frustration, borderline anhedonia, and even to depression.

Unhappy events challenge even the most optimistic people. They serve as the basis of pessimistic attitudes. How you handle unhappy events is the litmus test of your optimism; reactions to negative events in your life reveal to others how optimistic you are. At first blush no one likes to experience unhappy things. Negative acts are not very exciting. You probably have a tendency to avoid potentially negative happenings.

If you can't avoid an unhappy event, what do you do? Most people try to minimize the impact of the event on them. You may build a *shell* to protect yourself from any detrimental consequences. You may confront or attack the source of the unhappy event to reduce its strength. You may parry and deflect elements of the unhappy event in an effort to break it up and turn its impact in another direction.

But, suppose you can't avoid the unhappy event or even minimize its impact! What do you do then? Suppose your spouse moves for a divorce? Suppose you receive a pink slip and are separated from your company? Suppose you have an accident? Suppose you miss an important deadline? What then?

Hyatt and Gottleib studied situations where seemingly *smart* people failed, a sure sign of an unhappy event. A progression of five feelings occurred: shock, fear, anger/blame, shame, and despair.[2] Individuals who fail feel lonely, sad, and are without an obvious way to make things positive. Thoughts and actions associated with failure are based on what Snider calls "overgeneralized thinking."[3] This is the tendency to draw from unhappy events conclusions that go way beyond the verifiable consequences of the events. Johnson argued that "language spoken during moments of anger or despair or other relatively profound affective states appears to be particularly characterized by [all-inclusive] terms."[4] Burns cites "overgeneralizing" and "all-or-nothing thinking" as two of the "cognitive distortions" that form the basis of all depressions.[5] Lack of dynamism in an organization is often associated with pessimistic thinking.

When people are confronted with unhappy events—even a supposedly simple event such as being asked to stay late at work to complete a report—their thinking mode predisposes them to respond to that unhappy event in a particular way. Responses may range from fully pessimistic to neutral to fully optimistic, depending on how each individual thinks about the event. For example, a person might be turned down for a job he or she wanted badly. An all-inclusive thinking mode leads the person to think that unhappy things happen to him or her all the time, everywhere, and because he or she is just no good—a pessimistic response. A noninclusive thinking mode leads the person to feel and report that not getting that particular job allowed him or her to find something more suitable—an optimistic response.

Scholars and researchers have long been concerned about the effects of thought processes on our lives.[6] Thinking consists of an individual's predictions or decisions about events in the world.[7] Thinking style is a person's consistent way of looking at the world, making sense of it, and asking questions.[8]

MODES OF THINKING

A mode of thinking, in contrast, consists of the way people respond to events in their lives. This concept of thinking mode was derived in part from the observations of Stebbing that "thinking is primarily for the sake of action. No one," she asserted, "can avoid the responsibility of acting in accordance with his [or her] mode of thinking. No one can act wisely who has never felt the need to pause to think about how he [or she] is going to act and why he [or she] decides to act as he [or she] does."[9]

Two modes of thinking undergird our actions: all-inclusive generalizing and noninclusive generalizing. An all-inclusive generalizing pattern reveals a pessimistic mode of thinking. A noninclusive generalizing pattern indicates an optimistic mode of thinking.

Your thinking mode is a function of three feelings: (1) the feeling that you, as a person, are or are not the cause of the unhappy event (the source of events); (2) the feeling that similar unhappy events will or will not happen to you in the future (frequency of events); and (3) the feeling that unhappy events do or do not occur in all aspects of your life (extent of events). An all-inclusive, or pessimistic, thinking mode represents an ALL ME, ALL THE TIME, EVERYWHERE perspective. A noninclusive, or optimistic, thinking mode represents a MOSTLY OTHER THINGS, SOMETIMES, SOME AREAS perspective.

Pessimistic Thinking

One of the most disturbing aspects of an all-inclusive mode of thinking is the overall feeling of helplessness it brings to a person's life. Trotter concluded that there may be a link between helplessness and achievement, at least as expressed in the way individuals explain their performance.[10] One study of insurance sales people indicated that agents with a positive style were twice as likely as those with a pessimistic style to continue selling after a year.[11]

In another study, 618 employees working in the customer service department of a computer software company completed our measure of thinking mode. The frequency distribution of thinking mode scores ranged from a low of 1.00 to a high of 6.78 (on a scale of 1–7), with a mean score of 5.00. A regression analysis indicated that thinking mode scores predicted supervisor ratings of employee overall effectiveness at the 0.016 level of statistical significance, suggesting that effectiveness is likely to be associated with high scores (optimistic thinking) on the measure of thinking mode.[12]

Let us now discuss the three feelings associated with a pessimistic thinking mode in more detail. The first feeling is that you, as a person, are the cause of the unhappy event. People give one of two fundamental causes to account for unhappy events in their lives. Pessimistic thinking is based on the assumption that unhappy events are caused by your natural, habitual ways of doing things. When the cause of an unhappy event is attributed to faults with which you were born, there is just no way to make a change. You are unable to avoid unhappy events. You think, "I'm the reason why bad things happen. Any unhappy event that happens is my fault. I don't have what it takes to do things right." These kinds of statements and thoughts tend to disqualify you from doing anything good. You are disqualified from having any control over bad things that happen to you. These thoughts are called disqualifying personalizations.[13]

The second feeling is that similar unhappy events will happen to you in the future. You feel that unhappy events happen to you all of the time. In your mind, you feel doomed to experience unhappy events continuously. The inner talk that supports such a belief contains comments such as "I'm going to foul up again. I will never have opportunities. I am never happy with what I do. Things will continue to go wrong in the future."

When you engage in all-inclusive or pessimistic thinking, you project a feeling of impending doom. If you think that something bad is about to occur, regardless of what happens, you tend to interpret whatever happens in a way that justifies your thinking. This aspect of pessimistic thinking is called negative pygmallions.[14]

The third feeling is that unhappy events occur in all aspects of your life. You feel that unhappy events happen wherever you go, and that you are capable of doing only things that result in unhappy consequences. You think that you will do badly in everything you do. This aspect of pessimistic thinking is called frozen evaluations.[15]

It seems apparent that a dispirited and pessimistic thinking mode that incorporates disqualifying personalizations (source), negative pygmallions (frequency), and frozen evaluations (extent) predisposes people to respond to unhappy events in ways that signal helplessness tendencies. Being able to recognize all-inclusive thinking may aid you in eliminating unproductive and ineffective behaviors.

Thinking Mode Profile

The Thinking Mode Profile (TMP) has a format similar to the Attributional Style Questionnaire,[16] but has only six critical incidents, is without gender bias (e.g., missing an important social gathering), and represents only unhappy events. A copy of the TMP is included in the Appendix.

To complete the Profile, respondents are asked (1) to imagine that they experienced the unhappy event and felt discouraged, and (2) to explain briefly why the unhappy event occurred. Respondents are then asked to analyze the reason by providing an account for what happened.[17] Respondents mark a number from one to seven on each of three scales, indicating the extent to which (1) the reason had to do with their personal or habitual way of doing things, (2) the reason would be a cause of future failures, and (3) the reason would cause other unhappy events in the person's life.

Summing the numbers from the three scales and finding the mean score results in a thinking mode index score. The scales are structured so that high mean scores represent a noninclusive or optimistic thinking mode and low scores represent an all-inclusive or pessimistic thinking mode.

Optimistic Thinking

Optimistic (noninclusive) thinking is based on the philosophy that you can make the things happen that you want to take place. The three basic feelings comprising pessimistic thinking are dealt with in a slightly different way in optimistic thinking.

As an optimistic thinker, you feel that the cause of unhappy events is lodged in circumstances not associated with your inborn traits. You feel that unhappy events are caused by dumb luck, being in the wrong place, not trying hard enough, or not concentrating on the task. You are disorganized, for example, because you do not take the time to file things adequately. You could, but you just have other things to do.

For optimistic thinkers, bad things come from misjudgments, acts of nature, violations of a principle, or deliberate miscalculations. Rabbi Kushner attempted to help people understand this point of view by explaining that the "laws of nature treat everyone alike. They do not make exceptions for good people or for useful people."[18] Thinking about events that way, you should attribute unhappy events to natural processes that may be understood and dealt with, and avoided another time.

Why is it important to grasp the distinction between an internal orientation toward the cause of unhappy events and an external orientation toward them? The philosopher Johann Fichte provides an explanation. He says that you live in a world in which events just occur. You may take them into account or you may disregard them; you do not decide whether the events take place, but you do decide whether they are real or not. To be real simply means that you think that the events will make a difference in your life. Events are presented to you as unclassified, uninterpreted, nonmeaningful sensations. You have the opportunity and responsibility to classify, interpret, and make sensations meaningful; that is, you make them real. You decide what causes them and you determine how to deal with them by the reality you give to them.[19]

The question is not "why do unhappy events occur in your life?" but "what do you do after the unhappy event occurs?" Your life can be made more livable when you understand that it is possible for you to deal with events in a more effective way. Rabbi Kushner argues that God does not cause bad things to happen, but God does provide support to enable you to deal with the bad things by giving you strength and perseverance.

The thought processes that you use to make sense out of unhappy events determine whether you will take a pessimistic or an optimistic approach toward understanding events in your life. You may be better able to deal with the negative consequences of events if you see them as violations of natural laws, failure to perform skillfully, a lack of effort, or other circumstances that may not occur again or over which you may have some control.

Thinking about the sources of unhappy events as external causes leads you to be more optimistic.[20] You may be able to deal with them with greater perseverance and strength, and by doing so upend the unhappy event to create more dynamism in the workplace. As an optimistic thinker, you assume that the conditions of life are such that they may not repeat themselves soon or even ever. Limiting the number of unhappy events in your life allows you to feel more in control. Without disregarding reality completely, you think that unhappy events will in fact occur less frequently, allowing your mind to interpret unhappy events in a more positive framework.

Finally, as an optimistic thinker, you believe that unhappy events occur in limited areas of your life. If you have something unhappy occur at work, you believe that you will not have an unhappy event at home. You assume that an unhappy event is restricted to the specific circumstances associated with the negative consequence. By narrowing the consequences of a negative event to its immediate circumstances, you are able to respond to negative events one at a time without getting overwhelmed by them. You don't generalize one negative event to other parts of your life.

Optimistic thinking is strongest when the things that you want to happen seem possible; you will be most optimistic when you have a clear idea of what you want to accomplish. Then, you need to feel that you have the energy necessary to achieve your goal. Of course, you must also feel that you have the talents, skills, and abilities to achieve the goal. Finally, you must feel that if you exert your available energy and talents, you will be able to achieve what you want. If you have doubts about your abilities to meet these four requirements, you will begin to think more negatively and may ultimately adopt pessimistic thinking in your analyses of events that happen in your life.

Optimistic thinking is fundamental to enhancing the four core work perceptions—performance, opportunity, fulfillment, and expectations—that lead to the highest levels of dynamism in organizations. At this point let us touch on four steps that are part of an elegant strategy for making the achievement of goals possible, without creating problems in the process. The first step is to write down a goal that you would like to achieve or identify something you would like to have happen. The second step is to list the resources—equipment, money, space, materials—you need to get started. The third step is to identify the people—family members, co-workers, friends—who need to cooperate with you in order to achieve the goal; briefly describe why each person needs to cooperate with you. Finally, the fourth step is to determine what needs to be checked on to assure that you can move toward accomplishing the goal; of course, explain why you think you need to check on them.

Those four steps increase the likelihood that you will achieve your goal. If something does not turn out the way you planned, your optimistic thinking mode will look for alternatives. As a result, your perceptions of the workplace will be more positive.

SUMMARY

In this chapter we distinguished between pessimistic and optimistic thinking in terms of the overgeneralizing that people may indulge in when something negative happens. Three aspects of thinking mode were discussed: stable versus changing circumstances, global versus specific circumstances, and inborn, inherent characteristics versus natural, external processes as the causes of unhappy events in our lives. The relationship between making things possible and optimistic thinking was analyzed, and a four-step procedure for making things possible was explained. We pointed out that optimistic thinking—making things possible—and positive work perceptions were highly interrelated. Finally, we concluded that dynamism was very strongly related to and invariably enhanced by optimistic thinking—the view that things were possible to achieve—and that positive perceptions about a person's work performance, work opportunities, work fulfillment, and work expectations (aspirations) were invariably brought about by optimistic thinking.

NOTES

1. Seligman, Martin E.P. 1991. *Learned Optimism*. Milsons Point, New South Wales, Australia, p. 255.

2. Hyatt, Carole and Gottleib, Linda. 1987. *When Smart People Fail*. New York: Simon & Schuster.

3. Snider, J.G. 1968. Studies of All-Inclusive Conceptualization. *General Semantics Bulletin*, pp. 51–54.

4. Johnson, Wendell. 1946. *People in Quandaries*. New York: Harper & Row, p. 515.

5. Burns, David D. 1980. *Feeling Good: The New Mood Therapy*. New York: Signet Books, pp. 31–32.

6. Alexander, Hubert G. 1967. *Language and Thinking*. Princeton, NJ: D. Van Nostrand Company; Beardsley, Monroe C. 1950. *Thinking Straight*. New York: Prentice-Hall; Chase, Stuart. 1959. *Guides to Straight Thinking*. London: Phoenix House; Kushner, Harold S. 1981. *When Bad Things Happen to Good People*. New York: Avon Books.

7. Aiken, Henry D. 1956. *The Age of Ideology*. New York: Mentor Books.

8. Harrison, Allen F. and Bramson, Robert M. 1982. *The Art of Thinking*. New York: Berkley Books; Meyers, G. Douglas. 1991. Thinking Styles and Writing Group. *Bulletin of the Association for Business Communication*, March, pp. 17–20.

9. Stebbing, L. Susan. 1939. *Thinking to Some Purpose*. Baltimore: Penguin Books, p. 23.

10. Trotter, Robert J. 1987. Stop Blaming Yourself. *Psychology Today*, February, pp. 31–39.

11. Seligman, Martin E.P. and Schulman, Peter. 1986. Explanatory Style as a Predictor of Productivity and Quitting among Life Insurance Sales Agents. *Journal of Personality and Social Psychology*, pp. 50, 832–838.

12. Pace, R. Wayne, Stephan, Eric, Swenson, Michael J., and Jaw, Dar-Yu. November 1991. The Relationship between Thinking Mode and Employee Effectiveness. *Proceedings of the 56th Annual Convention of the Association for Business Communication*. Honolulu, Hawaii, pp. 73–79.

13. Burns, David D. 1980. *Feeling Good: The New Mood Therapy*. New York: Signet Books, pp. 31–32; Murray, Elwood and Barbour, Alton. 1973. Clinical General Semantics. *Journal of the American Society of Psychosomatic Dentistry and Medicine*, p. 20.

14. Haney, William V. 1979. *Communication and Interpersonal Relations*. Homewood, IL: Richard D. Irwin.

15. Burns, David D. 1980. *Feeling Good: The New Mood Therapy*. New York: Signet Books, pp. 31–32; Haney, William V. 1979. *Communication and Interpersonal Relations*. Homewood, IL: Richard D. Irwin.

16. Peterson, C., Semmel, A., Von Baeyer, C., Abramson, L.Y., Metalsky, G.I., and Seligman, M.E.P. 1982. The Attributional Style Questionnaire. *Cognitive Therapy and Research*, 6, pp. 287–299.

17. Thompkins, Phillip K. and Cheney, George. 1982. Account Analysis of Organizations. In Linda L. Putnam and Michael E. Pacanowsky (Eds.), *Communication and Organizations*. Beverly Hills, CA: Sage Publications.

18. Kushner. *When Bad Things Happen to Good People*.

19. Aiken, Henry D. 1956. *The Age of Ideology*. New York: Mentor Books.

20. Pace, R. Wayne. 1992. When Bad Things Happen to Good Semanticists. *ETC: A Review of General Semantics*, 49 (1), pp. 20–33.

Operating Styles: Sociability in the Workplace

A manager's operating style is generally regarded as the single most important factor in working successfully with employees.[1] Workers' consistent patterns of behavior interacting with others are their operating styles. However, in this book, the term "operating style" is used to refer to the special system described in this chapter, and the instrument that is included in Appendix.

STYLES WITH FOUR VARIABLES

Certain decisions that people make are predictable from what is popularly called their "style"; being able to predict people's decisions means you can understand how others may respond to a variety of conditions. It may be, also, that certain operating styles are more conducive to accomplishing certain types of goals. Thus, over many decades, researchers, scholars, and practitioners have been attempting to discover and describe people's styles of interacting with others.[2]

As far as we know, Hippocrates may have been the first individual to speculate about the factors that create a person's interaction style. He suggested that bodily structure and physiology determine a person's personality or habitual way of behaving. He described four personality types that were supposed to be the result of the predominant influence of one of the four "biles" of the body. Deese explains, however, that "there was, of course, no evidence for such a notion, and about the only remaining vestige of Hippocrates' types are the adjectives still in use to describe traits: phlegmatic, choleric, sanguine, and melancholic."[3] Littauer, nevertheless, developed an extensive analysis of behavioral styles using the four temperaments as their foundation.[4]

Carl Jung developed a system of types based on two *attitudes* and four *functions*.[5] The two attitudes are *introversion* and *extraversion*. Deese argues that "everyone now agrees, however, that the dichotomy [introversion vs. extraversion] does not serve as a useful typology."[6] The four functions—*thinking, feeling, sensing,* and *intuiting*—are, on the other hand, widely used as the template for style instruments. The thinking function is concerned with ideas. Through thinking, people try to comprehend the nature of the world and themselves. Feeling is the valuing function. Feelings give value to things and are responsible for emotions. Sensing is the perceptual or reality function and reveals concrete facts and information about the world. Intuiting refers to gaining knowledge from mystical experiences and unconscious sources.[7]

Deese suggests that since "our mental processes work by reducing the complexities of the world to simple schemes, type descriptions of personality will be with us in popular thought for a long time."[8] One of the most widely used instruments based on Jung's four basic functions is the Myers-Briggs Type Indicator.[9] They explain that Jung's theory posits that much apparently random behavior is actually quite orderly and consistent, owing to certain basic similarities and differences in the way people perceive the world and make judgments about it. If people differ systematically in how they perceive and in how they reach conclusions, it is reasonable to believe that they will differ in operating styles.

Paul Mok & Associates, now Mok-Bledsoe International, help clients identify their four styles using a Communicating Styles Survey (CST) that reveals an intuitor, a sensor, a thinker, and a feeler style.[10]

Kolb based his "learning styles" instrument on Jung's concept of personality types. Four learner activities were identified: thinking, feeling, watching, and doing. Combinations of each of these activities resulted in four learning styles: converger, diverger, assimilator, and accommodator.[11] Convergers are relatively unemotional and prefer to deal with things rather than people. Divergers tend to be emotional and imaginative and are interested in people. Assimilators excel in inductive reasoning and assimilating disparate observations into an integrated explanation, and they are less interested in people and more concerned with abstract concepts. Accommodators' greatest strengths lie in doing things, in carrying out plans, and in involving themselves in new experiences. They tend to solve problems in an intuitive trial-and-error manner.

Using a different database and methods, but starting from a Jungian theoretical framework, the Northwest Regional Education Laboratory in Portland, Oregon, created a leadership styles instrument from a behavior matrix that elicits data on four different styles: promoting, controlling, analyzing, and supporting.[12]

The Malone Training & Development Company of Akron, Ohio, developed the Behavior Style Survey, which provides information about four basic styles: director, persuader, analyzer, and supporter.[13]

The TRACOM Corporation of Denver, Colorado, markets the Social Style Profile, which reveals four styles: analytical, driving, amiable, and expressive.[14] These four are somewhat comparable to thinking (analytical), feeling (expressive), intuition (amiable), and sensing (driving).

Performax Systems International of Minneapolis, Minnesota, markets the Personal Profile System, a styles instrument based on the research of John G. Geier and the general theory of William Moulton Marston (inventor of the polygraph, the lie detector, and the Wonder Woman comic book character) from his book, *Emotions of Normal People.* Marston identified four primary emotions around which behaviors tend to cluster: dominance, influence, submission, and compliance. Geier verified a quartet of styles to which he gave the title DISC (dominance, influence, steadiness, and compliance).[15]

Although not derived from the same research and theory, there are obvious equivalents in the styles identified by Geier, Sayers, Oravecz, and Reid and Merrill. Dominance seems much like director, controller, and driving; influence shares features with promoter, persuader, and expressive; compliance has many of the characteristics of supporter, amiable, and intuition; and steadiness appears to be something like analyzer, analytical, and analyzing.

The most common leadership styles survey instruments are derived from the work of the Ohio State Leadership Studies[16] and the research of Blake and Mouton referred to as the managerial grid.[17] The factor of "initiating structure" accounted for a third of the total variation in leadership studies and "consideration" and "initiating structure" accounted for 83 percent of the variance, establishing these two variables as the most critical in leadership styles.[18]

A leader who earns a high score on consideration emphasizes promise, reward, and support as leadership techniques and acts in a warm and supportive manner, showing concern and respect for subordinates. A leader who scores low exhibits threatening, deflating, inconsiderate behavior and defines and structures his or her own role and those of subordinates toward goal attainment.

Reddin builds upon the two major dimensions of the Ohio State studies, although he calls them a task orientation (structuring) and a relationship orientation (consideration), but adds a third dimension—effectiveness—to the model. The result is a 3–D model of leadership styles with equivalent styles represented at different levels of effectiveness. There are eight styles at two different levels. The ineffective level includes the deserter, low on both task and relationships; the compromiser, high on both task and relationships; the autocrat, high on task but low on relationships; and the missionary, high on relationships but low on task. The effective level includes the bureaucrat, the executive, the benevolent autocrat, and the developer.[19]

Hersey and Blanchard use the Ohio State variables of consideration and structuring, but add a third variable of "maturity."[20] Later, Hersey substituted the concept of "readiness" for maturity.[21] As the level of maturity or readiness of one's followers increases, the leader is able to reduce the relationship behavior accordingly, resulting in a bell-shaped curve going through four leadership styles.

Maturity and readiness represent having high willingness and ability to take responsibility, and being experienced with the task at hand. Immature followers require a highly task-oriented leader, or one who tells them what to do. As followers mature, they require less direction, but need to be sold on actions, resulting in a selling style. As they mature, the leader progresses to a participating style, and eventually, with fully mature followers, a leader uses a delegating style, characterized by both low task behavior and low relationship behavior.

Fiedler and Chemers[22] look at leadership style from the perspective of followers, and arrive at somewhat similar conclusions. They suggest that combinations of factors comprising a leadership situation dictate the most effective leadership style. They deduced three situational conditions that account for a particular leadership approach or style: relations between the leader and followers, the structure of the task, and the positional power of the leader.

If for any reason the conditions are either highly favorable or highly unfavorable, that is, relations are either very good or very bad, the task is either highly structured or highly unstructured, or the leader's positional power is either very weak or very strong, then the leader's style should be more strongly oriented toward the task. If the conditions are ambiguous and the task is only moderately structured, relations are only fair, and positional power is moderately weak, then the leader should use a style much more strongly oriented toward relations.

Using the general line of thinking of the Ohio State studies, Blake and Mouton[23] extrapolated three organization universals on which their model of leadership styles is based:

1. Concern for production, or the degree to which the leader's concerns place high priority on the organization's productivity.
2. Concern for people, or the degree to which the leader feels and expresses personal commitment and accountability based on trust, shows regard for subordinates, and seeks positive social relations or friendships with associates.

3. Whenever a person acts as a supervisor or manager, concerns for people and production become intertwined and are expressed in vastly different ways, depending on the specific manner in which the two concerns are joined.

The Leadership Grid represents the model for how the two concerns—
for people and for production—find expression. The grid reflects five basic
styles usually referred to by numbers as well as by name; concern for tasks
appears first in the number.

9.1 Leadership style represents high concern for production or task and low concern for people. This is often called an authority-obedience style.

1.9 Leadership style represents high concern for people or relationships and low
   concern for production or task. This is often called a country-club style.

1.1 Leadership style represents both low concern for production and low concern
   for people. This is often called an impoverished style.

5.5 Leadership style represents moderate concern for both production and people.
   This is often called the organization man style.

9.9 Leadership style represents both high concern for production and high concern
   for people. This is often called the team style.

The Hill Interaction Matrix (HIM) characterizes a wide variety of behavioral phenomena and verbal content of group interaction. The categories
"make stylistic distinctions between groups."[24] According to the authors,
whether the categories involved in the HIM are valid "must remain with
the reader who can validate it against his [or her] experience with groups to
determine whether these categories are useful in the understanding and
management of groups."

Four styles were produced: confrontive, speculative, assertive, and conventional. Miller et al. extrapolated four variables that accounted for the
styles: emphasizes feelings, emphasizes thinking, emphasizes personal issues, and emphasizes relationship issues.[25] The four styles were characterized as follows:

Style I: Friendly, sociable, playful; keeps the world going.

Style II: Directing, persuading, blaming, demanding; usually used when you want
           to be persuasive or to control what is happening.

Style III: Tentative, expanding, elaborating, exploring, searching; a speculative
           style whose intention is almost to stop the world, reflect on it, and explore
           it.

Style IV: Aware, active, accepting, disclosing, caring, and cooperative; pursues the
           process of dealing with issues openly and directly; a committed style.

Miller et al. conclude that "if your intention is to socialize and participate
in some activities together, Style IV is too heavy. Style I would be better
here. If your intention is to direct and persuade, then Style IV doesn't fit. Try

Style II. If your intention is to explore tentatively and get a general overview of an issue, then Style IV is too focused. Style III is better for that." Style IV expresses a deeper commitment to deal with the issue. Style IV is best when you and your partner have an issue and want to work on it.

STYLES THAT VARY FROM FOUR VARIABLES

Harrison and Bramson began with "inquiry modes" and identified five styles, derived from the approaches to thinking of "certain seminal thinkers and philosophers" associated with major eras of time.[26] The idealist is associated with philosophy, government, and politics; the analyst reflects the foundations of Western intellectual methods; the realist represents thought and activity associated with scientific methods; the pragmatist is associated with nontraditional, progressive thinking and action; and the synthesist is grounded in the dialectical method and represents an integrative style.

Consistent with guidelines provided by most of the theorists, Harrison and Bramson explain that "each person is truly unique and never completely predictable." Their styles of thinking characterize only prototypes (or "ideal types"). No one is a total analyst or a total synthesist, yet knowing how much people have of each style makes it possible to predict a good deal about how they think about things.

Holland has identified six major personality orientations that comprise a "personality pattern," with the three strongest orientations constituting a person's main personality type.[27] The six orientations are realistic, investigative, artistic, social, enterprising, and conventional. Martin and Bartol argue that "a large body of research provides strong support for the ability of Holland's theory to distinguish among individuals in various college majors and occupations."[28] This suggests that individuals may be accurately categorized according to the six styles measured by Holland.

Styles can also be viewed from the perspective of Eric Berne and what is currently called Transactional Analysis.[29] Berne derived his styles from psychoanalytical theory and postulated three ego states—adult, parent, and children—as part of each person's behavioral repertory. James R. Noland[30] developed and distributes an instrument called Personalysis, in which responses are interpreted in terms of each of Berne's primary ego states and the four attributes that characterize each ego state. The adult ego state, for example, represents a person's preferred style of managing self and others and is organized around implementing, organizing, structuring, and planning activities. The parent ego state represents a controlling state and includes four styles: authoritative, bureaucratic, democratic, and self-directed. The child ego state represents a person's motivational needs and includes power, control, flexibility, and freedom. Wofford, Gerloff, and Cummins[31] infer six basic communication styles from Transactional Analysis theory, loosely derived from each of the primary ego states. The controlling style, the egalitarian style, the structuring style, the dynamic style, the relinquishing style, and the withdrawing style are distributed among the three ego states: parent uses controlling and structuring styles; adult uses egalitarian and dynamic styles; child uses relinquishing and withdrawing styles.

This summary of the major systems for classifying style represents the vast range of current thinking and reveals considerable similarity but some diversity in theoretical perspectives. The mere existence of the dozens of approaches to characterizing operating styles indicates the importance of the concept in the lives of organization members. The quality of interaction among supervisors, managers, and workers depends to a great extent on operating styles that encourage optimism and commitment in relationships. We cannot dismiss the significance of understanding, cultivating, and in some ways managing our operating styles to the best advantage.

OPERATING STYLES

The classification of operating style uses four dimensions: (1) sustaining tendencies, (2) initiating tendencies, (3) relational concerns, and (4) notional concerns. These dimensions combine to make a four-cell matrix of operating styles (Figure 7.1).

Initiating tendencies are revealed when a person takes the first step to begin something, and shows energy and direction in bringing about the action. A person with initiating tendencies is usually active, looks to get things done, and pushes things forward.

Figure 7.1
Operating Styles

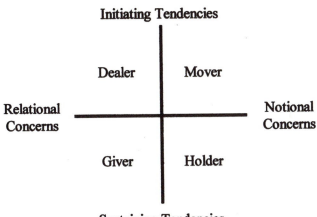

BEHAVIORAL OR STYLISTIC INCLINATIONS

Initiating Tendencies

Dealer	Mover

Relational Concerns — Notional Concerns

Giver	Holder

Sustaining Tendencies

Sustaining tendencies are revealed when a person gives support, endures without failing or yielding, and helps others to continue their actions. A person with sustaining tendencies is usually committed to minimizing conflict and promoting the happiness of everyone.

Relational concerns focus on the emotional connections between human beings. A person reveals relational concerns by placing value on people and caring for them. A person with relational concerns is people-oriented and nonaggressive.

Notional concerns focus on ideas, objects, and abstract conceptions. A person who reveals notional concerns places value on things and data, often appears aloof and cool, and may prefer to work alone.

Combinations of initiating tendencies and relational concerns produce a *dealer* style, whereas combinations of sustaining tendencies and notional concerns produce a *holder* style. On the other hand, combinations of initiating tendencies and notional concerns result in a *mover* style. Finally, combinations of sustaining tendencies and relational concerns result in a *giver* style.

Movers are very results-oriented and love to run things their own way. They are efficient, but are often viewed as unfeeling and threatening in their relationships with others. Movers make sure the job is done and are often impatient with others or policies that stand in their way.

Dealers are very diplomatic, socially outgoing, imaginative, and friendly. Dealers get things going, but may settle for less than the best in order to get on to something else. They have creative ideas but may be less likely to follow through to get a task done. Dealers tend to value information that gives them power to manage the situation so they can realize their goals in a socially acceptable way.

Holders are problem solvers and like to get all the data before making decisions. Some say they are thorough but others say they are slow. These people like to work alone, value conceptual skills, and may seem aloof and cool. They value information that allows them to make substantive decisions on the basis of fact and evidence.

Givers value interpersonal relations. These people try to minimize conflict and promote the happiness of everybody. They are seen by many as accommodating and friendly, while some see them as wishy-washy and nice. They like to please others, and rely on others to give directions about how to get their work done.

Operating style represents a holistic approach to understanding the patterns of interaction between people in workplaces. Having patterns in the way you interact with others provides a degree of predictability and confidence in what you say and do, making your interactions more comfortable. In terms of dynamism, however, it is the unpredictable, uniqueness, and challenge that produces energy and excitement. Thus, it may be important to look at your own style and see whether you can add some variety by shifting from your dominant style to a complementary style from time to time in order to maintain excitement in your relationships with colleagues.

Dynamism is enhanced through a fine combination of predictable style and interesting ventures into the slightly unpredictable arena of other patterns. You may cherish the opportunities you have to engage in some role taking and experience something other than your routine way of interacting. To get a brief analysis of your preferred style, complete the Operating Styles Profile (Appendix), which is a new, creative approach to identifying operating styles.

Metaphors

Metaphors structure complex situations by highlighting certain elements and obscuring others. They transport conceptions of the familiar to the less familiar and clarify topics for which we may not otherwise have language to express. Bednar and Hineline, in a review of the literature on the meaning and uses of metaphors, indicated that they are "a language device that influences both what and how we perceive." The "metaphor frames a particular image or 'picture' of reality and provides focus" while at the same time "provides a release from old, entrenched interpretations" that break away from traditional modes of thinking and behaving.[32]

Metaphors help us think by succinctly chunking together certain characteristics and transferring them from one thing to another without enumerating the characteristics, thus providing a compact and coherent whole. Metaphors can be highly memorable because they tend to be novel and vivid as well as succinct. For example, one way to understand how a person feels when trying to make sense of a difficult passage in a technical book is to explain that reading that book is like hitting something on the road while driving at night; you know that you've come across something, but you don't know exactly what it is.

The critical role of operating style in the enhancement of dynamism and vitality in organizations makes it important for you to have an accurate vision of your own style. This will give you some good information to build on when making adjustments, modifications, and shifts. You may not be able to change your habitual operating style a great deal; but with a clear idea of which style makes you feel most comfortable you may make small adaptations to make your style more amenable to others. At the same time, with a sense of your own style, you may anticipate how others will respond to you, allowing you to minimize negative effects.

SUMMARY

In this chapter, the concept of operating style was discussed and a variety of classification systems were reviewed. We introduced a model of operating style that includes four dimensions—initiating/sustaining and relational/notional—which result in a matrix of four distinct styles—mover, dealer, holder, and giver. As one of the elements of personal dynamism, a person's operating style is important to study and master.

NOTES

1. Whetten, David A. and Cameron, Kim S. 1995. *Developing Management Skills*, Third Edition. New York: HarperCollins College Publishers, p. 131.

2. Tannenbaum, Robert and Schmidt, Warren H. 1957. How to Choose a Leadership Pattern. *Harvard Business Review*, March–April, pp. 95–101; Fiedler, Fred E. 1967. *A Theory of Leadership Effectiveness*. New York: McGraw-Hill Book Company; Scott, Ian (Tr. and Ed.). 1969. *The Luscher Color Test*. New York: Random House; Holland, J.L. 1971. *Vocational Preference Inventory Manual*. Palo Alto, CA: Consulting Psychologists Press, Inc.; James, Muriel and Jongeward, Dorothy. 1978. *Born to Win: Transactional Analysis with Gestalt Experiments*. Reading, MA: Addison-Wesley Publishing Company; Kolb, David A. 1976. On Management and the Learning Process. *California Management Review*, Spring; Nelson, Darwin B. and Low, Gary R. 1981. *Personal Skills Map*. Corpus Christi, TX: Institute for the Development of Human Resources, Inc.; Hall, Jay, Harvey, Jerry B., and Williams, Martha. 1973. *Styles of Management Inventory*. Conroe, TX: Teleometrics Int'l; Robinson, Everett T. 1990. *Why Aren't You More Like Me?* Dubuque, IA: Kendall/Hunt Publishing Company.

3. Deese, James. 1967. *General Psychology*. Boston, MA: Allyn and Bacon, Inc., pp. 429–430.

4. Littauer, Florence. 1983. *Personality Plus*. Old Tappan, NJ: Fleming H. Revell Company.

5. Jung, Carl J. 1923. *Psychological Types*. New York: Harcourt Brace, Inc.

6. Deese. *General Psychology*.

7. Dushkin, David A. 1970. *Psychology Today: An Introduction*. Del Mar, CA:

8. Deese. *General Psychology*.

9. Briggs, Katharine C. and Myers, Isabel Briggs. 1976. *Myers-Briggs Type Indicator*. Palo Alto, CA: Consulting Psychologists Press.

10. Lynch, Dudley. 1976. Intuitors, Sensors, Thinkers, Feelers. *Texas Parade Magazine*, April, pp. 26–29; Lynch, Dudley. 1977. In Sync with the Other Guy. *TWA Ambassador Magazine*, March, pp. 28–31; Mok, Paul and Lynch, Dudley. 1978. Easy New Way to Get Your Way. *Reader's Digest*, March, pp. 105–109.

11. Kolb, David A. 1976. *Learning Style Inventory*. Boston: McBer & Company.

12. Sayers, Susan. 1978. *Leadership Styles: A Behavioral Matrix*. Portland, OR: Northwest Regional Educational Laboratory.

13. Oravecz, M.T. 1981. *Behavior Style Survey*. Akron, OH: Malone Training & Development.

14. Reid, Roger and Merrill, David W. 1987. *Social Style Profile*. Denver, CO: The TRACOM Corporation.

15. Geier, John G. 1977. *Personal Profile System*. Minneapolis, MN: Performax Systems International; Geier, John G. 1967. A Trait Approach to the Study of Leadership in Small Groups. *The Journal of Communication*, December, pp. 316–323; Marston, William Moulton. 1979. *Emotions of Normal People*. Minneapolis, MN:

Persona Press. With an Introduction by John G. Geier about the development of the Personal Profile System.

16. Stogdill, Roger M. and Coons, Alvin E. (Eds.). 1957. *Leader Behavior: Its Description and Measurement*. Research Monograph No. 88. Columbus, OH: Bureau of Business Research, Ohio State University.

17. Blake, Robert R. and Mouton, Jane S. 1964. *The Managerial Grid*. Houston, TX: Gulf Publishing Co.

18. Bass, Bernard M. 1960. *Leadership, Psychology, and Organizational Behavior*. New York: Harper & Row, Publishers, pp. 96–105; Korman, A.K. 1966. "Consideration," "Initiating Structure," and Organizational Criteria—A Review. *Personnel Psychology: A Journal of Applied Research*. Vol 19, No. 4 , Winter, pp. 349–361.

19. Reddin, William J. 1967. The 3–D Management Style Theory. *Training and Development Journal*, April, pp. 8–17.

20. Hersey, Paul and Blanchard, Kenneth H. 1974. So You Want to Know Your Leadership Style? *Training and Development Journal*, February, pp. 1–16.

21. Pace, R. Wayne and Faules, Don F. 1994. *Organizational Communication*, Third Edition. Englewood Cliffs, NJ: Prentice-Hall, p. 194.

22. Fiedler, Fred E. and Chemers, Martin M. 1974. *Leadership and Effective Management*. Glenview, IL: Scott, Foresman and Company.

23. Blake and Mouton. *The Managerial Grid*.

24. Hill, Wm. Fawcett. 1973. Hill Interaction Matrix (HIM): Conceptual Framework for Understanding Groups. *The 1973 Annual Handbook for Group Facilitators*. San Diego: University Associates, p. 160.

25. Miller, Sherod, Nunnally, Elam W. and Wackman, Daniel B. 1975. *Alive and Aware*. Minneapolis, MN: Interpersonal Communication Programs, Inc., pp. 209–211.

26. Harrison, Allen F. and Bramson, Robert M. 1982. *The Art of Thinking*. New York: Berkley Books, pp. 186–187.

27. Holland, J.L. 1971. *Vocational Preference Inventory Manual*. Palo Alto, CA: Consulting Psychologists Press, Inc.

28. Martin, David C. and Bartol, Kathryn M. 1986. Holland's Vocational Preference Inventory and the Myers-Briggs Type Indicator as Predictors of Vocational Choice among Master's of Business Administration. *Journal of Vocational Behavior*, 29, pp. 51–65.

29. Berne, Eric. 1964. *Games People Play*. New York: Grove Press, Inc.

30. Noland, James R. 1984. *Personalysis*. Houston, TX: Management Technologies.

31. Wofford, Jerry C., Gerloff, Edwin A., and Cummins, Robert C. 1977. *Organizational Communication: The Keystone to Managerial Effectiveness*. New York: McGraw-Hill Book Company.

32. Bednar, David A. and Hineline, Jaynette. 1982. The Management of Meaning through Metaphors. Department of Management, University of Arkansas. Paper presented to the Organizational Communication Division of the Academy of Management, New York.

PART II

THE STRATEGIES OF DYNAMISM

Competitiveness and Learning Organizations: A Dynamic Duo

Any changes we make in an organization are grounded in a philosophy of what is important to be achieved. In a free enterprise system one of the primary goals of organizations is to be competitive. To be competitive, an organization must provide products and services for which customers or clients are willing to pay a fair return or price. In the long run in a free enterprise system, competitiveness is measured by the ability of the organization to stay in business *and* to protect the organization's investments, to earn a return on those investments, and to ensure jobs for the future. The objective of managers is to use the elements of an organization to achieve the goal of competitiveness.

COMPETITIVENESS

The energy that workers devote to the organization may be one of the most critical factors in making certain that the organization is competitive. There is some evidence to suggest that the most competitive organizations are the ones in which all other elements of the organization encourage workers to achieve organization goals.[1]

External to the individual, four categories summarize most of the elements that are important in achieving competitiveness: (1) organization structure, which represents contacts between individuals and things; (2) organization guidelines, which direct decisions and actions; (3) work technology, which encompasses the work and how it is to be done; and (4) management and leadership practices, which are the ways organization leaders implement the structure, guidelines, and work technology (see Chapter 3).

PARADIGMS OF COMPETITIVENESS

Over the centuries, competitiveness has been measured by different criteria. For purposes of illustration, we will briefly discuss five different competitive paradigms. Six factors of each paradigm are considered: (1) the agenda, (2) the era in which the agenda flourished, (3) the agenda's competitive edge, (4) the agenda's key characteristics, (5) the basic need of the agenda, and (6) the agenda's technique (Table 8.1). For an earlier version of these paradigms, see Pace and Stephan.[2]

Craftsmanship. The first paradigm, which appears to have existed for almost 2,800 years, had the agenda of craftsmanship. The competitive edge was the absence of duplications, the key characteristic was artistry, the basic need was skilled individuals, and the essential technique was long apprenticeships.

Quantity. The second paradigm, introduced in many Western countries in the early 1800s and persisting until about 1969, had the agenda of productivity. The competitive edge was the elimination of shortages, and the key characteristic of this agenda was quantity. To avoid shortages, competitive organizations increased production by using assembly lines.

Quality. The third paradigm, with quality as the agenda, was introduced in the 1950s. A number of individuals, most notably W. Edwards Deming, led this movement. It reached its peak in the 1970s, but is still important in organizations that wish to be competitive. The competitive edge is the production and delivery of large numbers of perfect products and services; the key characteristic of this agenda is excellence. Quality improvement is the byword. Competitive organizations adopt a philosophy of total quality, in which they create products and provide services with zero defects.

Immediacy. The fourth paradigm was introduced in the middle 1970s by the creation of ways to quickly distribute information worldwide. The amount of time necessary for information to be disseminated around the world has been reduced to milliseconds. This paradigm has the agenda of immediacy. The competitive edge is no delays and the key characteristic is directness. The basic need of this agenda is improved systems, and the essential technique is process engineering. The goal is to produce and deliver large numbers of perfect products and services without delay. Competitive organizations realize that customers want to secure products or services in a form that is acceptable to them, and when they want them—immediately.

The immediacy agenda created an irreversible, revolutionary change in the competitiveness of organizations. Managers reexamined all aspects of their systems—structure, guidelines, management practices, and work technology—and discovered that teams and other alternative forms had to

Table 8.1
Paradigms of Competitiveness

	Paradigm 1 **Craftsmanship**	Paradigm 2 **Productivity**	Paradigm 3 **Quality**	Paradigm 4 **Immediacy**	Paradigm 5 **Customization**
Agenda **Era**	1,000 B.C. - 1,700 A.D. (2,800 years)	1800 - 1969 (169 years)	1970 - 1989 (19 years)	1990 - 1999 (9 years)	1999 - 2000 (6+ years)
Competitive Edge	No Duplications	No Shortages	No Imperfections	No Delays	No Unmet Needs
Key **Characteristic**	Artistry	Quantity	Excellence	Directness	Adaptation
Basic Need	Skilled Individuals	Increased Production	Quality Improvement	Improved Systems	Flexible Alignment
Essential **Technique**	Long Apprenticeships	Assembly Lines	TQM Programs	Process Re-engineering	Organizational Learning

be introduced in order to meet the immediacy criterion. Workers in this agenda also changed. They discovered that they had to become highly skilled, reliable, educated individuals who could understand and use the new forms of information technology and the information being made available, adapt to rapidly changing organization forms, and cooperate well with other workers. The cry was now for "collaborative individualism."[3]

To remain competitive, organizations reduced design and production cycles, improved the quality of products and services, improved relationships with suppliers, became responsive to customer preferences, and dramatically reduced costs. Some products and services were actually delivered with immediacy. For example, prescription eyeglass lenses were delivered in sixty minutes. Photographs were completed in sixty seconds through one-hour developing. Electronic cameras took and played pictures on a TV set seconds after they had been taken. Camcorders created instant movies. Personal computers and laser printers produced instant desktop publishing. Oil was changed in automobiles in ten minutes. Most travel agents made reservations almost instantly. People could withdraw money from their banks instantly through Automated Teller Machines. Facsimile (FAX) machines transmitted documents across the country in seconds. Electronic mail delivered messages in seconds between countries. Fast food outlets filled orders in twenty seconds. During athletic games, spectators had instant replays of the action on television.[4]

The ability to make and deliver products and services immediately is now a reality in much of the world; that ability determines which organizations will be competitive.

Developing immediacy requires a company to utterly revise itself, to control ever-more-sophisticated types of information, and to master new skills. The closer an organization gets to cost-effective instantaneous production of mass-customized goods and services, the more competitive it will be.

In competitive organizations seeking to provide products and services immediately, the workforce must be empowered to learn, innovate, and remove constraints in their production processes. They must eliminate unnecessary tasks and processes, thereby, reducing constraints and increasing flexibility and quality. Organizations that eliminate constraints can reduce lead time, use less space, use smaller equipment, and use people more efficiently and humanely. These benefits accrue not from large cost-reduction programs, but from tapping the talents and knowledge of employees.

Competitive companies must rely on workers skilled in problem solving and teamwork. Management's role becomes one of facilitating the processes, supporting the efforts, and taking a backseat when it comes to giving orders. People doing the work direct their own activities while managers make certain that the resources are available for them to compete.

Top managers give fewer orders because they are committed to letting the processes work and allowing workers to decide for themselves what should be done. If workers are making decisions about what they should do and are trained to do the right things, there is less of a need to have traditional middle management directing their activities. This is, of course, where professionals prepared in human resource training and development are making their greatest contributions. Human resource development professionals are needed to help workers acquire and enhance their abilities to be self-governing.

As management decisions become more team-oriented and as professionals and knowledge workers become more prominent, the distinctions between manager and nonmanager begin to erode. Managers must learn to operate without the crutch of hierarchy. Position, title, and authority are no longer adequate tools in a world where subordinates are encouraged to think for themselves and where managers have to work synergistically with other departments and even other companies. Increasingly, success depends on discovering sources of good ideas, figuring out whose collaboration is needed to act on those ideas, and producing results. In short, the new managerial work implies very different ways of obtaining and using power. Such a change forces managers to find new methods for motivating their people. Professionals in human resource development play a critical role in helping managers acquire new skills for vitalizing workers.

The Fifth Paradigm

Customization. These new conditions have created a fifth paradigm called customization. The era of customization may have begun in the 1980s or 1990s, but it is the agenda of the twenty-first century. It ensures that there are no unmet needs in customers. When customers want unique, tailor-made products that fit their interests, the most competitive companies respond to those requests. The key characteristic of organizations is now adaptation—not only to the environment but also to the forces within the organization that inevitably emerge when a new agenda looms on the horizon. The basic need is for flexible alignment. Finally, the fifth paradigm demands individual, workplace, and organizational learning. Learning-based organizations are most capable of adapting to any environment. They are robust survivors.

Learning Organizations

Few concepts have captivated organizational scholars quite as much as the learning organization.[5] In practice, however, the creation and maintenance of learning organizations has been difficult to implement. Nevertheless, the vision of organizations has been sufficient to continue inquiry into them and even to move the concept into a dominant position in both the theory and the practice of effective, competitive organizations. Chapter 9 will address the central role of learning in enhancing dynamism.

Learning organizations are, in fact, what most people call empowering work systems. We can say that the ideal work system to enhance dynamism in the workplace is a learning organization. It is becoming clear from efforts to transform traditional organizations into learning organizations that the process is not simple, but the value of making the transition is well worth the cost.[6]

Why Learning Organizations Contribute to Competitiveness

The bases of competitiveness have changed over time, and they will no doubt continue to change. The fifth paradigm may not even last as long as the other paradigms; however, learning is a paradigm that must be taken into account in the future, as the four preceding paradigms must be taken into account now. Competitiveness today requires that organizations show craftsmanship, productivity, quality, immediacy, and customization. Thus, though learning will certainly be eclipsed before long, it will not disappear.

Learning sustains competitiveness by allowing organizations to accommodate each new criterion for competitiveness. Thus, regardless of the new conditions, a learning organization can bring itself into compliance and respond to the new demands. Without the learning capacity, organizations will flounder.[7] In fact, learning organizations can not only respond to new requirements, but they can also raise the bar themselves and introduce their own standards to exceed current expectations. Without the learning capacity, organizations find that they are subject to responding, and seldom if ever take the lead. Learning organizations naturally evolve to keep up with innovations.[8]

The learning organization implements the contemporary competitive philosophy that enables organizations of all types to "unleash the power of the work force." As Jeffrey Pfeffer explained, "As other sources of competitive success have become less important, what remains as a crucial, differentiating factor is the organization, its employees, and how they work." Pfeffer offers an insightful explanation for why the people factor is so critical in competitiveness: "Achieving competitive success through people involves fundamentally altering how we think about the work force and the employment relationship. It means achieving success by working *with* people, not by replacing them or limiting the scope of their activities. It entails seeing the work force as a source of strategic advantage, not just as a cost to be minimized or avoided."[9]

It is the philosophy of the learning organization that ultimately turns one's attention to working with people. It appears that the shift from "how to change some processes to make people efficient" to "how to free people to learn for themselves and make the necessary changes themselves" may be the critical transformation in changing the focus of organizations from reengineering to the learning organization.

Learning Organizations

There is a difference between organizational learning and a learning organization. The difference lies in whether the focus is on learning or on organization. Organizational learning examines the kinds of learning that occur in organizations; the study of a learning organization seeks to discover what kind of organization results from focusing on learning.

Organizational learning means that an organization, as an institution, is able to retain information and efficiently distribute that information through its networks to solve problems as they occur and find new approaches to avoid future problems.

A learning organization, on the other hand, is where workers learn, develop meaning, acquire dignity, and make contributions of progressively higher quality to the institution. The organization can improve the key elements of the organization—its structure, guidelines, the work itself, and its management practices, as well as the mindsets of the workers. In a learning organization, workers acquire and share information and participate in making organizational decisions.[10]

Ask yourself these questions about your organization to see if you have what it takes to be a learning organization:[11]

Are creativity and innovation valued by the organization?

Does the organization's structure create energy and build commitment?

Do managers understand that learning and work are synonymous?

Do managers make managing the process as important as managing the content?

Do managers understand that knowledge alone is not learning?

What processes does the organization have in place to access and interpret information from the environment?

In what ways does the organization add value to the lives of its workers?

Do organization members understand how groups and organizations learn?

Does the allocation of resources reflect the value of learning?

Do workers understand their contribution to making organization improvements?

Four things are necessary for a learning organization.

An effective system for acquiring and sharing information.

Mechanisms and devices that create organizational memory.

Ways to engage in systematic problem solving.

A climate and culture that encourage new ways of working and managing.

One phase in the evolution of a learning organization is preparing workers to learn from their work. Workplace learning consists of reconstructing problem events and discovering what happened. Problem events are those in which an individual, a team, or the entire organization has failed to achieve a goal or some aspect of a goal. This is done in six stages:

1. Workers must recognize what happened and have a common understanding of the actions involved in the event.
2. Workers must make sense of what happened, an information-sharing task. They must understand why the event occurred, what precipitated the event, and what resulted from the event.
3. Workers must identify one or more goals that were *not* achieved as a result of the occurrence, the first step in problem solving.
4. Workers must be able to describe adjustments in the work system that would allow the system to *achieve* the goals, the second step in problem solving.
5. Workers must be able to codify or describe and store the reconstructed event so that the information can be retrieved and used in making other adjustments in the future, a step in the development of an organization's memory.
6. Workers must be able to make changes in the work system to allow the system to function more effectively; that is, they must be allowed to experiment and test out different ways of doing things.

Central to these six stages is *reflection*, the process of meditating on the meaning of an experience.[12] Reflection involves finding answers to seven questions:

1. What happened?
2. What precipitated the happening?
3. What were or could have been the consequences of what happened?
4. What is the significance of what happened?
5. What does the happening say about us, how we deal with others, and how the organization functions?
6. What should we do about what happened?
7. What else would be helpful to ask about what happened?

Workers can cultivate the reflection process by focusing more on what is happening around them and working out ways to describe what happened. Then, workers should share with co-workers stories about what happened, why it happened, and what might be done to avoid the happening in the future. Workers should be released—physically and psychologically—to experiment with new ways of improving organizational functioning. This means that workers must be free to speak openly, respect the reflections of others, and have some skill development making clear explanations, withholding judgment, and making their reasoning explicit.[13]

The significant observation that we can make about organizational learning is that the key or central principles and skills are closely allied to the release of organizational dynamism. We have only scratched the surface of what might be done to enhance organizational dynamism, but it is certain that the movement toward learning organizations is a major contribution toward achieving organizational dynamism.

SUMMARY

In this chapter, we have examined the five paradigms of competitiveness and analyzed the dimensions of learning organizations as they take their role in making organizations competitive.

We discussed four things necessary to move toward becoming a learning organization and we also examined the process of reflection.

NOTES

1. Smith, Alan. 1988. The "People Factor," in *Competitiveness*. Chicago: University Club of Chicago; Pfeffer, Jeffrey. 1994. *Competitive Advantage through People*. Boston: Harvard Business School Press; Barney, Jay B. 1995. Looking Inside for Competitive Advantage. *Academy of Management Executive*, 9 (4), pp. 49–61.

2. Pace, R. Wayne and Stephan, Eric G. 1996. Paradigms of Competitiveness. *Competitiveness Review: An International Business Journal*, 6 (1), pp. 8–13.

3. Limerick, David and Cunnington, Bert. 1993. *Managing the New Organization: A Blueprint for Networks and Strategic Alliances*. Chatswood, NSW: Business & Professional Publishing.

4. Davidow, William H. and Malone, Michael S. 1992. *The Virtual Corporation*. New York: HarperCollins Publishers.

5. Argyris, Chris and Schon, Donald A. 1973. *Organizational Learning: A Theory of Action Perspective*. Reading, MA: Addison-Wesley Publishing Company; Senge, Peter M. 1990. *The Fifth Discipline*. New York: Bantam Doubleday Dell Publishing Group.

6. Garvin, David A. 1993. Building a Learning Organization. *Harvard Business Review*, July–August, pp. 78–91.

7. Watkins, Karen E. and Marsick, Victoria J. (Eds.). 1996. *In Action: Creating the Learning Organization*. Alexandria, VA: American Society for Training and Development.

8. Mumford, Alan. 1992. Individual and Organizational Learning: The Pursuit of Change. *Management Decision*, 30 (6), pp. 143–148.

9. Pfeffer, Jeffrey. 1994. *Competitive Advantage through People*. Boston: Harvard Business School Press, pp. 8–10.

10. Watkins, Karen E. and Marsick, Victoria. 1993. *Sculpting the Learning Organization*. San Francisco: Jossey-Bass Publishers.

11. Martin, Susannne and Kehoe, Ben. 1990. Organisation Change: Developing a Learning Organization and Adapting to Change. *Training & Development in Australia*, 17 (1), March, pp. 7–12.

12. Schon, Donald A. 1983. *The Reflective Practitioner*. New York: Basic Books.

13. Dixon, Nancy. 1994. *The Organizational Learning Cycle*. London: McGraw-Hill Book Company.

9

Organizational Learning: Paradigm Five

For decades, educational psychologists and other learning specialists have studied the process of learning. We will structure this chapter around what they have discovered.

THE MEANING OF LEARNING

It is generally agreed that "learning is something that takes place inside an individual's head—in [the] brain" that "enables [them] to modify their behavior fairly rapidly in a more or less permanent way, so that the same modification does not have to occur again and again in each new situation."[1] An observer should be able to recognize that learning has occurred by noting some persisting behavioral change in the learner.

Learning can be called an *act*, but is usually called a *process* because, like other human processes breathing and digestion, it takes place whether we are concerned about it or not. Learning and other human processes are called *natural* since they are activated at birth and evolve over a lifetime.

Learning is associated with some living organisms; learning requires *information processing*, which goes beyond merely responding to some stimulus in the environment.[2]

An Information Processing Theory of Learning

The information processing theory of learning examines how learning actually works. It is applicable to both individual and organizational learning. The following concise explanation covers key principles that can be used in improving organizational learning.

Information processing can be understood as a simple system of inputs, transformations, and outputs (Figure 9.1).

In individual learning, sensory data represent the input. The input is transformed into neural messages and then transformed into messages stored as memory. To affect a person's behavior, messages must be remembered. The stored messages again become neural messages that affect the muscular structure. The resulting actions indicate that the learning process has been activated. The various transformations shown in Figure 9.2 are what we call learning processes.[3] As currently understood, the transformational process represents the way inputs become learning.

Five Message Transformations Involved in Learning

The process proceeds something like the following:

1. Stimulation from the environment affects sensory receptors and enters the nervous system, where it is coded into neural messages.

2. The neural messages are recoded into conceptual form and preserved in the short-term memory for a matter of seconds. An internal rehearsal process may preserve the messages in the short-term memory for longer periods of time.

3. If the messages are to be remembered, they are transformed again and stored in the long-term memory for later recall.

4. Messages that have passed from short-term to long-term memory may be brought back to short-term memory or a working memory for recall. It appears, also, that if new messages depend even partly on the recall of something that has been previously stored in long-term memory, that message must be retrieved from long-term memory to short-term memory.

5. Messages retrieved from memory—short-term or long-term—are moved to an action-response generator, which transforms neural messages and produces action. This action indicates that the information was processed and learning occurred.

Other Factors in the Transformation Process

Although the actions listed in Figure 9.2 are necessary for sensory stimuli to be transformed into learning, two other sets of messages appear to activate and modify the flow of messages: expectations and cognitive strategies or learning styles.

Learners have expectations about what they will be able to accomplish after they have learned something, which may affect how a stimulus is perceived, how it is coded in memory, and how it is transformed into action.

A separate transformation control center appears to determine how messages are coded when they enter and are retrieved from long-term

Figure 9.1
Model of Simple System

Inputs--Transformations--Outputs

Figure 9.2
Five Message Transformations Involved in Learning

Transformation 1
From Sensory Inputs to Neural Messages

Transformation 2
From Neural Messages to Conceptual Messages for Short Term Memory Storage

Transformation 3
From Short Term Memory to Long Term Memory Storage

Transformation 4
From Long Term Memory to Short Term Working Memory

Transformation 5
From Working Memory to Response Generator to Action

memory. Our cognitive strategies or learning styles often affect the manner in which messages are coded.[4]

Phases in Learning

Eight phases in formal individual learning have been identified.[5] The processes associated with each phase can be influenced by factors in the learner's environment. These factors may affect learners' expectations, attention, and coding practices. The activities intentionally arranged to influence the learning phases are what we call teaching, training, instruction, or the facilitation of learning. Knowledge of each phase in the learning process may give you a foundation for examining individual, team, and organizational learning.

Motivation Phase. Learners must be motivated or goal-oriented. Locke and Latham[6] have demonstrated that goal-directed action is essential for both survival and happiness, and that purposeful, goal-directed action is associated with highly motivated states. Goal-directed action, also called incentive motivation, urge for mastery, and achievement motivation, describes the natural tendency of human beings to reach for goals. Learners must perceive that the energy they devote to learning will help them reach an achievable goal. In the workplace, new goals encourage a person to grow. New goals are vitalizing.

Apprehending Phase. For learning to occur, learners must be able to respond to some stimulus or event in the environment. To do that, they must focus on specific aspects of the total environment that are relevant to learning. For example, if reading a text is the critical stimulus, learners must recognize that they are to attend to the language and meaning rather than to the type style and page layout; on the other hand, if the learners are artists or graphic designers, attending to the type faces and visual layout may be more relevant to their learning purposes.

Attending is both facilitated and deterred by a temporary internal state often called a mindset.[7] Once adopted, the mindset influences which aspects of a situation will be attended to. Mindsets lead to what is often referred to as selective perception, or the tendency to focus on some things and ignore others. If their mindset leads learners to focus on irrelevancies or to ignore critical elements, they may not learn in the most effective manner. In the workplace, employees often need to become more discriminating attenders to their situations.

In the workplace, learning is more often directed toward improving the functioning of the company. Past job experiences often contribute to mindsets detrimental to recognizing what needs to be changed and how changes could be made. Workers may need assistance in recognizing detrimental aspects of their mindsets.

Acquisition Phase. Once learners attend to and selectively perceive relevant elements, they can begin the actual act of learning, what Gagne calls the moment when a newly formed entity enters the short-term memory. A critical feature of this phase is that a transformation occurs in the perception; what is stored is almost never exactly the same as the original perception.

This means that the storage process actually distorts messages through simplification, regularization, embellishment, or amplification. This generalization may be particularly critical for workplace learning where critical tolerances must be accepted. Learners must be alert to the varying perceptions of individuals. Because greater retention of messages may occur by grouping perceptions, classifying them under previously acquired concepts, by using simplified principles, or by using a familiar scheme, learners should be encouraged to find a system for organizing their learning.

Retention Phase. At this phase, the perceptions, although altered by the coding scheme, move into the long-term memory. Because it is the least accessible to study, this phase is the least understood. Nevertheless, a number of generalizations may be made about the retention of perceptions.

1. Some perceptions may be stored with sharp clarity for many years and may be recalled in great detail under special circumstances, such as electrical brain stimulation or hypnosis. This capacity to retain perceptions is often referred to as super learning.[8]

2. Some perceptions may gradually diminish. One may be able to remember a general event but recall only a few details about it.

3. Old perceptions may interfere with new perceptions, confusing or crowding them out. If you have lived in several different places, you may confuse the house numbers or associate details of one house with another. It is likely that the interference occurs during the retrieval process. The capacity of long-term memory appears to be unlimited; long-term memory cannot likely be overloaded.

Recall Phase. The process of recall consists of retrieving messages, images, and perceptions from long- and short-term memory. Recall is usually facilitated by *cues.* Sophisticated learners supply their own retrieval cues, which allow them to function independently as learners.

Generalization Phase. The generalization phase of learning involves recalling what has been learned and applying it in a new and potentially different context. In training settings, this is referred to as the transfer of training. MacGyver, the main character in a popular television show in the 1990s, had recall and generalization abilities that were uncanny. In almost any dangerous set of circumstances, MacGyver could study the situation and use materials in the immediate vicinity to overcome the obstacles. In one episode, for example, he was able to reverse the coolant in a refrigerated room to trigger a signal for rescue. MacGyver regularly devised a working rule from a general principle to apply to the situation. In workplace learning especially, the creation of working rules may be the heart of the generalization and transfer process.

Performance Phase. In this phase, learners demonstrate that they have learned. This allows learners to recognize the products of their learning. The specification of behavioral objectives is an attempt to identify ways to recognize the products of learning. In setting new learning goals, learners target products and demonstrate their abilities to achieve them.

Feedback Phase. Feedback consists of obtaining information that a target has been reached. In many instances, the performance itself offers feedback. In other cases, another step beyond performance must be completed. Often, feedback comes from comparing the product with a model product. When, for example, has a person satisfactorily "paraphrased" a response to a comment from someone? The answer is not in the learner's response, but in the comparison with a model provided by the teacher, trainer, or facilitator.

LEARNING IN THE WORKPLACE

We have made brief references to how the phases of learning may affect learning in the workplace. At this point, we would like to focus on the things that are learned in the workplace. We will examine three types of learning: (1) individual learning, (2) team learning, and (3) organizational learning.

Individual Learning

Work-based learning focuses on understanding and performing (the know-what and the know-how) technical work skills.[9] Through work-based learning, organization members gain skills, knowledge, and attitudes.

The outcome of learning is human capabilities. Educational psychologists have identified five classes of learned human capabilities: (1) the acquisition of verbal information, (2) the development of intellectual skills, (3) the use of cognitive strategies, (4) the refinement of social attitudes, and (5) the refinement of motor skills.[10]

According to Watkins, work-based learning also deals with (1) acquiring knowledge about the organization where you work, (2) developing an understanding of one's relationship to the organization, (3) discovering how to enact a democratic culture, (4) facilitating shared cognitions, (5) manipulating tools, (6) developing contextualized reasoning, and (7) developing situation-specific competencies.[11]

Work-based learning involves learning how to learn from work experiences. This requires individuals to engage in self-directed and team learning. The outcomes of work-based learning are (1) to be able to change things, including behaviors and policies, when errors occur, and (2) to be able to change the underlying values and programs that created the behaviors and policies in the first place.[12]

Opportunities to learn are always present at work. The key is to enhance the learning atmosphere of natural work settings. The group that brings about work-based learning includes the individual worker, the worker's immediate supervisor, the organization's human resource development coordinator, and a learning facilitator (who may be outside the organization).

Workplace individual learning differs from other approaches to individual development because it recognizes that most of what organization members learn about their work is learned right where they do the work. Workplace learning takes advantage of the natural circumstances in a person's work life. It focuses on learning from a real-life job. Because individual workers learn from where they work in the organization, the organization benefits directly from change that occurs in the workplace. Finally, when learning is an integral part of the organization, the organization gets direct results in the shortest amount of time. Everyone benefits from individual workplace learning.

Team Learning

Team learning is based on the assumption that people in teams can learn more effectively than they might do alone. In many organizations learning is closely tied to teamwork. When the team is the usual structure for doing work, it is the natural place to introduce workplace learning. Through the support mechanisms of a team, organization members can learn how to innovate while working collectively. The ideal of individual collectivism may be achieved through team learning.

Dechant and others[13] identified four learning processes that characterize team learning:

Framing and reframing. Framing is the group's initial view of a situation, based on their past understanding of it. Reframing is the process of changing the initial view. To reframe, one must interpret the circumstances by challenging initially held views. Team reframing can only occur through a dialogic process in which all team members come to understand the mindset of other members, and then review their own mindsets. Ultimately, the team integrates all of the mindsets into a new mental model that is held collectively. The reframing process transforms mindsets so that relatively enduring behavioral change occurs.

Experimenting. Experimenting involves testing educated guesses. Another term for experimenting is action. Experimenting requires team members to agree on team actions. The very process of hypothesizing potential actions, deciding on a course of action, and agreeing on how to proceed brings about learning. Action may be taken in two or more ways. One of these is called exploratory experimentation, in which individuals try out new behaviors. A second way to take action is to implement a set of decisions to see how they would work.

Crossing boundaries. Boundaries are the limits of the team's actions. Boundaries can be physical, mental, or structural. The team moves ideas, views, and information to people and other organizational units beyond its initial boundaries. We often feel that there are both real and imaginary lines that establish a space in which activities occur, and beyond which one does not move. For learning to occur boundaries must be identified and deliberately challenged. To tap into the knowledge of someone in another area, it is necessary to cross some boundaries. Initially, crossing a boundary can be a disturbing experience, but it can also be exhilarating. Ultimately, boundary crossing results in more learning.

Integrating perspectives. Through consensual processes, team members integrate their views so that conflicting perspectives are encompassed within higher-order principles, without majority rule but through consensus. True learning—authentic changes in a person's mindset—may be a function of the process of integration. The collective construction of a new perspective is the most substantive form of learning.

Team learning requires a sharing of perspectives, information, and decision-making processes. Sharing in a team serves as the basis for organization-wide sharing that is essential to becoming a learning organization.

Organizational Learning

The move from individual learning to team learning to organizational learning is a cumulative process in which the basic principles of learning themselves are reframed to apply to a larger entity. The reframing process, however, must be done, as Kim suggests, without anthropomorphizing a nonhuman entity.[14] Organizations are more than collections of individuals. Organizational learning, likewise, is not just the collective learning of individuals, although organizations can learn only through individuals.

Clearly, though, the evolution from team learning to organizational learning may be less a difference in kind than a difference in degree; the move to organizational learning involves more institutional theory, issues, and functions than does individual or team learning. In this section, our goal is to sort out some of the critical features of organizational learning in an effort to distinguish it from team and individual learning.

The assumption may be made that organizations have mindsets in some way parallel to individuals' mindsets, and that organizations have memories in some way similar to individuals' memories. Organizations have information distribution systems comparable to the information distribution systems of individuals, and organizations take action and get feedback somewhat like individuals take action and get feedback.

Following these lines, organizational learning should occur in a manner similar to individual and team learning.

Source of Mindsets

A critical difference between individual learning and team and organizational learning is the source of the mindsets used in deciding what information is to be processed, how it is to be processed, how it is to be stored, and when information is to be processed.

The information-processing activities of individuals are governed by mindsets that are a function of individual personalities, attitudes, perceptions, and attributions. These four aspects of individuals combine to influence individual preferences and decision making.

The information-processing activities of teams are governed by group mindsets that are a function of common attitudes (beliefs, feelings, and intentions), perceptions, and attributions, often referred to as norms, or perceptions of acceptable actions. The tendency to associate with people who share common feelings, beliefs, and values strengthens team solidarity and exerts pressure on team members not to deviate from team norms.

The information-processing activities of organizations are governed by institutional mindsets that are a function of written and unwritten expectations of behavior (rules and norms), often called the culture of the organization or institution. Each organization has one or more cultures and subcultures that contain expected behaviors of those associated with the organization. An institutional mindset evolves from interaction among organization members over time. An organizational mindset begins to exist when the organization is perceived to have boundaries that distinguish it from other parts of the world, when decisions made in the name of the organization are not those of any specific individual, and when actions may be taken on behalf of the organization separate from that of any specific individual.

Some time ago, Berlo[15] explained that once a social system (organization) has developed, it determines the communication of its members. The organization affects how, to and from whom, and with what effects communication occurs among members of the social system. A style develops that is characteristic of members of the social organization. The organization develops ways of doing things, writing about activities, and talking about its work that are imposed on members of the organization. As individuals are immersed in the system, their unique behaviors adapt to the demands of the organization. Thus, Berlo argues that even if we do not know a person as an individual, we can still make fairly accurate predictions about the person from a knowledge of the person's status in the social system.

Weick has articulated a more contemporary version of the relationship between organizational talk and learning in organizations. He observes that "to manage meaning is to view your organization as a set of procedures for arguing and interpreting. In any organizational assessment, ask questions such as these: How do we declare winners of the argument? When do we interpret? What interpretations do we tend to favor (blind spots)? Whose interpretations seem to stick?"[16]

Thus, we find that organizations have processes for making sense of their own activities. Weick has reconceptualized organizations as less orderly than once supposed. However, he also suggests that "organizations may be anarchy's, but they are organized anarchy's. Organizations may be loosely coupled, but they are loosely coupled systems. Organizations may resort to garbage-can decision making, but garbage cans have borders that impose some structure."[17]

Key Issues in Organizational Learning

The concepts of organizational culture and communication are a solid foundation on which to build an understanding of organizational learning. Many of the concepts of organizational learning may be deduced from literature on culture and communication. The key issues of organizational learning may be summarized as follows:[18]

1. How the organization stores and retrieves information.
2. How the organization distributes information.
3. How the organization solves problems.
4. How the organization facilitates change through experimentation and action.
5. How the culture of the organization evolves and functions to deter or facilitate action.
6. How the organization encourages and maintains an innovative and energized workforce.
7. How the organization maintains stability in the workforce while becoming competitive.
8. How the organization cultivates a learning climate.
9. How the organization discovers more about itself as a learning organization.
10. How the organization functions in a global environment.
11. How the organization questions the underlying concepts of work.

Action Learning

Marquardt observes that "perhaps no tool is more effective in building a learning organization than action learning."[19] Meyer selected action learning as the process to use in developing strategies for the Department of Subways of the New York City Transit Authority in order to "grapple with the need to become increasingly flexible and responsive in a climate of change."[20] Three problems concerning overcrowding, train announcements, and a lack of teamwork were presented by the Senior Vice President. Groups were formed to reflect diversity of job function, gender, ethnicity, and age. Participants worked across divisional lines and generated fifteen solutions. All but two were at least partially implemented.

Mounting evidence shows that action learning is an effective tool for facilitating learning in organizations. Watkins and Marsick[21] published a casebook describing activities that companies used to enhance learning, many of which were action learning projects. Yorks, O'Neil, and Marsick observe that "action learning helps to build a critical mass of change agents who influence larger-scale change. Action learning represents a significant organizational intervention that can release considerable energy for change into the organization."[22]

Action learning has been defined as "a small group of people solving real problems while at the same time focusing on what they are learning and how their learning can benefit each group member and the organization as a whole."[23] This definition suggests the six components of an action learning program: (1) a significant problem; (2) within the authority of the team to resolve; (3) a somewhat diverse set or team of four to eight individuals with a facilitator to monitor progress; (4) team members formulate problem-resolving strategies through a questioning process; (5) take action in a real situation to implement the strategy; review the outcomes using reflection and compare what was expected with what actually happened; and (6) develop insights about themselves, their problem-solving processes, and the consequences of actions—that is, learning from their actions.

Since the process of reflection (learning from their actions) takes such a prominent role in action learning, we shall examine the process in a bit more detail. Reflection is defined formally as the process of meditating on the meaning of an experience. Seven questions should be answered during the reflection period:

What happened or is happening?

What precipitated the action or response to the action?

What are, have been, or could be the consequences of what happened?

What is the significance of the event for the team (good/bad, serious/trivial)?

What does the reaction or consequences say about the team in terms of how members deal with one another and how the organization functions?

What should be done about the response, event, or consequences?

What other questions would be helpful to ask about what happened?

Reflection often leads to the recognition that managerial problems are many-sided. Often, reflection reveals differences in organizational goals and leads to additional reflection on other organizational functions. Reflection also allows team members to acquire personal insights and become more sensitive to others.

Organizational learning may be defined as the process of reflecting on an event in order to:

Recognize what happened (share perceptions).

Make sense of what happened (share information).

Identify goals that were not achieved as part of what happened (identify problem).

Describe adjustments that allows the organization to achieve its goals (solve problem).

Codify what was learned and store for future use (develop memory).

Try out changes that may improve efficiency (experiment).

Action learning can contribute to making the elements of a learning organization—shared perceptions, information sharing, problem identification, problem solving, memory development, and experimentation—more effective.

Project Selection

The following is a critical list of questions to ask when evaluating possible projects:

In the project, will team members bring about significant change?

Is the project feasible given the time and skills available?

Are the risks of loss of reputation and money high enough to stimulate action without being too threatening?

Is the problem sufficiently ambiguous or open-ended to require imaginative and creative solutions?

Is the "client" sufficiently committed to the success of the project?

Is the implementation of actions within the authority of the management of the organization?

The results of the action learning process should be presented at a high-profile meeting involving key executives and senior managers. Both the project results and the lessons learned by the team members ought to be presented.[24]

SUMMARY

In this chapter, we took a preliminary look at the meaning of organizational and action learning and their relationship to organizational dynamism. We reviewed the concepts of individual and team learning. Learning was defined as the transformation of sensory data into information that results in persistent behavioral change. A conceptual model of learning revealed that at least five transformations occur as inputs are processed, prepared, stored, and retrieved to result in persistent behavior. Eight phases were identified in the individual learning process: motivation, apprehension, acquisition, retention, recall, generalization, performance, and feedback. Learning that occurs in the workplace was discussed in terms of individual work-based learning, team learning, and organizational learning. The critical skills of action learning were discussed.

NOTES

1. Gagne, Robert M. 1974. *Essentials of Learning for Instruction.* Hinsdale, IL: The Dryden Press, pp. 4–5, 17–19, 28, 34, 51–52.

2. Barrie, John and Pace, R. Wayne. 1998. Learning for Organizational Effectiveness: Philosophy of Education and Human Resource Development. *Human Resource Development Quarterly,* 9 (1), pp. 39–54.

3. Gagne. *Essentials of Learning for Instruction.*

4. Kolb, David A. 1984. *Experiential Learning: Experience as a Source of Learning and Development.* Englewood Cliffs, NJ: Prentice-Hall.

5. Gagne. *Essentials of Learning for Instruction.*

6. Locke, Edwin A. and Latham, Gary P. 1990. *A Theory of Goal Setting and Task Performance.* Englewood Cliffs, NJ: Prentice-Hall.

7. Fisher, Glen. *Mindsets.* 1988. Yarmouth, ME: Intercultural Press, Inc.

8. Ostrander, Sheila and Schroeder, Lynn. 1979. *Superlearning.* New York: Dell Publishing Company; Brown, Barbara. 1980. *Supermind: The Ultimate Energy.* New York: Harper & Row, Publishers.

9. Kim, Daniel H. 1993. The Link between Individual and Organizational Learning. *Sloan Mananagement Review*, Fall, pp. 37–50.

10. Gagne. *Essentials of Learning for Instruction*.

11. Watkins, Karen E. 1991. Many Voices: Defining Human Resource Development from Different Disciplines. *Adult Education Quarterly*, 41 (4), pp. 241–255.

12. Argyris, Chris. 1994. The Future of Workplace Learning and Performance. *Training & Development*, May, pp. S36–S37.

13. Dechant, K., Marsick, V., and Kasl, E. 1993. Towards a Model of Team Learning. *Studies in Continuing Education*, 15 (1), pp. 1–14.

14. Kim. The Link between Individual and Organizational Learning.

15. Berlo, David K. 1960. *The Process of Communication*. New York: Holt, Rinehart & Winston, p. 150.

16. Weick, Karl E. 1985. Sources of Order in Under-organized Systems: Themes in Recent Organizational Theory, in Yvonna S. Lincoln (Ed.), *Organizational Theory and Inquiry: The Paradigm Revolution*. Beverly Hills, CA: Sage Publications, Inc., pp. 109, 133.

17. Ibid.

18. Fiol, C. Marlene and Lyles, Marjorie A. 1985. Organizational Learning. *Academy of Management Review*, 10 (4), pp. 803–813; Huber, George P. 1991. Organizational Learning: The Contributing Processes and the Literatures. *Organizational Science*, 2 (1), pp. 88–115; Levitt, Barbara and March, James G. 1988. Organizational Learning. *Annual Review of Sociology*, 14, pp. 319–340; Field, Laurie and Ford, Bill. 1995. *Managing Organizational Learning*. Melbourne, Vic: Longman Australia Pty Ltd; Martin, Susannne and Kehoe, Ben. 1990. Organisation Change: Developing a Learning Organization and Adapting to Change. *Training & Development in Australia*, 17 (1), March, pp. 7–12.

19. Marquardt, Michael J. 1999. *Action Learning: Transforming Problems and People for World-Class Organizational Learning*. Palo Alto, CA: Davies-Black Publishing.

20. Meyer, Susan R. 1998. Action Learning as a Vehicle for Organizational Culture Change. *Proceedings of the Academy of Human Resource Development*. Baton Rouge, LA: Academy of Human Resource Development, March 11.

21. Watkins, Karen E. and Marsick, Victoria J. (Eds.). 1996. *Creating the Learning Organization*. Alexandria, VA: American Society for Training and Development.

22. Yorks, Lyle, O'Neil, Judy and Marsick, Victoria J. (Eds.). 1999. *Action Learning: Successful Strategies for Individual, Team, and Organizational Development*. Baton Rouge, LA: Academy of Human Resource Development.

23. Marquardt. *Action Learning*.

24. Boddy, David. 1981. Putting Action Learning into Action. *Journal of European Industrial Training*, 5 (5).

10

Techniques for Achieving Goals: Projects

In the last chapter, we focused on learning as a strategy for enhancing organizational dynamism. In this chapter, we will focus on techniques. Techniques are specialized procedures and methods used to accomplish desired goals. The basics of a science, a sport, or art are often referred to as its techniques. The techniques of football, for example, include how to run, block, pass, tackle, and hand-off the ball. A football team that effectively executes the techniques of football increases its likelihood of winning games. The ability of communicators to employ appropriate communication techniques increases their success. In the field of organizational change and development, our techniques help us achieve the goals of organization development.

The techniques for enhancing dynamism are myriad, as demonstrated by Nelson's book *1001 Ways to Energize Employees* published in 1997 by the Workman Publishing Company. However, the basic mechanism for creating long-term, sustained dynamism is called the PROJECT. Consistent with the philosophy expressed here, Rosabeth Moss Kanter declared in her book *When Giants Learn to Dance* that *"projects* that begin small and with *cultural goals* [emphasis added] often generate greater proportional financial returns than those with economic goals."

Projects may consist of just about anything that needs to be done. For example, during an annual sales meeting, employees of a Minnesota company constructed a playground for children in the area. The cost to the company was equivalent to the cost of eighteen holes of golf at a resort for each of the employees. Most projects may be on-site and involve ways to improve technical operations and productivity, in much the same way that a Cleveland,

Ohio, company has employees prepare detailed performance reviews of the organization to identify ways in which work processes can be improved, or they may be off-site, like the Fairfield Inn's partnership arrangement with Habitat for Humanity to build homes for low-income families.

Projects should be designed effectively so that their goals are clear and what is to be accomplished is described precisely. For convenience in referring to projects, they should be given a name. The rationale should be explained and a step-by-step procedure for completing each project should be enumerated.

An easy and effective way to initiate projects for enhancing dynamism is to create a projects steering committee (PSC). The first illustrative project describes the process by which a PSC might be organized. The projects that follow are illustrative of those designed to achieve natural work goals and revitalize the workforce in any company.

ILLUSTRATIVE PROJECTS

Project 1

Goal: To create a mechanism whereby employees can influence their work lives.

Project Name: Projects Steering Committee (PSC).

Project Description: Organize a steering committee to coordinate efforts of both management and employees to contribute to the company, other employees, the facilities, and the community. The central focus of the steering committee will be to review concerns expressed by management and employees. The steering committee will also be responsible for defining problems and forming problem-solving groups.

Rationale: Industry today is concerned by the apparent lack of workforce vitality. For many years society has placed great emphasis on the promotability of an individual within an organization. Vertical achievement has typically signified success, but American business has rarely faced the reality that vertical achievement is finite.

There comes a point in most employees' careers when promotions and the other material awards become trivialized, less frequent, and may even end altogether.

Judith M. Bardwick says that "plateauing is a controversial subject in American business, because facing it requires organizations to admit that the big rewards of promotion and money are available for a limited time only. Chances are [workers] will reach their promotion ceiling long before they retire."[1] Vertical achievements are limited and making these rewards available to everyone who earns them is nearly impossible. Instead there seems to be a general feeling of inability to progress. Therefore, management needs to promote growth in other ways, encouraging employees to develop their talents, skills, and ideas within their current work situation.

Creating a plant steering committee gives responsibility to employees at all levels to advance in their own careers and assist others in bettering their work lives.

Actions:

Step 1. Choose a chair for the steering committee from the senior leadership team. This person will be responsible for leading the committee and creating subcommittees to deal with each problem. The chair reports directly to upper management regarding those things discussed by the committee.

Step 2. Choose committee members from each department within the company (e.g., technical cells, engineering, office staff).

Step 3. Arrangements must be made for the committee to meet regularly, but to minimize the effect on their primary responsibilities, committees may meet before or after their shifts, or possibly during a lunch hour.

Step 4. Give those problems to the steering committee that do not require a decision from the senior leadership team. Allow them to discuss the concerns and define the problems.

Step 5. Give the steering committee authority to select sub-committees to address the individual issues brought to it. Subcommittees should be chosen in the same manner as the steering committee, with participants from all areas of the company. There should be no more than six individuals on each subcommittee.

Step 6. Place members on the steering committee for a limited time.

Positions within the steering committee should *not* be permanent. The chair person may be an exception. Change the steering committee frequently to allow many employees to participate. Those placed on sub-committees should serve only until the concern or problem is solved.

Step 7. Make sure each subcommittee reports to the steering committee frequently. The steering committee can report to the senior leadership team.

Project 2

Goal: To help employees feel optimistic about other each other and what they can accomplish.

Project Name: Plant Beautification.

Project Description: The plant beautification project will improve the work surroundings. Beautification can take place both within the plant and outside of the plant.

Rationale: Miller describes personal vitality as the desire and ability to perform effectively in life and at work.[2] In this program, employees will develop additional skills and feel a sense of accomplishment as they beautify the plant.

Vision: Employees will be energized by the appealing environment in which they work. Turnover and absenteeism will decrease, and the improved plant will enhance the recruiting process.

Actions:

Step 1. Appoint a committee for designing improvement projects.

Step 2. The committee could investigate, for example, how the lighting could be improved.

Step 3. Paint the walls of the plant white and add windows. This will improve the working area of the plant and invigorate the employees.

Step 4. Plant flowers around the outside of the building. If they are interested in planting the flowers themselves, the employees will feel a sense of pride in their workplace.

Step 5. Have employees paint their machines. This will give them a sense of ownership and motivate them to keep the machines in good working condition.

Step 6. Give all employees a hat to wear at work because they work with the company. This can contribute to the sense of teamwork and strengthen company pride.

Project 3

Goal: To encourage employees' confidence by showing them they are valued, respected, and appreciated.

Project Name: Open House.

Project Description: Sponsor a semi-annual open house in the company facilities.

Rationale: The open house will remind employees that they are respected by both the management and their families. The open house will encourage employees to prepare for the public presentations.

Vision: Employees should both value and feel valued by the company and community. Employees should feel a sense of pride in what they are doing.

Actions:

Step 1. Invite employees and family members to attend. Display projects and products created in the previous six months.

Step 2. Ask employees working in the computerized part of the operations to demonstrate technology and use of computers.

Step 3. Ask operations employees to show before and after pictures of products and explain exactly what is done to get products perfected.

Step 4. Ask engineers to show the design and function of products and explain their work.

Step 5. All employees should be present to explain their contributions.

Project 4

Goal: To encourage employees who are promoted to positions of leadership to acquire managerial leadership skills.

Project Name: Employee Leadership Excellence (ELE) Training.

Project Description: This course will ensure success for employees in leadership positions. This four-month course, taught via closed-circuit television from a local college or university, is completed in the company's Leadership Training and Development Center. Leadership skills are taught, practiced, and reviewed in each session.

Rationale: Eighty percent of those in leadership positions have been promoted from within the organization. Many have had little if any specialized training in leadership behavioral practices. The training currently given to new supervisors consists of a short orientation to the annual review to be completed on each employee.

This limited training offers little support. Through the current "Tuition Reimbursement Program," any employee may be reimbursed for college tuition for courses taken that are job related, or that progress the employee toward his or her degree. The amount of reimbursement is based on the grade the worker earns at the end of the course. This program places an emphasis on education. Training newly promoted leaders in leadership and management skills continues to emphasize education. It acknowledges that all employees need to be recognized as influential people: people expecting to succeed; people making alternative futures; people updating their missions; people who anticipate, adapt, and act.

Vision: The managers who complete this course will be committed to the company and their careers, and view the training as a way to make themselves more efficient producers. In addition, they will do all they can to develop other workers.

This vision must be supported from all levels within the company. The training program must be seen as an integral part of the ongoing training and development for leaders. It cannot be seen as a burden to bear to keep their jobs. For a new leader to grow through work, the training must stretch the individual and also be applicable to the work situation.

Actions:

Step 1. Appoint a Director of Human Resource Development to coordinate the program. The Director may initially choose to form a committee to assist in the planning and development.

Step 2. Contact a local university or college to initiate a closed-circuit course on managerial leadership skills, which could be contracted. Such a course would be far less expensive than hiring a professional to teach an on-site seminar. An Internet course could be used as well.

Step 3. The company Leadership Training and Development Center can be set up in an area upstairs currently reserved for large training groups. A portion of this room can be walled off and finished in order to create a classroom setting. Closed-circuit television and other equipment can be installed and the entire room can be secured when not in use.

Step 4. Once established, the HR Development Director would determine the course frequency. The course might follow the university semester schedule or be initiated as needed by the company. The director would decide how best to meet the needs of the company and the newly promoted employees.

Step 5. As courses are developed, other community businesses might become interested in sending their newly promoted employees to a similar course. The initial investment might be recuperated through small fees for those attending from outside the company.

Project 5

Goal: To illuminate possible work accomplishments.

Project Name: Employees on Site.

Project Description: The company should develop a system to help employees see the use of their products in the real world. Groups of employees could travel to locations where their individual products are used. This would give customers and workers a chance to compare product data, and share new ideas to improve products. This program could start locally and then, as the advantages are more readily visible, expand to reach customers throughout the continental United States.

Rationale: Customers want immediacy. One good way to encourage that response is to put the staff in direct contact with the customers themselves. This could improve the specifications of some products and also revitalize employees, increasing the attention they give to the manufacture of products and the delivery of services.[3] Employee enthusiasm is as critical a resource as the technology and financial support in the manufacturing process. Hackman and Oldham remind us that there are "three factors for . . . motivating Work: meaningfulness, autonomy, and feedback or knowledge of the results of work activities."[4]

Vision: By directly coming to know the customers' needs, workers can modify old products and develop new products more easily. The employees' abilities will expand to higher levels as they become more aware of the immediate needs of customers.

This program will enlarge possibilities and encourage a dedicated workforce.

Actions:

Step 1. Begin by contacting local and intrastate customers and proposing the Employees on Site Program as a way of enhancing services offered by the company.

Step 2. Each employee should travel once every three months, six months, or year to a location that uses company products.

Step 3. Each employee should spend a day with the customer's employees to find ways that improve the manufacturing process.

Step 4. Employees return to the company and report on the visit, and discuss with other employees how the manufacturing process might be improved.

Step 5. Office staff, including accounting, buyers, and ordering, could be added to this program to increase communication by contacting the customer directly to clarify information and orders. The customer's products would be manufactured and delivered in a much more timely manner, and feedback from the customer to the office staff would then be more open.

Project 6

Goal: Confirm individual contributions.

Project Name: Employee Recognition.

Project Description: The recognition program will acknowledge efforts made toward enhancing the appearance of the workplace and improving work conditions.

Rationale: Employees will value their work experience more when they are recognized for their contributions.

Vision: Employees will be invigorated by participating in a worthwhile activity where management expresses confidence in and respect for employees.

Actions:

Step 1. Recognize employees for their contributions to committees. The steering committee should choose employees to recognize for committee contributions since all committee activities proceed through the steering committee.

Step 2. An article of clothing with the company logo could be given to select employees as confirmation of their contributions. Specialized assignments could be recognized with appropriate gifts; for example, beautification committee members might receive gift certificates for a local restaurant.

Step 3. Committee members should identify employees who have improved work conditions. Committee members report to the committee leader, who can then give the employee a gift certificate and special thanks for their efforts.

Project 7

Goal: To enhance confidence, respect, and appreciation among employees.

Project Name: Seasonal Events.

Project Description: Sponsor two seasonal parties for employees and their families: a Christmas dinner and a summer barbecue.

Rationale: It is important that employees be recognized with guests present.

Vision: Employees will feel respected and valued by the company.

Actions:

Step 1. Give all employees an invitation with the option of bringing a guest.

Step 2. The Christmas dinner should be more formal, possibly being held at a reception center where there is enough room and available catering. Each unit should make a presentation recognizing the contributions of all their employees.

Step 3. The summer barbecue should be more informal. All employees and their families should be invited. A special committee of employees from all levels of the organization should plan the summer barbecue. All units should be given a budget and provide all the food, entertainment, and party favors, if any.

Project 8

Goal: To support activities beyond the boundaries of the company so as to advocate a sense of altruism and giving among employees.

Project Name: Community Services.

Project Description: Sponsor a series of community activities and services. This program would involve employees in mostly after-hours community volunteer activities.

Rationale: Community support creates a favorable climate for the development of productive employees by strengthening ties among employees, the organization, and the community.

Vision: When employees have the opportunity to expand the scope of their activities and services into the community on behalf of the organization, they become more responsive and committed to the organization.

Actions:

Step 1. Form a community services committee comprised of employees from all areas and levels of the company.

Step 2. The committee should investigate the possibility of sponsoring a basketball team or a softball team in a local city league.

Step 3. The committee should explore the possibility of company-sponsored events during festival days or the county fair.

Step 4. The committee should celebrate veterans by sponsoring programs on Veterans Day and Armed Forces Day. Veterans could be invited to tours of the facilities hosted by committee members.

A VISION FOR PROJECTS

Several illustrative projects have been outlined, but they should be taken as samples only.

The effective use of projects is possible only with the full involvement of organization members. The case of Applegate Health Care reveals how one company strategically implemented projects to respond to lost business and to energize its workforce.

APPLEGATE HOME HEALTH CARE

Dan, amiable CEO and President of a fledgling home health care group, had engineered an improvement in its financial status by securing a contract to provide health services for homebound government-funded clients. Eventually, the contract accounted for over 60 percent of the firm's income. Then, one afternoon Dan was informed that the contract had been canceled. He was distraught and angered at the thought of downsizing 60 percent of the workforce and starting all over again. After a fitful night, he decided to meet with employees and explain the situation to them.

At 11:00 A.M., employees assembled excitedly and crowded into the break room and hallway to hear news from Dan. Shocked and dismayed, they listened as he explained that the contract had not been renewed and that 60 percent of them would most likely need to be let go. Then, he turned the meeting over to a senior associate and walked back to his office.

The senior associate solemnly walked to the front of the room and, facing the group, he made a remarkable proposal. Employees should be given an opportunity to salvage the company and solicit new business. Consultants and associates knew the community and could make contacts for business that had not been touched as yet. All employees present were divided into working groups of five to six individuals and given the task of evaluating the proposition and how it might be approached.

The group broke for lunch and to tend to pressing business, but returned by 1:30 P.M. to continue deliberations. By 3:00 P.M., it was proposed that groups report to see how close they were in their ideas about what to do. As each group reported, it came clearer that the employees were committed to making the company viable. The following conclusions were reached:

1. A steering committee, consisting of the Director of Nurses, the Senior Aide, and the Director of Professional Services, should be organized to direct efforts.
2. Select teams should be created to solicit new business.
3. No employees were to be "let go" with the promise that business would be tripled soon.

The steering committee met with Dan in his office and presented the proposal. Dumbfounded, he pondered how he would pay the bills. The steering committee members assured him that employees would willingly take pay cuts until business increased. Reluctantly, he agreed to try the plan and carefully drove home that evening to reflect on why it might work.

During the next week, employees met and organized to continue operations. The company occupied rooms in a rented building that lacked regular maintenance. The outside of the building did not have appealing landscaping, which gave it the appearance of a run-down warehouse. Dan had repeatedly contacted the owner of the building about improving its external appearance, but to no avail. As business improved, an employee committee was organized to investigate ways to enhance the looks of the outside of the building. Eventually, the employee committee met with the owner of the building and negotiated an agreement where he provided the plants and the employees provided the labor to landscape the building. Employees were ecstatic, and on their own time completed the landscaping.

Other working groups focused on internal marketing and on how to proceed to replace the loss of 60 percent of the business. The internal marketing group investigated ways to improve employee morale without adding a lot of cost. Out of this came employee and community health fairs, summer picnics, and Christmas activities. They also helped to evaluate the employee benefit package and ended up emphasizing their value. They proposed implementing an employee newsletter to highlight great employee successes. The newsletter was designed to keep the home care staff, who worked in the clients' homes, informed of the company's progress and to keep them connected.

The business development group assigned tasks to a variety of staff members encouraging a more diversified market approach. Because of these efforts, revenues dropped only one month.

Applegate expanded its services from two cities to three rural areas to counter the impact of managed care contracts and large individual referral sources. The employees felt that they provided great home care services, and they would be easy to sell under the new arrangement.

Under the new arrangements, over a four-year period, home health visits increased from 18,791 to 74,302—a fourfold increase. During a report about the company, as part of a presentation at a local university, Dan described his job as primarily visiting offices in cities where Applegate had facilities and making sure that employees had what they needed to run operations. Employee perceptions of their performance, opportunities, fulfillment and expectations were positive, with scores in the high range.

ANALYSIS

In this instance, a traumatic event established an opening to make dramatic changes in Applegate. Nevertheless, dynamism may be enhanced by small changes and within the current organizational structure. Projects are a critical method for revitalizing the workforce and for increasing productivity. Projects create excitement because they encourage people to do better, move ahead, work free, and want more.

ACTION LEARNING AND PROJECTS

Action learning processes may be more compatible with a projects approach to change in organizations than other forms of organization development. One reason rests in the very structure of an action learning set or group. The set usually consists of four to eight organization members from different areas of the company with a moderator to monitor their progress. The set identifies a problem or a goal to be achieved and formulates a set of actions that can be used to reach the goal or resolve the problem. One or more members of the learning set then initiate actions designed to do something about the goal or problem.

A goal, and its associated actions, constitutes a project. The key to action learning is taking action. The key to effective project implementation is taking action. Without action, we have nothing to monitor and evaluate. After action has been taken, some consequences usually become apparent. If the action moves the set or team toward accomplishing the goal, team members tend to feel more confident, optimistic, and daring. If the action is thwarted or fails to move the team toward resolving the issue, team members tend to feel pessimistic, uncomfortable, and less willing to proceed.

Under any condition—success or failure—the team should meet and reflect upon what happened, why it happened, and what could be done to move the project forward. The process of meditating upon consequences and actions as a group is called reflection. The team attempts to discover what happened, why it happened, and what should happen next. In addition, the team seeks to learn from their actions—hence, learning from actions or action learning. To learn from an action means that you are able to identify and state an answer to each of the basic questions. Ultimately, the team should be able to develop a principle that helps explain what happened. The principle becomes the learning standard. When we can explain why something happened without being told, the reflection process is working.

As the team works, it should be looking for ways to codify and store the explanations and principles so that they can be used in the future. They should be located where they can be retrieved for use and in case team members are unavailable to provide their explanations. To codify means that you have devised a filing system, whereas to store something means that the file can be located where it can be found by someone else. When action learning occurs in a company, we often refer to it as organizational learning.

The action learning process allows the team to return to the project and work out the details so that another action can be taken to achieve the goal and solve the problem. Team members learn from their experience, the organization acquires information that contributes to sustained learning, and action moves projects along. With each success, enthusiasm builds and dynamism becomes apparent, with both individuals and teams sharing in the excitement.

SUMMARY

In this chapter, we presented a rationale for using projects to achieve natural work goals. Eight illustrative projects were discussed in detail and an example of how one company used projects to increase both productivity and organizational vitality and dynamism was presented. Building on those projects, an organization can establish a program for revitalizing its workforce.

We returned one more time to action learning as a process for advancing projects.

NOTES

1. Bardwick, Judith M. 1986. *The Plateauing Trap.* New York: AMACOM, p. 129.

2. Miller, Donald B. 1977. *Personal Vitality.* Reading, MA: Addison-Wesley Publishing Company, p. 19.

3. Taylor, James C. and Felten, David F. 1993. *Performance by Design.* Englewood Cliffs, NJ: Prentice-Hall, pp. 187–189.

4. Hackman, J. Richard and Oldham, Greg H. 1980. *Work Redesign.* Reading, MA: Addison-Wesley Publishing Company, p. 73.

11

Altra Teams: Beyond the Usual

The cover story of *Business Week*, July 10, 1989, focused attention on team-work with a question: The gains in quality are substantial—so why isn't it spreading faster?[1] According to our competitiveness chart, businesses were just moving out of the quality stage and its major technique, self-directed work teams, although many companies were just beginning to look over the guidelines to see whether they could afford to become more competitive using teams.

TYPES OF TEAMS

That cover story did a masterful job of summarizing the status of team-work as the 1990s approached. The story identified three types of teams, their structure and function, their results, their origin, and their prospects for the future. Let us briefly summarize the analysis.

Problem-Solving Teams

The first type of team was called the Problem-Solving Team. It consisted of five to twelve volunteers, both hourly and salaried, who were drawn from different areas of a department. They met for one or two hours a week to discuss ways of improving productivity, quality, efficiency, and the work environment. The team had no power to implement its ideas. Since they could come up with ideas to reduce costs and improve products, they were considered useful, but they could neither reorganize the work nor force managers to adopt a more participative style; thus, they tended to fade away after a few years. Problem-solving teams began with small efforts in the 1920s and 1930, but it wasn't until the 1970s that they began to flourish as part of the Quality Circles effort.

Special-Purpose Teams

The second type was called Special-Purpose Teams. Each team was relatively small, but it was able to design and introduce work reforms and new technology. The team met with suppliers and customers, linking what had been separate functions. In union shops, labor and management collaborated on operational decisions at all levels. The team involved workers and union representatives in decisions at higher levels in the organization. The result was the gradual development of a climate for productivity and quality improvements. This seems to have created a foundation for self-directed work teams.

Self-Directed Teams

The third type was called Self-Managing or Self-Directed Teams. Each team consisted of five to fifteen employees, who managed the production of an entire product rather than just subunits or parts. Members of the team learned all the tasks and rotated from job to job. They were considered to be multiskilled. Teams took over managerial duties, including scheduling work and vacations, ordering materials, and even, in some cases, hiring and firing team members. Self-managed teams increased productivity as much as 30 percent and substantially improved product quality. Teams made fundamental changes in work organization and the amount of control that employees had over their jobs. In many cases, supervisors were eliminated or became team coordinators, locating supplies and facilitating disputes. Self-managed work teams were used by a few companies in the 1960s and 1970s, spread rapidly in the mid-1980s, and appeared to be the wave of the future.[2]

Katzenbach and Smith described three types of teams they encountered in their studies: teams that recommend things, teams that make or do things, and teams that run things.[3] Teams that recommend things tend to parallel the problem-solving idea of people getting together to share information and make suggestions without having the authority or skills to implement them. Teams that run things have long been known as management teams, and should probably be called groups, since they mostly come together to make decisions. Teams that make or do things are what we usually call work teams; when they become self-managing, we often call them self-directed work teams (SDWT). These teams include people who are responsible for basic manufacturing, operations, marketing, sales, service, and new product development. Their activities are ongoing, so they have no completion deadlines. They do the work of the organization. Self-directed work teams have failed when team members fail to understand that the controlling mechanism of work teams is the work itself. Thus, Ketchum and Trist reasoned that "while individual character traits are not to be ignored, there is a strong relationship between behavior on the job and the way work is organized. We create the workplace, and the workplace creates us."[4] Teams created because of the way the work must be done are the only ones that are called work teams.

A work team is a group of workers responsible for creating a product or handling a process in an organization. The work team plans the work, completes it, and takes care of regular supervisory tasks. The team is accountable for production, quality, delivery, costs, statistical controls, motivation, and coordination with other teams and departments. The work team is governed by the work itself, not the other way around. The work team is charged with responsibility to manage itself, increase the skills of team members, and improve the process, the products, and the service the team provides.[5]

To create work teams—self-directed or otherwise—the work is changed so that it must be done by a team. To be self-directed, the team must be responsible for all aspects of the work of the team. When the work is changed so that a team must do it, work teams are created automatically. If the work must be done by one, then avoid the idea of work teams. Work teams require continual training and assistance to improve their technical, social, and administrative skills.

Self-directed work teams have improved the quality of products and services while dramatically reducing costs. As a result of becoming self-directed, work teams experience the vitalizing quality of some aspects of autonomy and other natural work goals. Unfortunately, as self-directed work teams become institutionalized and routine, they begin to lose much of their vitalizing strength. At that point, it may be appropriate to move to the next level of teamwork, which we call Altruistic or Altra Teams.

ENHANCING DYNAMISM WITH ALTRA TEAMS

The organization that wishes to endow its workers with vitality and enhance dynamism must make some systemic changes and place workers in a position to achieve more of their natural work goals. The changes should do more than create a permissive climate; the changes should enable workers to work better. One way to restructure some aspects of the work system is to implement altra teams.

Altra teams are based on the assumption that workers are more productive when they share responsibility for the development and success of others. The mission of altra teams is to help members of another team achieve four goals. These goals are:

1. To develop perceptions of self-efficacy, or strong feelings that they can perform well. Employees who experience a sense of personal mastery see themselves performing well; this goal is summarized by the phrase "doing better." The altra (altruistic) team is charged with the responsibility of assisting their bene (beneficiary) team to do better.

2. To see themselves as influential, exercising power, and receiving recognition for their efforts; this goal is summarized by the phrase "moving ahead." The altra team is charged with the responsibility of making certain that their bene team is influential and is recognized for that influence.

3. To engage in activities that allow them to feel creative; this goal is summarized by the phrase "working free." The altra team aids the bene team to do its work in ways that free them in their thinking.

4. To raise their aspirations and goals and to anticipate being able to get more out of life and their work experience; this goal is summarized by the phrase "wanting more." The altra team is charged with raising the sights and standards of the bene team in order to achieve more demanding goals.

By assuming responsibility for another team, the altra team discovers that it is also strengthening its own processes; in fact, it may derive more from the relationship than the bene team does. Through feelings of altruism—a concern for other human beings because they are human—the altra team acquires more than a benevolent attitude; they develop a passion for aiding others that is a source of intense energy. Bois refers to altruism as the equivalent of cosmic propulsive energy. Altruism can permeate all other activities to become the dominant passion that propels workers into higher states of energy. Altruism emerges from optimistic thinking and an authentic concern for others.[6]

From the perspective of a bene team, altruism may involve just being a friend. A friend is an advocate and defender. Friendship means having good fellowship. Friends have authentic respect for one another. They sacrifice for one another.

Altra teams follow a process consistent with the underlying values of friendship and altruism (see Figure 11.1). They base their decisions on carefully gathered data. In an altra team of five members, two serve as a data-gathering subunit. Their task is to gather information from the bene team about things that are keeping it from achieving the four objectives: to do better, to move ahead, to work free, and to want more. The data-gathering subunit returns with the data from their inquiry, and brings one member of the team being helped. The newly restructured altra team reflects on the information and attempts to understand what the bene team is attempting to achieve, and the methods they are using. The bene team member provides additional information and helps define problems.

All members of the altra team participate in analyzing the information and formulating specific recommendations for how the bene team can more effectively achieve the four goals; they also include recommendations

Figure 11.1
Process of Altra Teams

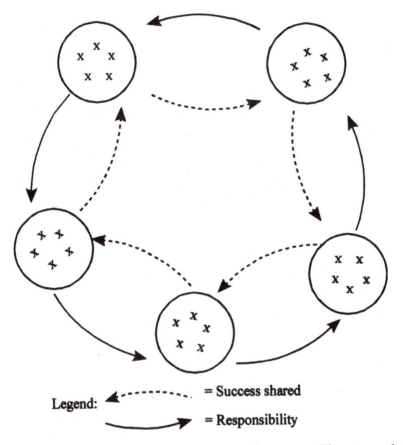

Legend: ← - - - - - - - -   = Success shared

   ——————————▶   = Responsibility

for how the altra team can be of assistance in the process. Then, two other members of the altra team report back to the bene team, accompanied by the bene team member from the data-collecting subunit. The new bene team then formulates a plan for improving their team's efforts to achieve its goals.

When the bene team appears to have a grasp on the plans, the altra team members return to their own teams. Throughout the work period, one or more members of the altra team monitor the bene team to aid them in improving their work processes. This continues throughout any work period.

What Do Altra Teams Achieve?

Let's examine this question in the light of a definition of a team offered by Katzenbach and Smith. They explain that a team is "a small number of people with complementary skills who are committed to a common purpose, a set of performance goals, and an approach for which they hold themselves mutually accountable."[7] Our definition of an organization is a system consisting of a small number of altra teams with complementary skills who are committed to a common purpose, a set of specific performance goals, and an approach for which they hold themselves mutually accountable.

Each element in the definition has significance for altra teams, but three issues are particularly important at this time: commitment to a common purpose, specific goals, and mutual accountability. Commitment to a common purpose gives meaning and brings emotional energy to altra teams by helping them to focus on challenging aspirations. Specific performance goals help a team keep track of its progress, and mutual accountability extends the concept of stewardship to the value of placing service above self-interest. In the past we may have thought of stewardship in terms of individual responsibility for resources, but altra teams are accountable for other teams and, ultimately, for the larger institution.

The overriding value of altra teams is that they replace self-interest, dependency, and control with service, accountability, and partnership. Altra teams enable democracy to thrive, economic success to be shared, and ethical and spiritual values to be part of the everyday work experience. Altra teams do not, of course, solve all work-related problems; however, self-directed work teams themselves implement a new paradigm of organization structure and meet many of the criteria for improved operations.

In their book about reengineering business processes, Hammer and Champy identify several characteristics of best practices in business process redesign. When a company reengineers its processes, many of the changes involve teams. Altra teams add a power, a new dimension to the concept of teams—enhanced dynamism. Alliances are built, trust is encouraged and rewarded, and altruism is demonstrated to be a very important value.[8]

Altra teams are designed to build vitality into your organization. They go one step beyond self-directed work teams. Your company may not be totally ready for altra teams, but they are a goal toward which you can work. At the beginning of reorganization, employees may have a great deal of optimism, but when the process actually begins there may be more confusion than clarity and team members may not see the future as clearly as they had hoped to. Usually, the team leader takes charge and gives the impression that everything is going to be fine, which often brings the group together but results in loyalty to the team rather than to the organization. True self-directed teams have a more loosely coupled system with collaborative individualism. Testing out altra teams too early may interfere with the full transition to authentic self-direction, but they often open up teams and allow them to experience what altruism in the workplace can be like. The thrill is difficult to describe, but the energy is there.

SUMMARY

In this chapter, we discussed the formation of teams and features of contemporary self-directed work teams. We traced the evolution of work teams and suggested that an appropriately timed introduction of altra teams could refocus a selfish or fiercely loyal team to experience authentic altruism in the workplace. The process of managing an altra team was diagrammed and described. All teams are not equal; the teams that work for you are best. If you want to walk the edge and experience more energy in the workplace, forming altra teams is the way to go.

NOTES

1. Hoerr, John. 1989. The Payoff from Teamwork. *Business Week*, July 10.

2. Orsburn, Jack D., Moran, Linda, Musselwhite, Ed, and Zenger, John H. 1990. *Self-Directed Work Teams: The New American Challenge*. Burr Ridge, IL: Irwin Professional Publishing.

3. Katzenbach, Jon R. and Smith, Douglas K. 1993. The Discipline of Teams. *Harvard Business Review*, March-April, pp. 111–120.

4. Ketchum, Lyman D. and Trist, Eric. 1992. *All Teams Are Not Created Equal*. Newbury Park, CA: Sage Publications, Inc., p. 7.

5. Hackman, J. Richard and Oldham, Greg R. 1980. *Work Redesign*. Reading, MA: Addison-Wesley.

6. Bois, J. Samuel. 1978. *The Art of Awareness*. Dubuque, IA: Wm C. Brown, pp. 248–251.

7. Katzenbach and Smith. The Discipline of Teams.

8. Hammer, Michael and Champy, James. 1993. *Reengineering the Corporation*. New York: HarperBusiness.

12

Pragmatics and Sociability:
Enabling Style

Pragmatics concerns the effects of symbols and language on human behavior. When people want to achieve a goal, they marshal their resources and arrange them in the most effective way. When the goal involves creating a sense of optimism in the workplace, symbols provide a very powerful starting place.

LANGUAGE TECHNIQUES THAT ENHANCE OPTIMISM IN THE WORKPLACE

E-Prime Language

Some simple solutions look elegant. Thinking, speaking, and writing in E-prime language overcomes pessimism in the workplace in a sublime way. Although the theory of E-prime language may appear complex, the technique exemplifies a direct way to confront pessimism (see Chapter 6, "Thinking Modes"). E-prime language consists of the whole of the English language minus the inflectional forms of the verb "be."[1] The following verb forms do not exist in E-prime language: am, are, is, was, and were, plus shall be, will be, have been, had been, shall have been, and will have been, at more complex levels. For purposes of this discussion, we focus on the basic forms of the verb "be"—is, are, was, were, and am.

The verb "be" primarily expresses state of being. To say that you "are" something means that you exist completely and totally in that state. In other words, when you use some form of the verb "be," you assert that something exists in a particular state or condition. The verb "be" also has other uses, however, such as an auxiliary in the formation of tenses in the statement "We are studying." In this case, the verb "are" means that we exist totally and completely in the state of studying; however, studying more accurately represents an activity in which we engage. Thus, for accuracy, we could say, "We engage in the activity of studying." Two other uses bear most directly on the issue of negativism in the workplace. We refer to them as the "be's" of identification and projection.[2]

Identification. When you think, speak, or write the sentence "Andy is a manager," you link two nouns—Andy and manager—and imply that one exists as the other. A simple analysis may demonstrate that we have an impossible situation.

If we mean that the word "Andy" exists as the word "manager," we should realize that one word can't exist as another word; they exist independently of one another. On the other hand, the verb "be" in this context serves as a synonym for the phrase "called or classified as." If we mean that the word "Andy" refers to a category of nonverbal individuals, whom we recognize as eating, sleeping, working, and we use the word "manager" as an abstraction at the strictly conceptual level, then we must assume that the nonverbal object "Andy" exists as the concept "manager," which also appears quite impossible. How can something nonverbal exist as something verbal?

We could analyze other combinations, but with somewhat equal futility: The word "Andy" exists as the object manager; the object "Andy" exists as the object manager. The problem rests in assuming that words exist as things. Why use language that perpetuates falsehoods? Why not simply say, "Andy works in the role of manager?" Why not think and express the thought more accurately by avoiding the "is" form of the verb "be?"

Predication. We call the final negativistic use of the verb "be" *predication.* To predicate means that you declare, assert, or affirm that some quality exists in some person or thing. This use of the verb "be" implies that qualities or characteristics exist in things and encompass them completely. In reality, sensory impressions arise in people who describe them using language. For example, the comment "The work deadline was disgusting" implies that a deadline possesses some quality called "disgusting." In reality, the person making the statement only labeled the perceptions as disgusting and projected the quality onto the deadline. This "be" of predication brings together nouns and adjectives implying that disgust somehow exists in the deadline. The "be" of predication serves as a synonym for the term "appears or judged." Thus, thoughts such as "the dress is beautiful," or "the manager is crude," or "the office is exotic" reveal the speaker's judgments about the dress, manager, and office, but say nothing about them directly.

When used to express negative judgments, the "be" of predication becomes particularly ominous. To say, "I am a failure," projects a judgment onto yourself suggesting that you caused the failure and that your entire life consists of failure. We could say the same of other judgments like "stupidity," "awkwardness," and "incompetence." None of those projections ring true in the face of reality. By asserting their truth in the form of all-inclusive generalizations, you validate them and become the judgments.

Eliminate the Verb "Be." Kellogg and Bourland urge more frequent use of E-prime language in thinking, speaking, and writing because it "reduces hidden assumptions," "fosters a world view in which the user perceives situations as changeable rather than static," and "indicates possibilities rather than certainties."[3] In sum, eliminating the verb "be" may vitalize your thinking mode, turning negative thinking into positive, optimistic thinking. As one begins to think of the world as changeable, problems as solvable, and people as active, happy events occur more often and life reveals more opportunities and greater fulfillment.

Let us look at other ways to change your thinking by eliminating the verb "be." Take the all-inclusive generalization: I am a failure! State the thought without using the verb "am." You could think to yourself, "I feel like a failure" or "I seem like a failure." This effectively removes the verb "am," but the thought still reeks of all-inclusiveness because of the term "failure." To avoid all-inclusive generalizing, you need to change the entire idea. You actually need to restate the idea of "failure" so that it describes the actual behaviors involved in the nonverbal, unhappy event that caused the feeling you call "failure." In school it might involve missing more items on a test than any other student who took the test. In this case, "I am a failure" translates into the thought "I missed more items on the test than other individuals who took the test." How would you correct the situation so as to feel less like a failure? Miss fewer items on the next test! How would you correct being a failure? The answer to this question may not leap out so clearly.

Now, take the disqualifying personalization "I am not worthy, I am capable of doing only bad things," and restate one or both parts of the statement without using the verb "be." How would you think the thought about being worthy and not being capable? What do they mean? Would you think, "I behaved badly" or "I lack adequate self confidence" or "I do things that others look down upon" or "I did not meet the expectations of my colleagues" Give the most precise explanation of why you feel capable of doing only bad things.

Take the following all-inclusive thoughts and translate them into E-prime language.

1. My boss is an incompetent jerk. [Eliminate the "is" verb and rephrase the term "incompetent jerk."] Tentative translation: My boss makes different decisions than I do.

This statement reveals why you disagree that your boss is incompetent while couching the idea in language that encourages positive feelings.

2. That is a stupid idea. [Eliminate the "is" verb and rephrase "stupid idea."] Tentative translation: That idea tends to encourage inefficiency. This

statement indicates why you prefer some other idea and provides an opportunity for the person who offered the idea to modify it without offense.

3. I am incompetent. [Eliminate the verb "am" and rephrase the term "incompetent."] Tentative translation: I dislike not being able to think of some creative ideas. This statement offers a suggestion for why you seem to feel negatively about yourself, making it possible to seek some remedies.

4. I am never happy about what I do. [Eliminate the verb "am" and rephrase the term "never happy."] Tentative translation: I just did not do well in that last presentation.

This statement eliminates the overgeneralization expressed by "never" and indicates a possible source of unhappiness.

5. You are ugly. [Eliminate the verb "are" and rephrase the term "ugly."] Tentative translation: I prefer slightly shorter people. This statement changes the negative evaluation into a description of your preferences, which more accurately expresses the idea.

6. He is the most obnoxious person I have ever met. [Eliminate the verb "is" and rephrase the terms "obnoxious person" and "have ever met."] Tentative translation: You probably recognized that this statement expresses a judgment. You might substitute the term "seems like" for the verb "is." The result would read: "He seems like the most obnoxious person I have ever met." That change certainly softens the statement. However, a more accurate translation might read: "His behavior seriously offends me." Rather than saying that he "is something," the statement indicates that the speaker feels affected by the other person's behavior in some intense way. This may be the thought that the speaker had in mind in the first place.

To experience thinking in E-prime language, write a page in your personal diary indicating how you feel about your own use of all-inclusive generalizations. Then, write a one- or two-page biographical sketch of yourself. Attempt to write every sentence in E-prime language. You may find several sentences where the E-prime version sounds overly awkward, but consider any reduction in the number of "be" verbs a step in the right direction.

Kellogg and Bourland provide a number of suggestions for using E-prime language:[4]

1. Use a variety of general substitutes for the "be" verb: seems, appears, feels, acts, looks.

2. If you find it difficult to compose a sentence in E-prime, narrow the statement. For example, "Everybody is smart!" might read as "Everybody makes $250,000 a year" or "Everybody scored 160 on an IQ test." You can see the ridiculousness of "everybody"in all-inclusive statements.

3. Replace the static "be" verb with an action verb. For example, rather than thinking that "Jack is a manager," think "Jack manages the shoe department."

4. Ask questions more directly and precisely; for example, if you ask, "Is the President in?" translate the question to "May I speak with the President?"

5. Mentally rehearse statements before you say them. Nod your head, look intelligently interested, and occasionally utter filler sounds such as "I see," "yes, indeed," and "perhaps" as you translate sentences from all-inclusive generalizations to E-prime language.

6. Practice translating the all-inclusive generalizations of others into E-prime language during conversations, then reflect back to the speaker the original idea only in E-prime language.

7. When you begin writing and speaking in E-prime language, you may find yourself in midsentence before you realize that you have set yourself up to use a "be" verb. In such a case, stop and rephrase the idea another way, seeking to begin the sentence with the real subject of the sentence. For example, if you find yourself saying, "The report was prepared by Lilly," make Lilly the subject of the sentence and restate it as "Lilly prepared the report." The translation changes the thought from the passive voice to the active voice, which most writing specialists prefer anyway.

8. Watch for dreaded contractions, such as I'm [I am], she's [she is], it's [it is], and you're [you are]. In a be-verb linguistic environment, alertness brings about greater sensitivity and more opportunities.

9. Enlist the support of a friend, colleague, or spouse to monitor your speaking and writing. Give them a quarter for every b-verb they identify in your conversations and papers.

Consistently using E-prime language represents a difficult task. The urge to use be-verbs feels overwhelming. You may discover that basic thought patterns develop habitually over the years and resist reorientation. That does not invalidate the new ways. It merely demonstrates the strength of our habits.

Seven Other Techniques

We shall now discuss seven other techniques for reducing pessimism in the workplace. Since the way you think about people governs the way you react to them, you should steadily respond to others with greater optimism if you follow these suggestions.

Use Indexes. We call the first of these techniques "using indexes." Since all-inclusive generalizing groups and categorizes people, giving the impression that they possess identical characteristics, you might use numerical indexes to reduce or eliminate that tendency. This technique involves distinguishing between individuals in classes of people, such as railroad workers, college professors, high-tech employees, managers, and even Republicans on specific characteristics. That means linking each person with a number or by using a given name when talking about characteristics. When you say that "workers in the chemical industry show little concern for the public interest," we assume that you know something about every worker in that industry; that may not ring true, since workers in the chemical industry have different concerns about the public interest.

Though most workers in the chemical industry probably have a great deal of concern about the public interest, the one or two whom you have contacted may have less concern than you would like. Thus, you should say, "Employees Bob, Bill, and Bing have less concern about the public interest than I would like them to have," to avoid conveying the wrong impression of workers not included in the generalization. Bob, Bill, and Bing represent indexes in the same way that saying Employee 1, Employee 2, and Employee 3 does. Indexing gives our talking and writing and thinking a more optimistic tone by refusing to obscure individual differences with categories, generalizations, and stereotypes.

Using Dates as Indexes. Dates remind you that no two times share identical features. Dates highlight differences in individuals and objects over time. To use the dating technique, add a date to each statement about people, objects, and events. For example, rather than saying, "All of the meetings we hold are rotten," you could say, "I felt uncomfortable during the [March 23] meeting." The consistent use of dates in conversations and reports, or just simply the awareness of the dates, reminds you that circumstances change over time.

Using Plurals. Many people experience anxiety when trying to avoid sexist language in their writing. In addition, some confusion occasionally develops over the consistent use of verbs and pronouns. Maybe your talking and writing reflect confusion when you try to explain that "an individual tries on their new shoes" so as to avoid the "his or her new shoes structure." Plurals avoid several forms of awkward sentences, such as "an associate ought to discover [his or her or their] own insight." The better sentence states that "associates ought to discover their own insights." Speaking in plurals helps us distinguish between experiences, an important consideration in avoiding overgeneralizing.

Each of us has felt many loves; to acknowledge this fact through the use of the plural term "loves" suggests that love 1, 1989, and love 2, 1999, represent different loves.

Using Hyphens. Traditional, all-inclusive generalizations tend to verbally separate many things that cannot be separated in reality. Our language permits such expressions as "biological background," and "cultural background," but in the lives of people, they experience only "biocultural backgrounds." Likewise, "emotional-intellectual" and "socioracial" reactions represent reality more clearly than does either term alone. By using hyphens more often, we remind ourselves that events in the world have more interrelatedness than our language enables us to indicate.

Using Etc. In a world that changes constantly, we may not represent with words everything that happens with, to, and between people and events.

This means that much may be left out and unsaid. The use of etc. alerts our thinking to this unlimited universe of events that goes without comment, and reveals a humility and modesty of statement appropriate to mature people.

Using Quotation Marks. Many statements contain words that refer to things that we cannot verify with our senses. Such words represent exclusive, personal knowledge, and need some way to indicate their special meanings. Using quotations marks in writing and using some kind of inflection or gesture when speaking allow us to call attention to those personal meanings and signal to others to be on guard in their responses because of potential differences in meanings. In conversation, you might "crook" a finger in a quotation-mark form to suggest that listeners might not get the same meaning from a statement that you intend. By using quotation marks, you may disclose to others that you may be using certain words with special meaning.

Using Qualifiers. What we know and say about people and events rests largely on observations that omit and distort details. The most accurate statements express the degree to which statements actually describe observations. Through the use of verbal qualifying terms, you can express your judgments about how confidently you describe your own thoughts and the behaviors of others. Qualifiers such as "it seems to me," "one possible way," or "as I understand the situation" indicate that additional information might contribute to a fuller understanding of the situation. In short, the use of verbal qualifiers provides for a realistic view of this world in which uncertainty plays a conspicuous role.

These eight language techniques help a person to deal with the tendency to overgeneralize and express a pessimistic view of life. Although you should avoid making a display of yourself, scrubbing the "be-verbs" from your thought processes will allow you to deal more effectively with pessimistic thinking and convert your interactions with others into an optimistic mode.

SOCIABLE OPERATING STYLE

Dynamism may be enhanced in an organization by a generally sociable pattern of interaction. People who react to others with enthusiasm, flexibility, attentiveness to others, and a positive sense of optimism tend to build an atmosphere of energy around them. Zimbardo studied "shy" people for several years and concluded that they often just do not have the energy to act in a positive manner. The heavy burden they carry as a result of anxiety, boredom, and passivity generates more fatigue than physical labor. He says that they "need to get *moving* and discover their untapped sources of energy."[5]

Lack of action, or what appears as withdrawing and passive behavior, characterizes shy people. They discover untapped sources of energy when they start greeting others with "Hello," "Hi there," and "Good to see you around." These little acts of kindness and acknowledgment generate energy. Zimbardo suggests that to feel energy, shy people need to develop vocal styles appropriate to the mood of the situation: forceful when needed, interested at times, concerned when concern seems to reflect the mood, and angry or tender as dictated by the moment.

In an earlier chapter we talked about operating styles—ways of interacting in the workplace. The Operating Styles Profile[6] identifies four styles of interacting. These styles have some of the characteristics of habits. They can take control of us and persist even when they shouldn't. Some styles seem to exude energy and respond to enthusiasm more naturally than others: Dealers respond well to people who show enthusiasm, and movers like friendly and enthusiastic people. Holders prefer diplomatic people, and givers like people who emphasize personal relationships. A sociable operating style encourages and supports sustained energy output in an organization, more than an unsociable or antisocial style. People react with energy to energetic people.

In his book *Feeling Good*, Burns explains that negative thoughts cause self-defeating feelings and actions.[7] Positive thoughts energize and enhance organizational dynamism. The language techniques described above counter cognitive distortions that lead to depression. Operating style and thinking mode may be different sides of the same coin. They mutually reinforce each other in optimizing an energetic organizational climate.

In his book *The Positive Principle Today*, Norman Vincent Peale writes, "It is a pathetic fact that multitudes of people actually drag through life in a dreary sort of way, having little or none of the zest and enthusiasm which should normally characterize a human being." His tenth principle for keeping the positive principle going is "the fabulous secret of energy and vitality thinking," which means by simply thinking energy and vitality, your energy and vitality increase.[8]

Donald Smith, on the other hand, in his book *How to Cure Yourself of Positive Thinking*, examines the downside of positive thinking and the mystifying fact that the bulk of positive thinkers don't really get the rewards touted for them. He says that the reason positive people fail is that they begin with a completely false premise: that goodness is a thing—a commodity—that they can acquire like a piece of property. The reality is that goodness is merely the absence of badness. This view says that "whatever energies are already flowing around us are essentially and basically good," and that what we need to do is give a "swift kick to the things that make us unhappy, rather than to spend our lives in a fruitless pursuit of something that we already have if we would just permit it to surface."[9]

From this view, sociability and optimism evolve naturally from the absence of unhappy events in your life. If negative things do not happen, you haven't acquired anything, but you have freed yourself to be happy. Dale Carnegie presents a somewhat similar idea in his book *How to Enjoy Your*

Life and Your Job when he describes the work of Charles Schwab, who was paid a million dollars a year to manage the Andrew Carnegie industries. Why did Schwab get paid so well? Schwab says, " I consider my ability to arouse enthusiasm among the men the greatest asset I possess, and the way to develop the best that is in a man is by appreciation and encouragement."[10] By showing sincere appreciation, people's natural energy and enthusiasm can be released. You can't give people vitality; all you can do is communicate with them in ways that release the energy and enthusiasm.

In his book *Family Communication*, Sven Wahlroos says that emotionally healthy people can take an interest in and invest enthusiasm in people and things around them, which in turn makes their own lives more enjoyable and rewarding. You can recognize emotionally healthy people by the way they talk, which reveals their enthusiasm and excitement.[11] We can conclude that a sociably enthusiastic operating style establishes a foundation for the revitalization of others and of your self. When you remove or minimize unhappy things that obstruct your interactions with others, you have a greater likelihood of enthusiastic communication.

SUMMARY

In this chapter, we described language techniques for enhancing optimism in the workplace. We offered E-prime language—the absence of all forms of the verb "be"—as a reasonable antidote to overgeneralizing that leads to pessimism. We offered several suggestions for ways to include E-prime language in your speech and writing. We described seven other techniques for reducing overgeneralizing in language. Finally, we offered advantages to maintaining a sociable style of interaction and an optimistic view of life.

NOTES

1. Bourland, David, Jr. 1965/1966. A Linguistic Note: Writing in E-Prime. *General Semantics Bulletin*, 32/33, pp. 11–14.

2. Lee, Irving J. 1941. *Language Habits in Human Affairs*. New York: Harper & Row.

3. Kellogg, E.W., III and D. David Bourland, Jr. 1990. Working with E-Prime: Some Practical Notes. *ETC: A Review of General Semantics*, 46 (Winter), pp. 376–392.

4, Ibid.

5. Zimbardo, Philip G. 1977. *Shyness: What It Is. What to Do about It*. Reading, MA: Addison-Wesley Publishing Company.

6. Pace, R. Wayne, Stephan, Eric G., and Mills, Gordon. 1996. Operating Style: A Profiling Tool. *The Take Charge Assistant*. New York: The American Management Association.

7. Burns, David D. 1980. *Feeling Good: The New Mood Therapy*. New York: Signet Books.

8. Peale, Norman Vincent. 1976. *The Positive Principle Today: How to Renew and Sustain the Power of Positive Thinking*. Englewood Cliffs, NJ: Prentice-Hall, pp. 184, 187.

9. Smith, Donald G. 1976. *How to Cure Yourself of Positive Thinking*. Miami, FL: E.A. Seemann Publishing, Inc., pp. 13–14.

10. Carnegie, Dale. 1970. *How to Enjoy Your Life and Your Job*. New York: Simon & Schuster, p. 97.

11. Wahlroos, Sven. 1974. *Family Communication*. New York: New American Library.

13

The Whole Nine Yards in Easy Steps: Meeting the Challenge

When you try to enhance dynamism and vitality in organizations, you must come to grips with the manner in which change occurs in your organization. You may need to reflect deeply on why employees do not feel passionate about their work and the organization. Everyone need not feel excessively exuberant about the workplace every day; however, workers should feel energized rather than discouraged about coming to work.

This book has provided a basic theory of why workers fail to push the organization's competitiveness. The theory is simple: Organization members feel energized when they have a clear sense that they are accomplishing four goals at work:

Doing Better—workers must feel that they are cultivating their talents and work skills. Doing better is also known as having self-efficacy, or feeling confident in your ability to do your work at a high level of excellence.

Moving Ahead—workers must feel that they influence people and decisions in the organization. To move ahead, workers need to feel that they are improving their status in the organization, that they are increasing their knowledge and influence.

Working Free—workers must feel that they are doing something meaningful and that they can take the initiative and use their own ideas to solve problems.

Wanting More—workers must feel comfortable aspiring to great things. Wanting more means that workers feel they can expect greater economic rewards, but more importantly, they feel they can meet the other goals—doing better, moving ahead, and working free.

Workers can instill these four fundamental perceptions by setting natural work goals. A worker usually has two kinds of goals. The first, technical goals, arises from the technical processes of the organization and focus the attention of workers on what the organization is trying to accomplish. Technical goals are imposed on workers, although certain work schemes, such as self-directed work teams, often allow workers to instigate technical goals, as long as the goals are within the expectations of management. Unfortunately, technical goals fail desperately to meet any of the workers' natural goals.

Natural work goals focus primarily on what workers want to achieve at work. They are derived from the core character of human beings, which lies in people's abilities to think, to infer conclusions, and to further their own happiness and well-being.

The power of natural work goals was hinted at by John W. Gardner when he said, "Everyone has noted the astonishing sources of energy that seem available to those who enjoy what they are doing and find meaning in what they are doing."[1] Natural work goals give purpose to actions that strengthen company commitment.

Spurts of energy can be triggered in other ways, but for only a short duration. The inability to achieve natural work goals leads to uncommitted, lethargic, and selfish workers. When management blocks natural work goals, they may find some compliance, tempered by listlessness, but they will more often meet resistance.

That's the whole nine yards in a nutshell. Energy stems from workers' perceptions of their performance and the extent to which they can do better (P), the influence and opportunity they experience in the organization (O), their significance and ability to work free from constraints (F), and to what extent their aspirations are realized (E). Those perceptions are heightened by the achievement of natural work goals.

The evidence is overwhelming: The single most important factor in the productivity of organizations is how easily employees can achieve natural work goals. If you continually facilitate efforts to achieve natural work goals, you will permanently enhance productivity. This may require implementing an organization change program. Here are some steps that you could take to initiate such a program.

EASY STEPS TO ENERGIZE EMPLOYEES

Teach Your Employees about Natural Work Goals

This will help overcome some prevalent misconceptions about "motivation," or why people do what they do. Most people have been exposed to the idea that people are motivated by something called "needs," which are considered part of our genetic makeup. Instead, workers should learn that they can release energy by identifying natural work goals and achieving those goals, not by trying to satisfy some need. Goals direct intensity, and sustain actions, while the satisfaction of needs merely leads to lethargy, which is the last thing an organization wants. Workers must discover the relationship between sustained energy release and the achievement of natural work goals.

Help Employees Select One or Two Natural Work Goals to Achieve

This is very nonthreatening because it doesn't involve modifying the technical goals of an organization. However, you need to focus your goal-setting activities on natural work goals and provide the structure and process for employees to achieve a small number of natural work goals. This will allow workers to feel the excitement of doing things that they want to do, while enhancing their stature in the organization. Achievement of the organization's technical goals will follow naturally.

Identify Activities that Could Be Used to Achieve the Goals

In Chapter 10, we explained a number of plans that could be used to achieve natural work goals. With employees, brainstorm some ways in which they might meet each goal they select. Follow the sample programs in Chapter 10.

Make Programs Consistent with the Culture of the Organization

Just about every successful organization reports having a fairly strong culture associated with that success. Since organizational culture has such a powerful connection to long-term effectiveness, it is a good idea to make sure that any effort to introduce new programs is at least minimally consistent with the current culture. Over time, the new programs may affect both the climate and culture of the organization, which in turn may affect individual perceptions of POFE, making it highly desirable to be mindful of both the climate and the culture in introducing new ideas.

Prepare Specific Steps to Implement Activities

Your organization can implement the processes of change much more easily when you have identified some precise steps to take. Most people are more comfortable with new projects when they see a step-by-step plan for bringing the projects into fruition.

Confirm the Success Each Time a Goal Is Achieved

One of the most powerful responses you can give to the successful achievement of a goal is confirmation, not to be confused with rewards. Rewards are tangible indications that a person or an act is better than some other person or act. You give rewards for winning races because the winner ran the fastest; you give rewards to actors because someone thinks they are better than other actors; you give rewards to children who complete more requirements than other children. However, you should provide confirmation to everyone who achieves a goal—any goal. Don't give rewards in the workplace; they simply irritate the people who don't receive them. Let the goal achievers know that you appreciate their achievements, and that achieving those goals was a good idea.

Have All Employees Take a Regular Vitality Break—a VB

Every day employees should spend some time identifying ways to improve their performance, find opportunities, derive greater fulfillment at work, and meet their highest aspirations. During that period of reflection, they will identify other natural work goals and continue to energize the workplace. The break can consist of these simple steps:

Stop what you're doing.

Relax for a few seconds.

Visualize your work setting.

Scan the setting until you identify a goal.

Write down the goal.

Stand up, raise your hands high, and say, "I can do it!"

WHAT MANAGERS CAN DO TO BEGIN

Because managers currently have greater control over the work setting than employees do, it is important for managers to initiate the move toward an environment in which employees can achieve natural work goals. Managers can encourage employees by doing a few basic things:

Start by Including a POFE Evaluation in Your Employee Appraisal System

Make the POFE perceptions part of your formal employee reviews. The questions should include these ideas: What could we do to help you improve your performance at work? What could we do to increase your opportunities at work? What could we do to make your work more fulfilling? What could we do to help you meet your expectations and how can we encourage you to aspire to get more from work in the future? The answers to these questions may very well identify important natural work goals. Managers can then assist employees by providing resources and support toward achieving the natural work goals.

Experiment More; Go Ahead and Do Something; Start a Project

The biggest difficulty in moving ahead is the first step. If you as a manager can authorize a project and some expenditures to get it started, the project will get started more quickly and directly than it would otherwise. Nevertheless, always check on the results of projects by having workers report back on what happened. Pay attention to the reports for ideas that could result in new projects, and keep adapting processes and projects that bring better results.

Arrange the Elements of the Work System to Release Workers' Energy

This is a prodigious task, so work with only parts of the organization at the beginning; this requires less effort. In Chapter 3, we identified five elements of a work system—structure, guidelines, the work itself, leadership practices, and the individual worker—and some of the negative effects that they perpetuate. Identify places in your organization where these negative effects deter vitality. After you have identified these, there are four steps you should take. First, modify policies, eliminate rules, and cut work practices that restrict employee autonomy. Second, refine individual leadership practices to enable employees to make more decisions. You may want to take a look at the operating style of managers and lay out a plan for bringing more sociability into their interactions with others. Third, restructure the work and the work system to highlight collaborative individualism and maximize the use of teams. Fourth, have employees adopt new ways of doing their work, especially based on their own analyses and conclusions.

Manage the Change Process to Achieve Maximum Effectiveness

This involves several subtasks.

First, create a readiness for continuous change. Prepare managers and workers to anticipate adopting new practices that allow them to reach their POFE goals.

Second, start at the top; obtain support from the most senior person who has the credibility, control of resources, and position power to make the change to natural work goals and POFE a reality.

Third, make the decision to implement new procedures within the context of the organization's strategic plan; link changes to department, divisional, and company-wide strategic plans.

Fourth, seek to underpromise and overdeliver so that expectations do not become unrealistic. Failed promises turn out to be the single most de-energizing aspect of any change effort.

Fifth, involve workers who will be affected most by the change. In fact, the processes outlined for implementing energizing projects require that workers be involved in the decisions from the very beginning. If you follow those suggestions and procedures, workers will be involved.

Sixth, get a commitment from top management for dollars, time, and physical resources to implement the projects. Inadequate resources indicate that top management isn't interested in making changes.

Seventh, use steering committees, explained in Proposal 1, Chapter 10, to oversee projects. An appointment to a temporary steering committee tends to elicit support for the project.

Eighth, keep everyone informed about the status and effects of projects. Highlight the ways the project will benefit the individual.

Ninth, start small and work big by creating small successes at the beginning. Successful projects become models for expanded efforts. Even the most enthusiastic people tire of supporting new projects if no payoff is seen within a reasonable time.

That's the whole nine yards.

MORE GENERAL STRATEGIES—YARD TEN

If we were dealing with football, ten yards would be a more appropriate ending. Given some liberty to stretch the comparison, let's take a look at the next yard for a moment. Every change effort should be placed in a framework so that it moves forward with some sense of rationality. Several alternative frames are usable, including organizational development, sociotechnical systems, human resource development, persuasion, behavioral modification, culture, and action.

Action Learning

Action learning captures the philosophy and methods that seem compatible with this change process. At its core, action learning holds that organization members can learn or develop principles that guide decision making by taking direct action. Then they can reflect on that action to discover guidelines for improving both their own lives and the functioning of the organization. We sometimes refer to "taking direct action" as "having an experience," since both imply deciding to do something. Action learning begins with the decision to take some action, but it is greater than just having an experience; it focuses on goals to be accomplished in the workplace. As individuals take action to reach their goals, they can learn from what they did. As you'll discover, though a group facilitates learning, the learning that occurs turns out to be individual learning. Hopefully, all members of the group will learn from the process, but they should learn in such a way as to link effective action with the learning that takes place.[2]

The second element of action learning involves a group of people, often called a "set," who meet together for a concentrated period of time. The set helps members to learn from their experiences as they explore issues and exert pressure on one another to form sound judgments about future actions. This process is called "reflection."

Reflection is based on a simple model of problem solving that says that a problem is the difference between the way things are and the way we think they ought to be. The process of problem solving follows three steps: (1) phrase the goal you want to achieve, (2) identify the barriers keeping you from achieving the goal, and (3) take the actions necessary to surmount the barriers and achieve the goal.

Members of the set help each other to work through the process of identifying a goal and the barriers to its accomplishment. The goal is refined by asking challenging questions. Helpful questions free the mind to think about alternative ways of defining the goal and the barriers. Three questions are often helpful at this stage: What are you trying to accomplish? What is stopping you from accomplishing it? What can you do about moving ahead?

Three other questions examine the conditions surrounding the goal: (1) Who knows what you are trying to do? (2) Who has a vested interest in accomplishing the goal? (3) Who has control of the resources to accomplish the goal?

This questioning phase clarifies the goal and the barriers. Some barriers not identified earlier are often raised at this point. In the action learning process, the goal should be solidified in the questioning stage.

The next phase is, of course, to decide how to surmount the barriers and achieve the goal. It is an absolute necessity for the set member to take action. There can be no learning unless some action is taken. To encourage action, set members could ask the focal person, What are you going to do before the next meeting? How can you move forward to achieve this goal? What is the most important thing for you to do to get started?

I live on a golf course and have discovered from watching the golfers who pass our deck that the way to learn to play golf is to get a set of clubs and hit a ball. Now, you won't learn how to play golf by just hitting a ball. In your action set, once the meeting has adjourned, you should go out and take some action, then reflect on that action in order to derive some principles for improving the action.

It is after you have acted that the actual learning process begins. Though you may have discovered some interesting things from the goal and barriers identification phase, you haven't actually learned what it takes to achieve the goal. Only after taking action can you meet to initiate the reflection process.

The first task is to get a clear concept of what actually took place. Some questions that could be asked are: What happened? What is still happening? What triggered the reaction? What are the consequences of what happened? What could be other consequences?

The second task is to brainstorm ideas about what to do next. What should be done about what happened? What changes should be made? How will the changes be made?

The third task is to prepare the next set of actions. What are the most pressing sub-goals? What are some possible next steps? What could get in the way of achieving the goal? What do you need to get from this meeting?

To facilitate this third task, the person pursuing the goal should make a short presentation about what happened when action was taken. The group should listen to the presentation, and then ask questions about the action. Sometimes, by using overhead transparencies or a flip chart, you can accept questions and comments as you introduce issues. Be sure to focus on the consequences of what happened, when the action was taken, and explain developments since the last meeting. The presenter has no need to defend ideas or win any arguments. The set members are there to assist, not to refute, the presenter. However, the presenter should share plans for action before another set member presents or the meeting is adjourned.

The meetings will be more productive if set members have some information about the problem. It is also very helpful if set members can agree to maintain confidentiality around their comments so that everyone has the freedom to speak openly. Naturally, respect must be maintained for any ideas presented and any questions asked. The set should be small enough—up to nine members—to allow for face-to-face discussion and questioning. All set members must be willing to engage in collaborative decision making, even to changing their minds when a reasonable alternative is presented.

To assist in the action learning process, ask a person who may not be involved with the set to serve as the facilitator. The facilitator's job is to help participants reflect on the action learning process. The facilitator is not an expert, and should not be a chairperson who controls what happens. The facilitator is there to help set members be honest with one another, to help connect ideas, and to focus on what could be learned.

SUMMARY

In this chapter, we briefly reviewed the four work perceptions and the role of natural work goals in the vitalizing process. Nine specific steps that endow workers and organizations with dynamism were also discussed. Additionally, some specific suggestions for how managers might get started with revitalization programs were introduced. Finally, we discussed action learning as an approach to introducing organization changes.

NOTES

1. Gardner, John W. 1963. *Self-Renewal.* New York: Harper & Row, p. 16.
2. Marquardt, Michael J. 1999. *Action Learning in Action.* Palo Alto, CA: Davies-Black Publishing.

14

Confirmation:
Evidences of Dynamism

The worst bankrupt in the world is the man who has lost his enthusiasm. Let a man lose everything else in the world but his enthusiasm and he will come through again to success.

> H.W. Arnold

Every man is enthusiastic at times. One man has enthusiasm for thirty minutes, another man has it for thirty days, but it is the man who has it for thirty years who makes a success in life.

> Edward B. Butler

When enthusiasm is inspired by reason; controlled by caution; sound in theory; practical in application; reflects confidence; spreads good cheer; raises morale; inspires associates; arouses loyalty, and laughs at adversity, it is beyond price.

> Coleman Cox

It is energy—the central element of which is will—that produces the miracles of enthusiasm in all ages. Everywhere it is the mainspring of what is called force of character and the sustaining power of all great action.

> Samuel Smiles

Nothing is so contagious as enthusiasm.

> Edward Bulwer-Lytton

WORK PERCEPTIONS AND NATURAL WORK GOALS

Workers' perceptions, not reality, determine how well their natural work goals are achieved. Perception is the process by which individuals interpret their experiences in order to give meaning to their lives. None of us perceives things directly; we simply interpret what happens to us and call it experience. What we perceive ("see") affects how willing we are to devote energy to our work. A person's interpretations are heavily influenced by personal characteristics, such as beliefs (what we accept as true); often, our beliefs are so strong that we see what we believe happened instead of what actually happened. Our feelings and values (positive and negative judgments) also affect our perceptions.

Both research and the experience of living in organizations indicate that four basic perceptions serve as the indicators of an employee's vitality and energy output. In the context of strategies for enhancing organizational dynamism, let us briefly review the role of the core work perceptions. Each set of perceptions represents a cluster of natural work goals to be accomplished. Hence, at the end of each section, a paragraph describes the evidence that the goal has been achieved. The evidence indicates how workers ought to feel and what they should be doing if the workplace supports positive work perceptions.

Performance

Workers' perceptions of performance represent how well they think they are able to do functional and behavioral work tasks. Functional tasks are the technical aspects or mechanics of the job. Behavioral tasks are the interpersonal skills of a job, such as resolving conflicts, managing time, motivating others, managing groups, and working independently.

The degree to which people feel that they can perform well affects their actual performance. Individuals with high self-esteem appear to be more confident in their ability to perform. Individuals with proper experience and skills try to cultivate their talents and maximize their successes in order to excel. Positive perceptions of performance ("I'm sure I can do it") or self-efficacy lead to putting more energy into work. The effort that results from positive performance perceptions accelerates productivity. When workers perceive themselves as performing incompetently, that is, doing work that fails to create valuable results but consumes time, energy, and resources, they feel frustrated. Workers then reduce the effort they put into doing their work.

Evidence of Goal Attainment. Employees report having high confidence in their work ability. They have expertise in depth in certain areas and can learn to do other jobs in the organization. They report being able to use their talents and skills in a wide variety of tasks.

Opportunity

When meeting the goal of opportunity, workers perceive that they are able to progress. If they think, for example, that they may receive a promotion or a salary increase, they will tend to feel that they have opportunity in the organization. On the other hand, if workers feel that they are not able to advance in the organization, they will feel that they lack opportunity and they will not be energized.

In our research, the most consistent predictor of promotions and salary increases was the evaluation by an employee's manager of the employee's opportunities in the organization, and not the employee's performance evaluations. Employees nearly always reported having opportunity in the same degree as perceived by their managers.

Evidence of Goal Attainment. Employees report having considerable influence on organizational decisions. Employees receive recognitions for their contributions and feel that they are growing personally. They work together and share their expertise. Employees have a sense of loyalty to others and a sense of community in the organization. They are confident, focused, and clear about their roles and responsibilities.

Fulfillment

To achieve fulfillment, workers must feel able to make innovative contributions. The clearest indication of fulfillment is the feeling that people are able to do things in their own ways.

Evidence of Goal Attainment. Employees report having great autonomy. They exhibit high levels of initiative, and are free from external controls and constraints. Employees report that they take calculated risks. They believe that their contributions are meaningful and significant. They use their own ideas, solutions, and plans to evolve new approaches to problem solving. They report exhibiting their creativity and imagination.

Expectations

The beginning of our careers is composed, to some extent, of a set of expectations rooted in a series of perceived promises. A promise is some assurance—real or imagined—that someone or something (often the organization) will give us or help us accomplish something in the future.

Employment itself is a form of promise. When we get a job, the assumption is tentatively established that the future may turn out the way we imagined it would. Continued employment reinforces the promise. Advancement on the job enables us to confirm that the promises underlying the agreement of employment are being fulfilled. If things go well, we become confident that the promises were sincere. Although some occasional setbacks may occur, on the whole, a career that progresses systematically appears to be based on sincere promises.

So expectations represent what people think they can achieve and promises are the assurances that lead to expectations. Thus, the belief that one's highest aspirations will be achieved by working in an organization encourages workers to devote energy to their work. Downsizing represents a failed promise.

Even more important to dynamism is the fact that, within reason, the higher the expectations are, the greater the results will be. People tend to grow when they have high expectations. In one sense, we become what we aspire to become, we achieve what we aspire to achieve. If we cease to have high expectations, we deny our right to have full personal growth. For people to become highly successful, they need to set difficult and challenging goals. Difficult goals produce higher levels of performance than easy goals or low expectations. The ultimate conclusion is that organization members must be helped to see that they can aspire to greater things and to feel assured that their highest expectations will be realized.

Evidence of Goal Attainment. Employees report that they feel that their future in the organization is constantly getting better. Employees want more for the organization and for themselves. Employees share their expanded aspirations with one another. Personal aspirations are matched with the realities of work. Employees believe passionately in limitless possibilities for the organization and for themselves.

The competitiveness of an organization in today's customization era depends on its ability to provide large numbers of customized, flawless products and services without delay. In order to move into the customization era, workers must be managed so that they can work with energy and feel dynamism. Customization requires workers who are constantly learning.

WHAT DO COMPANIES DO TO DEVELOP DYNAMISM?

Paul W. Ivey urged us to "study the unusually successful people you know, and you will find them imbued with enthusiasm for their work which is contagious. Not only are they themselves excited about what they are doing, but they also get you excited." Our plan is to describe some companies in which dynamism has played a critical role in both the success of the company and the commitment of employees.

These are not only instances in which company practices have engendered widespread enthusiasm in the workforce, but these are some of the places in which working is a real treat. Jeffrey Pfeffer, for example, identified the five top-performing firms in the United States, the ones that provided the greatest returns to their stockholders from 1972 to 1992, each of which returned over 15,000 percent on their investments. One was Southwest Airlines, which not only returned 21,775 percent but also had fewer employees per aircraft (79 to 131), flew more passengers per employee (2,318 to 848), had more available seat miles per employee (1,891,082 to 1,330,995), turned around 80 percent of its flights in 15 minutes or less where other airlines averaged 45 minutes, and provided an exceptional level of passenger service. Pfeffer notes that "much of its [Southwest Airlines] cost advantage comes from its very productive, very motivated, and . . . unionized work force." The other companies were Wal-Mart, Tyson Foods, Circuit City, and Plenum Publishing. Pfeffer concludes that "as other sources of competitive success have become less important, what remains as a crucial, differentiating factor is the organization, its employees, and how they work."[1]

Analysis: Great companies inevitably endow employees and the workplace with dynamism. It is a factor that distinguishes great companies from good companies. When employees work with dynamism, they are more productive and more credible. Customers love to do business with people who show dynamism in their behavior.

TOP TEN COMPANIES

Levering and Moskowitz's 100 best companies to work for in America illustrate the effects of dynamism. In listing the top places to work, they observed that "even as workplaces have been traumatized by layoffs, job burnout and the shift of health insurance costs to employees, the very best workplaces have gotten better."

Levering and Moskowitz's main questions to employees of companies they were studying was: Do you enjoy working here? Why? In a cautious caveat, they explain that "it's tempting to generalize that good workplaces are superior because they help companies succeed. And nearly all the companies we profile are highly successful. But it's a temptation we want to resist, because it demeans the central thrust of our work, which is that there is something to be said, in and of itself, for providing a meaningful, healthy workplace."[2] Their top ten companies were Beth Israel Hospital, Boston; Delta Air Lines, Atlanta; Donnelly (glass), Holland, Michigan; Federal Express, Memphis; Fel-Pro, Skokie, Illinois; Hallmark Cards, Kansas City, Missouri; Publix Super Markets, Lakeland, Florida; Rosenbluth International, Philadelphia; Southwest Airlines, Dallas, Texas; and USAA Insurance, San Antonio, Texas. What characterizes these companies is that they are places where people thrive.

Analysis: A close look at companies that are considered to be part of any group of excellent organizations reveals that employees are endowed with enthusiasm, put a great deal of energy into their work, and, as a result, they enjoy what they do and bring dynamism to the workplace.

BEN & JERRY'S

Patricia Aburdene, coauthor of the book *Megatrends 2000*, says that Ben & Jerry's Homemade Inc. "is the new model of the corporate form that we will see created in the 1990s and into the 21st century." Ben & Jerry's is located in Waterbury, Vermont, with premium ice cream sold in 38 states. Alice Houghton, a production worker, is on the Day Care Committee, the Safety Committee, and the Fruit Feeder Task Force, which studies the fine art of smashing Heath Bars and other goodies and blending them into ice cream. Lisa Carpenter, also a production worker, persuaded her husband to leave his family's dairy farm and work with her. She says, "It's what a job should be. It's not just making money, but doing good things." *USA Weekend* explains that "every day, she can choose which production task she'll do. Every day she runs the risk of getting a free back rub or having a hilarious run-in with the company's Joy Gang."[3]

Analysis: Ben & Jerry's is a classic example of ways to enhance dynamism in an organization. Although some of the practices go beyond the expected, the model projects an appeal that captures the imagination. Every company has the potential for identifying unique, provocative activities that demonstrate to employees that enthusiasm is contagious and underlies sustained competitiveness. Nearly all of the imaginative actions have embedded in them a sense of fun, which often goes with dynamism. Chrysler CEO Robert Eaton and Vice Chairman Robert Lutz repeatedly explain that uptight executives don't feel comfortable at Chrysler because everybody is a little wacky. They say that people should have fun and encourage some creative wackiness.

JOHNSONVILLE FOODS

Ralph Stayer, CEO of Johnsonville Foods, Inc. of Sheboygan, Wisconsin, writing in the *Harvard Business Review*, explained the revitalization process that moved his company from "wallowing like buffalo to flying like geese." He first started by looking for a book that would tell him how to "get people to care about their jobs and their company." But, the search was fruitless. He reflected that no one could tell him how to wake up his own workforce. He had made the company, so he had to fix it himself. "I hadn't really built the company all alone, but I had created the management style that kept people from assuming responsibility. . . . If I was going to fix what I had made, I would have to start by fixing myself."[4] What he visualized for Johnsonville Foods was a company that could sell the most expensive sausage in the industry and still have the biggest market share.

What he saw was an organization where people took responsibility for their own work, for the product, and for the company as a whole. Johnsonville Foods was financially successful, but employee attitudes were startlingly poor. A survey indicated that employees saw nothing for themselves at Johnsonville, that they simply had jobs with little commitment. He realized that he had focused entirely on the financial side of the business and had viewed people as dutiful tools to make the business grow. The employees had no stake in the company and no power to make decisions or control their own work. If he wanted more commitment from employees, he had to involve them in the business. Early efforts to delegate responsibilities failed miserably. He learned that employees had to expect responsibility, want responsibility, and even demand responsibility. He needed an environment in which employees insisted on being responsible.

One problem area illustrates how Stayer began the revitalization process. He was told that workers in one plant disliked working weekends, which they did often to meet schedules. He asked them if they had measured production efficiency and if they had tried to get workers to take responsibility for the problem. With survey data, they discovered that machine downtime hovered between 30 percent and 40 percent, most of which was caused by lateness, absences, sloppy maintenance, and slow shift startups. Once workers began to see that they were the source of the problem, they cut downtime to less than 10 percent and had Saturdays and Sundays off.

Stayer, in addition, discovered that expectations have a way of becoming reality, so he decided to break down traditional pictures in employees' minds of what managers do and how subordinates behave, so they changed the words used. "Employee" and "subordinate" were changed to "member of the organization" and "coordinators" or "coaches." They stressed the need for coaching skills and de-emphasized technical experience. Whenever a person was promoted to coordinator, word was sent around that the promotion was for demonstrated abilities as a teacher, coach, and facilitator. Eventually, Stayer scheduled himself out of meetings, forcing others to make decisions without him.

At one point, Johnsonville Foods was confronted with a problem and an opportunity. They could take on new temporary business and saddle themselves with a cancellation of the contract and big layoffs or a new capacity for a market they no longer had. This was a problem for all of the organization members. A meeting of the entire plant was called and members were asked three questions: What will it take to make it work? Is it possible to reduce the downside? Do we want to do it? Teams in each area of the plant were asked to discuss the questions and develop a list of pros and cons. Each team chose one member to report its findings to a plantwide representative body to develop a plantwide answer. The small groups began to meet immediately and within a few days their representatives met. The discussion moved back and forth between the representatives and the teams. Eventually, they decided that to take on the additional work, the plant would need to operate seven days a week, new members would need to be hired and trained to take new shifts, and efficiency would need to be increased to get more from their current capacity. They also decided that to maintain the new contract, they would need to improve the quality of the already top-quality products and make sure that the quality of their own products did not fall. By the end of two weeks, the employees decided to take on the new business.

Stayer reported that, left to the traditional decision process, Johnsonville would have turned down the new business. The results surpassed their best projections. Quality improved faster than anticipated in both product lines. In their early enthusiasm, they had played down the technical aspects of the business, encouraging everyone to become a coordinator. When good salespeople became coordinators, they lost sales. Thus, a career team recommended that Johnsonville set up dual career tracks, one for technical careers and one for coordinator careers. The career team agreed to own the problem and fix it. Now, teams of Johnsonville organization members met to discuss next year's capital budget, new product ideas, product schedules, and quality and cost figures. Their sales, margins, quality, and productivity far exceeded anything they could have imagined years before.

Without belaboring the obvious, the leadership at Johnsonville Foods shifted their focus from technical goals to natural work goals in order to revitalize employees and the organization. In every instance in which great progress was made, actions affected the perceptions of organization members so that they wanted to do better, move ahead, work free, and want more. Their workforce was more optimistic and made the company more competitive.

Analysis: Johnsonville Foods stands as a classic instance of revitalization gone right. Stayer struggled, but captured the essence of natural work goal accomplishment and the role that work perceptions play in the way in which employees understand their jobs and respond to challenges. Letting organization members lead and make decisions fully implements the idea of working free. The change in organization language to eliminate superior/subordinate roles shows how language styles affect dynamism. Most important, however, is the realization that CEO's and upper-level managers have a responsibility to help organization members experience dynamism, for their own good and for the good of the company.

> Management's job is to find out what it is doing that keeps people from doing a good job, and stop doing it.
>
> Peter Drucker

PERSONAL REFLECTIONS AND CASES

We asked individuals from around the country to reflect upon and describe practices in their organizations that affected the level and intensity of dynamism. The personal incidents and cases selected for inclusion in this section join thousands of others in revealing the positive effects of dynamism in bringing about organizational success. Just as major professional sports organizations have learned that a team that plays with enthusiasm may overcome differences in talent and ability, to win, other organizations of all types will be more successful when their employees work with enthusiasm and experience high levels of dynamism.

JEFF LIGHTBURN, TRICON GLOBAL RESTAURANTS

The symbol "YUM" certainly conjures up the thought of great-tasting food, but it's also quickly taking on the connotation for being a flavorful culture at Tricon Global Restaurants.

The company is an excellent case in point of an organization that's created a culture where everyone across its business "makes a difference." Through its YUM culture, it clearly sets expectations for its people, provides countless opportunities for personal fulfillment, and recognizes and celebrates the performance of its associates.

Although Tricon's culture is only four years old and is still in the formative stages, it's one that's comprised by three well-known brands (Pizza Hut, KFC, and Taco Bell) that have thrived for decades.

On October 7, 1997, PepsiCo spun off its restaurant businesses, enabling Tricon to become a separate company. In doing so, Tricon set about creating a new culture that focused solely on becoming a restaurant operating system, rather than remaining part of a diverse consumer retail portfolio. Under the PepsiCo umbrella, the three brands essentially operated autonomously, and at times even viewed one another competitively. That all changed with the formation of Tricon.

From its inception, Tricon's senior leaders knew they had a unique opportunity to bring Pizza Hut, KFC, and Taco Bell together in a powerful way, and to differentiate the company through its culture around the world in more than 100 countries. They knew that individually the brands would succeed, but together they represented a restaurant system powerhouse that few could duplicate. Many franchisees, who before only operated restaurants under one brand, would now operate restaurants under two or all three of Tricon's brands. The stage for significant future growth was set.

Creating the YUM culture would be a way to unite people of different backgrounds and diverse beliefs—a culture based upon common principles that everyone could share and aspire to follow. Tricon's goal is to put a YUM on customers' faces the world over, and to do so, the company knows it first must put a YUM on its own people's faces. That's where its formula for success and culture come into play.

FORMULA FOR SUCCESS PUTS PEOPLE FIRST

Tricon's Formula for Success makes building people capability its highest priority. The formula is this: When you "put people capability first, satisfied customers follow and then we make more money."

[Tricon Global Restaurants, Inc. (NYSE:YUM), based in Louisville, KY is the world's largest restaurant owner with more than 30,000 company-owned, franchised, and licensed restaurants in over 100 countries and territories. The company's brands—KFC, Pizza Hut and Taco Bell—are the global leaders of chicken, pizza and Mexican-style restaurant categories, respectively. Total worldwide system retail sales for the brands were over $22 billion in 2000.]

Gregg Dedrick, Tricon's Executive VP for People and Shared Services, describes the commitment to building people capability this way:

One of our "Founding Truths" and one of our key strategies is putting people capability first. This means we must support our employees by giving them the tools they need to be successful, and then reward and recognize them for that success. We all know when we do that, satisfied customers and profits follow.

Why is that? Because the restaurant industry is a highly people-driven business—one where success with the customer depends on enthusiastic, well-trained, service-driven teams. So our challenge is not only to attract great people, but also to retain and motivate them, particularly in our restaurants. To do that, we're creating a unique work environment where everyone counts and knows they make a difference. In fact, our goal is to build an ownership and recognition culture that drives the best results in the industry.

How are we doing this? First, by encouraging everyone to think and act like owners and to be accountable as owners. That means understanding how our actions and ideas have an impact with customers and on the bottom line.

Second, we're making recognition a key part of our operation. Recognition shows you care, and in this demanding quick service business, if you don't care, people leave. So every day we celebrate the achievements of our people, which builds commitment and puts energized, motivated teams on the frontline serving our customers.

Ownership and recognition take numerous forms across Tricon. All company employees are encouraged to purchase shares of Tricon stock through the 401K program, and when they do, the company supplements those investments. As well, Tricon views its Restaurant General Managers as being its #1 leaders, and each year the RGMs and other above store leaders are presented stock option grants based on their individual performance and contributions.

Recognition is driven deep both informally and formally. Restaurant teams regularly celebrate their success in-store, while each brand president personally bestows special recognition on people who've distinguished themselves. Pizza Hut has the "Big Cheese" award, Taco Bell the "Pepper" award, KFC the "Floppy Chicken" award, and TRI (international) the Globe Award. Chairman and CEO David Novak even has his own personal recognition that's called the "YUM Award"—a set of chattering teeth—to salute those who walk the talk.

"We're bringing our unique culture to life in a number of other ways as well," Dedrick adds. "For example, we established our YUM Leadership program, where franchise and company leaders gather with David Novak to learn how to coach and build teams with a common agenda. We've also cascaded our core values of accountability, excellence and teamwork— what we call our How We Work Together principles—throughout our entire system."

HOW WE WORK TOGETHER PRINCIPLES—COMMON GROUND, COMMON FOCUS

Eight commonly shared principles guide how Tricon's 725,000 associates around the world work together.

1. *Customer Mania*: We not only listen and respond to the voice of the customer, we are obsessed to go the extra mile to make our customers happy.
2. *Belief in People*: We believe in people, trust in positive intentions, encourage ideas from everyone and actively develop a workforce that is diverse in style and background.
3. *Recognition*: we find reasons to celebrate the achievements of others, and have fun doing it.
4. *Coaching and Support*: We coach and support each other.
5. *Accountability*: We do what we say, we are accountable; we act like owners.
6. *Excellence*: We take pride in our work and have a passion for excellence.
7. *Positive Energy*: We execute with positive energy and intensity. We hate bureaucracy and all the nonsense that comes with it.
8. *Teamwork with Positive Conflict*: We practice team together, team apart after collaborative debate.

Aylwin Lewis, Tricon's Chief Operating Officer, describes how common ground and synergy are being achieved in creating the system's new culture.

Best-practice sharing is a key element of the way we do business. One of our primary challenges is to formalize best-practice sharing across the globe and to learn from both inside and outside of the company. In beginning our journey, we've looked outside of the company and bench marked some of the most successful businesses in the U.S. to learn from them and incorporated those learnings into our own business.

Internally, our greatest success story is demonstrated through CHAMPS—which stands for Cleanliness, Hospitality, Accuracy, Maintenance, Product Quality and Speed. CHAMPS is our umbrella operations program for training, measuring and rewarding our employees' performance against customer standards. Not too long ago, we were a restaurant system with three great brands but many different procedures and training processes. So, we went to work to weed out redundancies, leverage learnings and create a uniform approach for everything from the way we train our people to how we cook our food.

The beauty of CHAMPS is that it's a best practice that emerged from our international side of the business—where the program was developed and became a tremendous success in driving consistency in the restaurant experience and improving customer satisfaction. Now, we're applying this program domestically to ensure that our customers receive the same level of superior service and food quality at all our restaurants. Going forward, we're absolutely committed to becoming true Customer Maniacs—being so maniacal about satisfying our customers that we think about it all the time.

YUM CULTURE PROVIDES LIFE SKILLS

In putting people first, Tricon also recognizes that it is striving to accomplish more than creating customer maniacs—it's aspiring to teach restaurant team members life skills that will benefit them for years to come.

Says David Novak,

Through our training and development, we want to provide jobs that help people acquire life skills in at least four key ways.

First, we're teaching people about the importance of customers—how to look at things with empathy and to see the world from our customers' perspective. This will help us in how we relate to people in the future, whether it be a business setting or in just about any circumstance.

Second, we teach listening as a leadership skill—how to listen to our customers and respond. It's one of the attributes of a great leader. How many times do we see people who derail, or miss important opportunities, because of poor listening skills? How many times do good listeners get the best from their teams?

Third, we teach how to successfully sell or produce something—especially in exceeding customers' expectations where possible. Exceeding expectations always separates us apart from others and demonstrates an ability to take on more responsibility. The sooner we see this in life, the better.

Finally, we teach our people about the power of teamwork—how we can accomplish much more together rather than apart. This is especially true when we're trying to recover and win back customers. After all, who doesn't make a mistake? When we do, we will teach our people how to recover with the right attitude of a Customer Maniac.

Teaching these life skills is another way that we're bringing our How We Work Together principles alive. All these lessons will help you in any walk of life, and we'd like to see the jobs we provide for our people become a great base to build upon.

THE FOUNDATION IS SET

Novak believes Tricon is well positioned to achieve significant growth in the next decade, and to become one of the most admired companies and place were people would like to work.

We're a company on a global mission. From Mexico to Malaysia, and Boston to Bangkok, we've become obsessed—even maniacal—about satisfying customers better than any other restaurant company in the world. We're creating lifelong customers with food you crave, comeback value and customer-focused teams. And we're committed to making our jobs the best in the world for people who are committed to quality food and satisfying customers better than anyone.

Stepping back, we are a significantly stronger company now than we were when we were spun off by PepsiCo nearly four years ago. We've more than doubled ongoing operating earnings per share, reduced debt by $2.2 billion, improved restaurant margins over three full points, reduced our general and administrative expenses by over $50 million, improved ongoing operating profit 32% and grown system sales 8%.

What's really important, is the fact that we've put all the building blocks in place to drive future consistent performance, and Tricon has all the characteristics to become one of the world's great companies over time: Leading Brands, a proven International business, tremendous cash flow for reinvestment and the leaders around the world to make it happen.

We know that by building the capability of our people, Customer Mania will result and the profitability that will make Tricon a great investment and a lasting YUM Dynasty will follow.

Analysis: Tricon Restaurants is setting the standard for dynamism in its industry. Tricon has discovered that enthusiastic, well-trained, service-driven employees make the company successful. Their global workforce clearly seeks to do better, move ahead, work free, and want more. Tricon confirms energized, motivated performance with recognitions. The eight principles for how to work together highlights positive energy.

MARK H. FERGUSON, RAYTHEON

Raytheon Company specializes and excels in the design, development, and manufacture of electronic components used in a variety of military, defense, and commercial applications. It is organized into business units, which focus on specific product lines. The business units, known as segments, are: Electronic Systems, Command Control and Communications, Aircraft Integration Systems, Technical Services, Commercial Electronics, and Raytheon Aircraft Company. Products range in size from jet aircraft, missiles, and ship self-defense systems, to radars, lasers, and state-of-the-art electronic components.

Raytheon has operations across the United States, in Canada, the United Kingdom, and other international locations. Its customers include the United States' military and many international countries. The Louisville, Kentucky, site, with approximately 230 employees, is part of Raytheon Missile Systems (RMS), Tucson, Arizona. RMS is the global leader in the design and manufacture of missile systems, which are used around the world. The Louisville facility manufactures, repairs, and overhauls the Phalanx Close-in Weapon System, which is part of the Surface Navy Air Defense Product Line that specializes in ship self-defense.

WHAT PRACTICES ENCOURAGE EMPLOYEES TO DO BETTER?

A couple of years ago, Raytheon initiated a culture change campaign centered on employees doing their jobs better and improving processes that focus on important tasks and eliminating waste. The initiative is simply entitled "Raytheon Six Sigma" (RSS). This initiative was to be more than a statistical measure of the company's performance, but a new way of thinking. The RSS thrust is not just a method for collecting and analyzing technical data, but a systems approach to improving any process, whether it is manufacturing or administrative. Resulting outcomes highlight value-added tasks important to the user and customers of that process. A goal of this culture change, from the CEO's perspective, is that he would like to go to any site and ask the question "How do you solve your problems?" The answer he wants to hear is "We use Six Sigma." For many, this is an old name given to old programs such as "Total Quality Management," "Quality Circles," "Statistical Process Control," "Reengineering," and the like. But it is of such strategic importance to the CEO and the company's day-to-day success that "specialist" certification is required for employees who want to advance into higher levels of management.

Other practices include a suggestion program called "Bureaucracy Busting." Employees are encouraged to submit ideas that improve processing times, and eliminate signatures that constitute an "easy kill."

Raytheon has implemented a process called HR Review. This is not a review of the Human Resources department, but a review of the human resources—the people. The HR Review Toolkit includes such things as Performance Development process (annual reviews and performance improvement plans), Most Promotable Women and Minorities, High Potential Employee Reviews, New Leader Assimilation, 360-degree feedback, and Succession Planning. By using these tools, managers are able to focus efforts on retaining employees who show promise in running the company in the future as well as getting feedback on their own performance from peers, customers, and direct reports. Taken as a whole, it is a strategy that Raytheon uses to become an "employer of choice" and that delights its workforce.

Many Raytheon employees are organized in a "matrix" fashion. For example, the engineering function has engineers who support a specific program such as Phalanx. The engineer receives his or her assignment from the Phalanx Program office, not the engineering department. However, the engineer's home department is not the Program office, but the engineering department. This matrix organization is a mixed blessing. It provides flexibility and versatility to the engineers who want experience on different programs, making them well rounded while keeping them challenged. However, the home department retains the authority to promote, rate, and review the engineer's performance. The assigned department has input but not the decision. This works well most of the time, but has resulted in differing views between the work department and the home department with the employee being caught in the middle.

From a personal standpoint, my manager allows me to make the decisions that impact the day-to-day operations of Employee Services, but he also expects me to follow up and follow through by reporting back to him on those things that affect the site. I have found that when managers allow employees to do their jobs while requiring an accounting, they find excitement in dealing with the challenges they face because they experience personal growth and development.

WHAT OPPORTUNITIES ARE THERE TO MOVE AHEAD?

Raytheon is a global company. During the past four years, many company cultures have been combined into one. The current company is made up of four former competitors: Raytheon, E-Systems, Texas Instruments Defense, and Hughes Aircraft Company. Each of these four companies also merged with other defense companies such as General Dynamics, Loral, and the U.S. Government. One of the initial primary goals of the CEO was to establish a "One Company, One Philosophy" culture. To do this, all of the existing policies and procedures were reviewed to determine which would be kept.

Although this effort is ongoing, one practice that has bubbled to the top is intercompany transfers and compensation structure. Raytheon has standardized all of its job titles and compensation structures into one. All job openings within the company are posted on the intranet. This allows employees anywhere in the company to know what jobs are available in any given location. They can apply on-line and, if they are successful, be transferred to that new location with the cost of the relocation paid by Raytheon. This type of system allows employees to become more mobile as the industry requires more flexibility in assignments. It also allows employees to gain new experience, with which come higher-level duties and more independent responsibility. Plus, the company has one more method of retaining key talent.

On a personal front, I have been entrusted with the authority and freedom to manage a team of people responsible for a variety of services: Human Resources, Environmental, Health, and Safety, Training, Security, Facilities, and Administrative Support. Two years ago, each of these functions reported to a different manager. However, there were issues that arose in each function that ultimately came back to Human Resources. My frustration was that while I could give advice or suggestions, I had no authority to implement them. Since each function was staffed with only one person, putting them all together made sense. I suggested the idea to the site manager (who is also my boss) and he not only agreed to it, but was also instrumental in making it a reality. Although my goal was not to get a promotion from it, that is what happened.

Since then, being the manager of the Employee Services team has challenged me in other areas with which I was previously only familiar. It has taken me beyond my experience and training in Human Resources. I was able to hire an HR Generalist and assign many of the daily duties to her. This has opened up the opportunity for me to learn new things and put into practice the leadership points I used to preach when I was a management trainer early in my career. I like the freedom I have to "run the show." I take great satisfaction in knowing that I have the latitude to make decisions and be influential, but also knowing that I will be held accountable. Knowing that I will be held accountable for services that affect the entire site generates enthusiasm to do a job well and to the satisfaction of the customer.

The opportunities I have had to move ahead were allowed to happen because I asked and because I have a trusting relationship with my manager. This reaffirms that I am expected to recognize problems and provide solutions. It creates credibility, which leads to more opportunities.

WHAT ALLOWS ME TO WORK FREE?

I have the ability to alter my work schedule, which allows me to focus on my job, the freedom to do my job, and be trusted to do the right thing. Communication always needs to be improved. I have discovered that by keeping the right parties informed about what is going on, they feel more comfortable in allowing me to take care of what I am charged to do. In large measure (though not always) only higher-level managers control the extent to which the company can encumber an employee or an organization, which may be different for different employees. The more an employee can prevent his or her boss from looking bad or the more an employee can ease the burdens of his or her boss, the more freedom to make decisions is allowed. This assumes, to some extent, that the employee has attained a certain level of competence and can be relied upon to do good work.

The organizational structure at Louisville, in addition, allows employees at lower levels to be influential and visible as if they were at higher levels in different parts of the company. Although my level would be considered an experienced level, my duties and responsibilities sometimes equate to a senior manager. This is an excellent training opportunity for anyone who wants to move ahead.

Bureaucracy does exist, however, because we are tied to Tucson. Local site policies may allow more flexibility, but they have to be balanced with the larger policies of the corporation. This can lead to delays caused by a lack of understanding of what takes place in both locations. It requires coordination on both ends, a skill that needs to be developed by many employees.

WHAT MAKES ME WANT MORE?

My senior managers are sufficiently confident in themselves to allow me to do my job. Because I have the opportunity to interface with executive management at the local level as well as those visiting the facility from Tucson or other parts of the company, I get to know other people and increase my network of contacts.

Senior managers at this site allow me to influence them and consider me part of their team. This is a critical factor because I feel like I am making a difference, not only for them and the employees, but also in what is right for this site. The increased visibility does carry with it increased scrutiny, which also provides an opportunity for learning and additional experience.

In the end, what has worked for me is that attitude accounts for much of enjoyment: I try to accept the bad days and savor the good. That is not to say that employee relations in general are not frustrating; negative employees take their toll. But I have found that if I can make the best with what I have, regardless of the company's rules and bureaucracy, the employee-friendly policies are icing on the cake.

Analysis: The Raytheon practices of "bureaucracy busting," "HR Reviewing," matrix structures," "one company, one philosophy," use of teams, and an attitude of "run your own show," lay a solid foundation of dynamism in individuals and the organization. These practices encourage employees to do better, work free, move ahead, and want more.

GREG GOATES, SENIOR FLEXONICS, KETEMA DIVISION

Our employees are vital to our projected growth and their "can do" attitude and involvement is truly a way of life for us. To achieve our full growth potential will require that we remain focused on meeting our customer's requirements.
> Tom Brooks, Former Vice President & General Manager,
> Senior Flexonics Ketema Division

THE GLOBAL MARKETPLACE

American corporations face external pressures that are different from any other period of world history. The North American Free Trade Agreement and the formation of the European Economic Community are two examples of many economic initiatives that have generated tremendous business pressure and are forging a new world economy. We recognize that in order to survive and thrive in the postindustrial global economy, we need to become far more flexible, effective, and productive—to provide ever-increasing levels of quality goods and services in faster turnaround times and for less cost

Ketema Division is part of the Aerospace Group of Senior Flexonics North America with headquarters located in Bartlett, Illinois, and ultimately Senior Engineering plc. in Rickmansworth, England. Ketema Division is located in El Cajon, California, and in 1999 employed 656 people in a

360,000-square-foot facility on 25 acres, equipped with a full range of metal fabrication (sheet metal forming and machining) capabilities. Ketema Division forms exotic metals into complex geometries with very tight tolerances, then into parts and subassemblies that become aerospace jet engine (military and commercial plane) applications, space applications consisting of cryogenic valves and ducts for rockets, reusable launch and space shuttle vehicles, and support commercial applications in the land-based gas turbine market. Ketema Division is AS9000 and IS09001 certified and has National Aerospace and Defense Contractors approved manufacturing processes.

OUR STRATEGIC PLAN

Ketema Division is addressing the challenge of globalization and the changing market needs that conditions create in three significant ways. First, we are training our employees in critical skills and competencies required by our customers to be competitive in a global market. Second, we are looking at the organizational structure to determine the most effective and efficient ways to meet varying customer needs in different market segments, and third, we are creating an engine of continuous improvement in driving cycle time and variation down, all the while maintaining the highest levels of quality in every process throughout the division.

In 1999, Ketema Division completed a 21-month training initiative designed around the philosophy that learning must occur at both the worker level, in terms of understanding their impact on the outcome of the product as a whole, and at the executive level, where they need a paradigm shift around their responsibility to facilitate learning and promote employee empowerment in the organization. Goal 2000 training in total included 75,000 class/lab hours and 25,000 on-the-job training (Structured On-Site Training) hours and involved every employee with a minimum of 60 hours of training in skills critical to the strategy and their position within the division. Goal 2000 training included a module entitled High Performance Work Please—Ketema 101, which addressed the business knowledge requirement for all employees. It also included several different levels of leadership skills training (tactical, strategic, team, and facilitation) for all employees in leadership roles. The result of this training was that even our shop employees could articulate our business goals, mission, and values, which pleased and, quite frankly, surprised visitors who were touring the facility. Our employees were enthusiastic about their work because they saw how what they did added value to our products. They even took more pride in their work.

To become a process-centered organization, Ketema Division embarked on a several-year process to completely redesign the organizational structure to focus on critical processes and the customer value stream. The initiative was called Focused Simplicity, how we engineer what we do to make sure that people can focus on what's important to the customer and uncomplicated work. In 1998, Ketema Division began developing a detailed blueprint to describe the type of organization articulated in the Ketema Vision: Business Units, Cellular Manufacturing Teams, Process Teams, and Support Teams. The overall goal was to get as many people as possible into a Business Unit, Manufacturing Cell, or Process Team, and reduce the number in the traditional manufacturing functions. Ketema identified eight businesswide processes that were critical to the customer value stream. It formed focus groups made up of customers and suppliers for each one of those critical processes. Through a facilitated group process, each focus group identified a team charter, roles in the customer value stream, goals, measures, and inputs and outputs. A Blueprint for Focused Simplicity was created to capture all of the work from each of the groups. The process was repeated with each of the business units and the support teams.

The year for building the new organization was 1999, where, as the various teams finished their blueprint columns and presented them to executive staff, the new work teams were officially chartered and deployed. Parallel with this effort the company reorganized the manufacturing functions into work cells following lean manufacturing principles and co-located the professional and technical support out on the shop floor in the manufacturing cell teams in a new 100,000-square-foot facility. A new midmanagement-level position called cell leader was created with the idea that they become minigeneral managers with control over all of the resources required to make the specific parts assigned to their cell.

During the change from a traditional manufacturing structure to business units and process teams, employees were given control over the changes, resulting in more employee buy-in and contribution to the division. As a new team was launched, employees were more excited about the change than about resisting the change. At about the same time, a "Gotch Ya" employee recognition program was introduced. The purposes were to encourage high levels of acknowledgment and recognition, to create a positive and motivating environment that supported the change effort and provided the optimum environment for change.

The Gotch Ya program encouraged employees to acknowledge their teammates for implementing one or more of the division's values (customer needs are our opportunities, employees are our most valuable asset, do what you say you're going to do, we're in business with our suppliers, give consideration to your surroundings, and continuously and creatively challenge paradigms). Acknowledgments were given by filling out a slip of paper posted on boards located around the shop. The acknowledging employee presented the slip to the employee who demonstrated the value and personally acknowledged the person for his/her support and identified the behavior that represented the value. The employee could then take the slip back to any of the boards and put it in a jar for a monthly employee drawing. Each month twenty employees were publicly acknowledge for what they had done in an all-company e-mail, and by leadership of the division in a ceremony at lunch break. Each employee recognized received a $20 bill. Employees recognized had their pictures taken and placed on a Gotch Ya board located in the lunchroom.

To confirm Ketema Division's ongoing commitment to continuous improvement, it adopted two specific strategies that helped refine the new process organization, improve the cycle time, and reduce variation. Those strategies are lean manufacturing and six sigma quality. The lean enterprise is one in which every process is judged by its contribution to the customer "value stream," and anything in the process that doesn't contribute to value is eliminated as "Muda" (Japanese for waste). Another critical lean principle is "flow," which maximizes the output of any given process by producing only what the customer requires—no more, no less (no mass manufacturing or batch processes)—and finding ways to decrease process cycle time.

SIX SIGMA IS A SISTER STRATEGY TO LEAN

While lean focuses on process flow and waste elimination, six sigma focuses on variation reduction in processes. Six sigma is a statistical unit of measurement that means a standard deviation from a mean. Six sigma represents a plus or minus three standard deviations and accounts for 99.9 percent of the errors in a process. Unlike other quality programs such as TQM, best practices, and Kaizen, the six sigma method is a disciplined system of using extremely rigorous data gathering and statistical analyses to pinpoint sources of errors and ways of eliminating them. Instead of the fuzzy goals of continuous improvement, six sigma projects are based on customer feedback. Improvements that have a significant customer impact are given top priority.

Shop floor employees were involved in the training and deployment of continuous improvement initiatives by going through a rigorous assessment center. Fifteen employees were trained by General Electric, one of Ketema's customers. The fifteen trained employees initiated teams in the new manufacturing cells. Monthly leadership progress meetings were held where team leaders reported on what they had achieved. This created a great deal of employee excitement as they were able to show results achieved by their efforts.

Lean manufacturing Kaizen events were scheduled each month with the goal of eliminating waste and improving process flows on the manufacturing floor. Each Kaizen event involved cell employees as well as other employees from other areas in the division. During the week, employees on a team analyzed the process, identified waste, made recommendations, and implemented changes in the process. Each member of the team presented part of the results. It was amazing to see the excitement generated among team members as they saw firsthand how the ideas they came up with were implemented during the Kaizen event. Team members were acknowledged for their contributions with a lean logo shirt, which they wore proudly to work.

The cumulative effect of all the change processes was evident when the Ketema Division, out of fifty divisions worldwide, was recognized as the Senior Division of the Year in 1999. The reasons given for recognizing the Ketema Division were the enthusiasm of employees, the spirit of the teams, and overall business effectiveness. In fact, corporate engineering brought a planeload of investors over to America to tour the plant. They actually acknowledged the difference in feelings that the employee involvement program had created at Ketema Division.

In summary, Senior Flexonics Ketema Division is meeting the challenge of globalization and the changing market needs by operationalizing our mission statement. This means being market-driven in our strategies, customer-focused in our employee training, flexibly organized in organizational process and structure, and committed to continuous improvement through creating an engine of continuous improvement that drives cycle time and variation down, while maintaining the highest levels of quality in every process throughout the division.

Analysis: The Ketema Division of Senior Flexonics has discovered that the power of enthusiastic employees is a critical factor in competitiveness. Their goal to project a "can do" attitude and employee involvement is fully compatible with the principles of dynamism. The process of restructuring around teams and seeking to maintain the highest standards implements a dynamism philosophy that encourages employees to do better, move ahead, work free, and want more. Ketema is doing an exceptional job of achieving lofty goals that unleash power in the workforce.

DOUGLAS HOLYOAK, ANDERSEN

What makes my job so enjoyable?

I came to Arthur Andersen over twelve years ago with the intent of working for two years, gaining valuable experience, and placing the firm's name on my résumé. While there have been peaks and valleys in my twelve years, overall it has been a very rewarding experience. My responsibilities are limited to a "back office" view, meaning that I am in the training group and never see the whites of the clients eyes. Nevertheless, because of my exposure to the professionals who work with the clients, I have been able to observe steady and real change within the firm. Below are a few of those observations.

Printed by permission of the author and Arthur Andersen, Inc.

I started my Andersen career in 1989 with Andersen Worldwide and was assigned to projects that supported a newly created business unit— Andersen Consulting. In 1994, Andersen Consulting (now Accenture) put all of its training, development, and delivery resources, including me, into Andersen Consulting. In 1999, I transferred to the other business unit, Arthur Andersen, thus completing my tour of the Andersen entities. My comments reflect my *total* experience at Andersen. With essentially the same cultural and historical development, my observations apply to all three firms.

FIRM'S VALUES ARE IN LARGE PART CLOSELY ALIGNED TO MY PERSONAL VALUES

Stewardship, integrity, family, high-quality client service, development of the individual and firm, and leadership are the firm's values. When I come to work, I'm not asked to compromise who I am to behave differently. I believe that the firm's values attracts employees with similar values. I can honestly say that the people with whom I am honored to work is the number one reason I stay with the firm. They are some of the finest people I have associated with in my life. Of course, there have been some rare exceptions to that claim. These talented, values-driven professionals have inspired me to be a better employee and human being.

TALENTED PROFESSIONALS WITH A WIDE RANGE OF SKILLS AND DEPTH OF EXPERTISE

Most positions within the firm require a college degree, making this a highly educated workforce. Degrees include M.B.A., J.D., computer science, accounting, business, economics, English, organizational behavior, and instructional design/technology. While most employees have a bachelor's degree, there are a significant number of master's and doctoral graduates as well. It's not hard to find specialists in the firm to answer complex and mind-numbing questions. This has always led to better educational products and client services. Where it's appropriate, the firm allows the individual to gain more education in evening programs. In my case, I was granted a rare opportunity to earn my master's degree in computer science from Northwestern University. I was awarded a half-tuition grant from the firm and spent two years on the Evanston campus learning how to design and develop educational software.

ONGOING AND STEADY COMMITMENT TO PROFESSIONAL DEVELOPMENT (OVER $500 MILLION ANNUALLY)

Professionals in the United States, who are certified public accountants (CPA), are required to maintain and upgrade their skills regularly, specifically 120 hours in any three-year period and a minimum of 20 hours a year. The firm has invested millions in a world-class training facility located in St. Charles, Illinois, employing over 500 training development and delivery professionals. In addition to the Center for Professional Education, which is capable of housing and training approximately 1,800 people a week, each local office around the world sponsors hundreds of training courses.

LEADERS WITH COURAGE TO DO WHAT IS ETHICAL AND MORAL

Working with leaders who are ethical and do the right thing not because they'll get caught, but because it's the right thing, is refreshing. They don't try to cut corners or get away with anything. They put the time into the legal issues to stay within the law and serve the clients with sound, legal, and compliant advice.

CONSTANT CHANGE, NEVER SATISFIED WITH YESTERDAY'S SUCCESS

What worked yesterday in the marketplace may not satisfy our clients today. Andersen has long been recognized as a leading accounting and audit firm. Yet, as the marketplace shifts with the economic tide, so the firm shifts its organization and product offerings to meet the marketplace demands. This requires an attitude of change, nimbleness, and perseverance. When the financial audit became a commodity resulting in marginal value to the client, the firm changed its approach to auditing; instead of looking backward and agreeing with historical facts and figures, the audit methodology, called The Business Audit, takes a proactive view of the processes that generate the financial statements and identifies where processes could be improved. The result is improved processes that generate better financial data.

THE OPPORTUNITY TO REINVENT ONESELF WITHOUT LEAVING THE ORGANIZATION

The ability to move from auditing to tax consultation to financial systems implementation to financial operations outsourcing, from training design to knowledge manager to client engagement, to partner represents opportunities to move ahead. I have known many people who began their career working at the Center for Professional Education in the western suburbs of Chicago. As they learned more about the firm's products and services, they expressed interest in and qualified for positions in other parts of the firm. For example, one individual started his career developing interpersonal skills, moved to another part of the firm supporting outsourcing businesses, and eventually became the partner over human resources within North America. Another person, who has a Ph.D. in education, assumed responsibility for a very technical curriculum line, then retooled himself to become an expert in quality. He spent three to four years working with clients to help them improve their processes, and now sits on the executive committee for learning and professional growth. Others have moved from auditing clients' financial statements to designing and implementing financial systems for clients.

WELL-DEFINED GROWTH POTENTIAL

Career paths are very well defined within the organization. I know what my career path looks like and when I might be considered for promotion. I know what is expected of me and what it takes to get promoted to the next level.

RESPECT FOR THE FAMILY AND THE INDIVIDUAL'S NEED TO BALANCE WORK AND PERSONAL LIFE

When I first started with the firm, I had to adjust to a number of rigid culture and personnel policies. This included all personnel reporting to work by 8 A.M. and leaving no sooner than 5 P.M. Of course, there was sensitivity to family emergencies, but the starting time was strictly enforced. As the 1990s progressed, the emphasis on families and personal time increased. Stephen Covey's training and book *Seven Habits of Highly Effective People* influenced leadership in a positive way. Flexible work arrangements were introduced into the offices, meaning professionals in the St. Charles office could now start their day as early as 6:30 A.M. or as late as 9:00 A.M. Professionals can also choose to work four ten-hour days and take the fifth day off or work four nine-hour days and take an afternoon off. The firm also introduced a travel policy that recognized the tremendous sacrifice professionals make as they serve clients. Simply stated, professionals may leave their residences no earlier than 7:00 A.M. on Monday morning and return home no later than 9:00 P.M. on Friday evening.

CHALLENGING BUSINESS PROBLEMS DUE TO GLOBAL PRESENCE

As I develop a five-day training event that will be attended by 4,000 professionals, I must, for example, constantly take into consideration the learning styles of dozens of cultures, professionals who speak over twenty languages, and representatives of approximately eighty countries. What works in one culture or country may not work in another. The local customs and business practices may vary from one region of the world to another. For example, auditing standards, accounting principles, and tax regulations vary greatly from one country to another and the training design must account for these differences. Equally challenging is developing a common methodology that is used by professionals to sell products.

OPPORTUNITY TO INNOVATE AND BE CREATIVE

I have been involved in numerous projects in which we were given creative license to develop interactive and improved learning environments, both in the classroom and on the computer. I have worked with professionals in graphic design, video and television, multimedia, facilities management, assessment and measurement, communication, production, and training delivery. Each has contributed significant insight to the creative process and made the final learning environment engaging, valuable, and enjoyable. Related to the firm's belief that the development of the individual is paramount, leadership hires talented and creative professionals to ensure that investment is maximized.

EXPOSURE TO PARTNERS, THE FIRM'S OWNERS

This has been important to me. I have learned that the partners' view of the marketplace, the firm's strategy, and skill domain is invaluable. I have gleaned much from their experiences, and their attention to the learning environment has resulted in stronger, more credible courses.

VALUING DIVERSITY TO CREATE UNIFIED SOLUTIONS

The essential challenge all businesses face, in my opinion, is to take advantage of the wide variety of experiences (both personal and professional), cultures, ethnic groups, academic research, and business savvy to create a strategic vision and achieve that vision with products and services. I believe, for Andersen, this is best exemplified with the statement "one firm, one culture, one vision." It's our ability to create unity with the diversity that makes this such a great place to work.

Analysis: This case has revealed very clearly how important achieving natural work goals can be to a vitalized environment. Goals that encourage and assist employees to do better, move ahead, work free, and want more from their work are illustrated very nicely by the Arthur Andersen case. Excellence in work, learning and advancement, independent decision making, and a sense that one can get more from work and life in this environment make a convincing argument for the role of dynamism in highly successful organizations.

DOUGLAS SPRING, LAS VEGAS METROPOLITAN POLICE DEPARTMENT

ENTHUSIASTIC WORK ENVIRONMENT

The Las Vegas Metropolitan Police Department provides police services to all of the unincorporated areas of Clark County and the City of Las Vegas. With approximately 4,000 employees, LVMPD is the largest law enforcement agency in Nevada and the tenth largest police agency in the United States. In 1974 the Sheriff's Department and City Police Department joined together to form one metropolitan police department.

As the Executive Director of Personnel, I report directly to the Deputy Chief of the Human Resources Division. The Deputy Chief reports to the Undersheriff, who reports to the Sheriff. I am one of two civilians (the Comptroller is the other civilian) who are considered part of executive staff to make decisions for the department as a whole. I am responsible for a comprehensive personnel management program and have directors of Labor Relations, Selection and Classification, Payroll, Health and Safety, and a lieutenant over recruiting and background investigations reporting directly to me.

My enthusiasm is simple to explain. It rests on three important principles. First, I work for a department that is committed to values. Employees' performance is based on how well they pattern their behavior after the Department's values. We use an acronym to help us remember the values—"I CARE"—which refers to Integrity, Courage, Accountability, Respect for others, and Excellence. The interesting part of working for LVMPD is that the Sheriff (chief executive officer) is not only committed to these values, he lives by them and sets the example. He expects all members of his executive staff to do the same. What could be a very political environment is controlled to some extent by these values.

Second, what I do as the Executive Director is valued by the Department. Since I started working for LVMPD four and one-half years ago, I have made several significant changes to the way we recruit, select, and background our employees. These changes were readily accepted by the Department and implemented. My opinion is requested regularly and I enjoy the opportunity to meet with the executive staff on a daily basis to discuss Department issues and problems. LVMPD is one of the fastest-growing law enforcement agencies in the nation. Owing to its growth and the sensitive nature of a police officer's job, I am compelled to ensure that all employees who are hired meet our high hiring standards and qualifications. The Personnel Bureau could make or break the credibility of the Department by who is hired. Tell me that isn't valuable?

Finally, the Department provides me with an opportunity to grow. I am given opportunities to participate in professional organizations and law enforcement committees. These organizations and committees set policies that affect not only my Department but the human resources field nationally. For example, I am a member of the Major Cities Chiefs' Human Resources Committee. All the major city police departments participate in this committee, which yearly prepares a report on critical issues facing law enforcement. As a member of the committee, I am able to learn from other great departments and make a difference for my profession.

The best example I can give of the Sheriff's commitment to the agency is his leadership. He is an elected sheriff, but as soon as he was elected, politics went out the window. He has been known to promote those who do not support him and even discipline some of his best supporters. In an environment that could easily be autocratic, Sheriff Keller expects a democratic/participatory approach to management and decision making. We recently completed a comprehensive strategic planning effort that resulted in our current values, goals, and objectives. This was no small task and the Sheriff demonstrated complete commitment to its completion and implementation.

Analysis: These personal reflections highlight the critical role that employees' perceptions of the organization about what it allows and encourages them to do influence deeply the level of enthusiasm and dynamism they experience. The importance of appropriate values and living by them affects employee perceptions of the organization and intensifies the experience of dynamism.

CAMILLE B. COUCH, GLENDALE FEDERAL SAVINGS

As a training and development intern at Glendale Federal Savings, I embarked on an experience that, to this day, has positively impacted my life as a person, an employee, and an employer. My predecessor had also been an intern and had recently been hired in a permanent position. He had made entry into my position difficult—big male shoes that probably no one in the company expected I would be able to fill. At twenty-five years of age, I looked sixteen, at least according to my new manager.

So, with uncertainty on the part of my manager, he asked me to identify a training need in the company and put together a workshop to meet that need. I assessed the needs of the employees and came up with a stress management workshop. The program was very successful. I received a lot of positive feedback from my manager and others in the organization. It began looking as if it wouldn't be necessary to fill someone else's shoes.

With my initial success, I was given the opportunity to help implement a sales training program. The vendor of the program required that I be certified in order to facilitate it. I felt overwhelmed with the volume of material to learn and the skills needed to facilitate the program.

Again, my manager and others were available to help me, but they also stood back and allowed me to learn at my own pace. I was an active participant in creating the schedule that ultimately led to mastery in facilitating the program.

After reaching the point of being able to run the program, I was given the great opportunity to be master certified. A master-certified instructor trains other people to teach the program. The company invested a lot of time and money in me to contribute to my success. In so many ways, I received the message that I was a valued person and a valuable player in the company.

My internship ended and I was offered a job to stay with the company. I took it. In time, another position came up that was a horizontal move, but in a very technical job. Although I am not a detail person, especially when working with numbers, I thought a challenge would be good. I took over a position dealing with 401K benefit plans for the employees.

I was to experience a lesson that has stayed with me and served me to this day. I struggled in the job; it was difficult. The time came for a performance review. I now had a woman manager. I respected her. She was brilliant and anything she touched seemed to turn to gold. I was also a little fearful of her. I was nervous about the review.

I had come to believe that if I were perfect enough in life, I might be loved and accepted. My grade point average in school was nearly perfect. In every job in which I had worked for years, I excelled. So, as we discussed my performance and I looked at the review, I was shocked to my core. She had checked the box that stated "needs improvement." It didn't matter that in reality, I did need improvement. How could I face myself or others if I hadn't measured up? I was crushed. I cried.

I can still see us sitting in the restaurant talking about it. My manager told me about herself and about her mistakes and imperfections. She was very honest and open. This woman, who seemed to walk on water, made herself appear real and vulnerable. I understood. I had respected her before; now I respected her and adored her. She remains a person whom I consider a friend and mentor. I worked in the job and did what I could to improve. I was supported by my manager. When the chance came, though, to go back to the training department, I jumped at it. But I did so not to run away, but for a better opportunity and for a better fit.

The time came when I had an assignment to evaluate a business to see if we wanted to use their training program. In the process of evaluating them, they sized me up and asked me if I wanted a job. The job would take me into a whole new industry and would provide a great opportunity for growth. When I accepted it, my manager at Glendale Federal supported me and let me know that she, and the company, wanted the best for me.

After about a year and a half, I was approached by my original Glendale Federal manager to come back to Glendale Federal. I would be taking on a big project. I would also be gaining a sizable increase in salary. I accepted.

Once again, I was given big responsibilities. I headed the training portion of a state-wide program that was funded in part by the state of California. I put together assessment tools to evaluate the progress of the program, became involved in creating training videos, worked with other employees to insure the success of the project, and traveled extensively to implement the program. Over and over again, the company provided opportunities for me to find challenge and growth as a person and as an employee. I will be forever grateful and awed by a company and by managers who helped me be all that I could be.

Analysis: This incident traces the impact of organization practices on an individual's dynamism and reveals how even a single negative moment can have devastating effects on enthusiasm. It also shows how managers should respond to employees to revitalize them. The development of individual talents has a powerful impact on worker perceptions and produces profound effects on the dynamism of individual organization members.

BRUCE PRIDAY, HALLMARK CARDS, INC.

Hallmark Cards, Inc. of Kansas City, Missouri, is a corporation that is committed to helping foster personal growth and development in their employees. Hallmark, for example, is one of the few corporations in the world that sponsors a company band.

Don Shaffer joined Hallmark Cards as a Human Resource Manager after teaching high school band for over twenty years. Don's enthusiasm and love for music prompted him to put an announcement in Hallmark's employee newsletter during the summer of 1992 to invite Hallmark employees with musical talent to show up for a band rehearsal during the lunch period. Over sixty employees showed up, and the Hallmark Band was formed. Hallmark provides a place for the band to rehearse, instruments, music, and band uniforms.

The band has enabled a creative and recreational outlet for the employees, and a chance for band members to meet other employees in other parts of the company. The Hallmark Band rehearses during the lunch hour once a week, and they perform several times throughout the year at concerts for Hallmark employees, families, and the community.

Each December, the Hallmark Band performs a Hallmark Family Night Holiday Concert for employees and their families, complete with a sing-along and a visit from Santa with gifts for all of the children.

The band has instilled employee loyalty and pride, and the band members have enthusiastically appreciated the opportunity to further develop their musical talents while pursuing other professional careers.

Another example demonstrates how a corporation can motivate and reward employees in nontraditional ways, while at the same time provide a meaningful service to the community. Hallmark Cards encourages employees to be actively involved in providing community service. Through

Hallmark's Voluntary Involvement Pays (VIP) program, employees who volunteer twenty-five or more hours over a six-month period to a nonprofit organization are eligible to receive $200 for their organization.

For years, I've served as a boy scout leader. My scout troop has benefitted from the VIP program by receiving $400 a year from Hallmark. This money has enabled the troop to buy much-needed camp equipment and it has allowed underprivileged boys from the troop to attend scout camp.

Analysis: The Hallmark Cards incidents are only a few of the many ways that this company attempts to assist employees in achieving natural work goals in their workplaces. Providing confirmation of the value of voluntary contributions to the community through financial donations to community organizations and supporting a band with uniforms and other necessities clearly demonstrate that positive work perceptions evolve as natural work goals are achieved.

SUMMARY

In this chapter we presented criteria for determining the extent to which appropriate work perceptions have evolved in an organization to exhibit effective levels of dynamism. A group of cases and personal reflections were reported to illustrate dynamism practices and their effects on organization members. We demonstrated that sustained dynamism brings with it long-range organization and individual effectiveness and success.

NOTES

1. Pfeffer, Jeffrey. 1994. *Competitive Advantage through People: Unleashing the Power of the Work Force*. Boston, MA: Harvard Business School Press, Chapter 1.

2. Levering, Robert and Moskowitz, Milton. 1993. *The 100 Best Companies to Work for in America*. New York: Doubleday.

3. Clurman, Carol. 1990. More Than Just a Paycheck. *USA Weekend*, January 19–21, pp. 4–5.

4. Stayer, Ralph. 1990. How I Learned to Let My Workers Lead. *Harvard Business Review*, November–December, pp. 66–83.

Afterword

Life has become very complex and demanding for most of us and the ability to cope with rapid change can seem difficult. Working in some companies is almost too demanding, leading to attitudes that are negativistic and depressing. We have all heard the mantras "more with less" and "I needed it yesterday." What are we to do in these times of rapid, unceasing change to keep our spirits up and remain enthusiastic and energized about the future? I have been intrigued by these questions for many years now. I have wondered how people can help others acquire and maintain an optimistic outlook that results in commitment, dedication, and the investment of higher levels of energy to a cause while being challenged with the complex demands of an ever-changing world. I have found that Wayne Pace's insights on what he calls "dynamism" have been most helpful and effective.

Several years ago Wayne taught me about four perceptions: I am doing better, I can move ahead, I am able to work free, I can get more. He helped me to understand that people who really believe these things about their life are vitalized and bring an enthusiasm for work and achieving goals that distinguish them from the average employee. He challenged me to adopt these perceptions in workplace and adapt my leadership approach so that I would influence others around me to acquire these perceptions. The results have been very encouraging.

In 1994 I began work with Parker Aerospace as a performance technologist for the Control System Division Commercial. Parker is a Fortune 200 company with eight operating groups. CSD-C is the largest division within the corporation. This division manufactures hydraulic actuators for commercial airplanes. Within the aerospace group there is a wonderful culture of exploration and innovation. When I interviewed for the job I was excited by the ideals of the "new enterprise." Parker had decided to bring all commercial work to CSD-C. This meant that the workforce and cultures of three different organizations would be joined together. The company recognized that there were as-yet-unanswered questions concerning culture, leadership, teamwork, and other issues that can influence organization effectiveness. There was an opportunity to become part of an organization whose lofty goals were to become "world class" and the recognized best in its market niche.

As the performance technologist for CSD-C, I was given the opportunity to work in this "new enterprise" with company leadership to influence the perceptions of employees and bring about needed important changes. Early in the change process we invited team leaders to have their members complete questionnaires concerning issues of vitality. Without a doubt, team leaders who listen to their team members and act on their ideas, who provide recognition for success, and who help team members see that their contributions are making a positive difference have teams that are more vitalized than those who do not.

In 1998 I was given the challenge of building a team that could provide a response to both the technical and social learning needs of the division. Four interns from the Instructional Technology Department of a local university were brought in to develop a means by which machinists could understand what they did and did not know about machining. Several assessment tools were developed and a program implemented to help machinists determine specifically what they needed to learn to be more successful in their jobs. In the learning plan, we were careful to build in the principles of vitality. Participating machinists understood that their individual learning plans were a means by which they could become better, be able to move ahead, and to work with more freedom, because others would have confidence in their abilities. By mastering these skills, they would become eligible for other considerations down the road. Many of the machinists became excited and looked forward to working with their new mentors and improving their abilities.

On the Human Performance and Learning Team, the people who are my colleagues truly understand their work life in the context of the four perceptions. Let me explain. Each of the team members has a perception that what he/she is doing is significant and unique. The members of the team are allowed to make independent decisions. They enjoy the empowerment of a self-directed work team. Customers help the team to understand that it is meeting their needs and because of their recognition and praise, the team feels that it is doing better and moving ahead. The team has aspirations of becoming a profit center and generating income for the division. Intrinsically each team member wants more. Recognizing the team's efforts and the results they were providing, company leadership determined that the remaining interns should be invited to join Parker and receive full-time status. The team has continued to grow and flourish.

The team has a quarterly "renewal" off-site and interacts with professors from the university. The team has developed a can-do attitude, takes risks, experiments, explores, and has earned the respect and admiration of the plant leadership and team members. Because the team is vitalized, there is a very high level of dedication and loyalty. The team is highly committed to helping the division understand its performance needs, discovering learning solutions, and developing the competencies they need to be successful. The principles of dynamism, when applied to human performance technology, help ensure that performance becomes more than results; commitment, enthusiasm, and dedication become the extra bonus!

When people cannot see that they are performing well, when they cannot see that they have opportunities, when they feel unfulfilled or believe their expectations have little chance of being realized, they become lethargic, they are less committed, they reserve their energy for places outside of work and leave their enthusiasm at home. We are told that technology is not necessarily a competitive advantage, because any organization that chooses to can go out and buy the same machines, equipment, or software. Any organization can pay for a lean manufacturing guru or an efficiency expert. Any organization can access a plethora of training and development interventions to help with literally thousands of different developmental challenges. But if there is little enthusiasm in the workplace, lip service commitment, and/or low energy, the impact on a business's competitive advantage could be the company's demise.

The experts of our day insist that the only real competitive advantage is an organization's ability to learn and adapt faster than its competitors. Think of the edge a company would have if the employees learned with enthusiasm, if they brought real commitment and dedication to the learning journey, if they were genuinely excited and energized about learning and changing. The key is in leadership and in leaders who have the know-how to influence the perceptions of their team members. When people come to Parker to visit, they comment on the friendliness and enthusiasm of the workforce; they can see and feel a difference.

Several of our competitors' employees have quit their former jobs, leaving behind far more generous benefit packages, to join Parker. They share their perceptions of a workplace that is oppressive, of possibilities gone awry, of opportunity doors that are now closed. Their perceptions of Parker are of a company that is successful and will continue to be successful. They perceive that the company is performing well and is getting even better. They perceive that they can bring their knowledge and talents to the workplace and make a difference. By coming to Parker they have shown that they want something more than what their former workplaces could offer.

These perceptions do not just happen; they are influenced by leaders who understand that having a workforce of dynamic, vitalized people is a superior way to operate. They understand that helping organization members see that they are performing better, that they are moving ahead, that they are working free, and that they are getting more is a competitive advantage that increases employee retention, encourages employees to embrace learning, generates a willingness to change, and improves performance. The next frontier for organizations is the understanding and nurturing of human vitality. Once the systems for technological advancement are in place, once the learning and adaptation methods are embraced, leadership must become adept at being vitalized and influencing the vitality of every member of their organization because enthusiasm and commitment are every bit as important as learning and change. Keep your eye on Parker Aerospace's Control System Division Commercial. We are technologically advanced, we are learning new opportunities rapidly, we are continuously improving, and we are vitalized. The future is ours as we look upon the horizon of discovery and the possibilities for continuous breakthrough ingenuity!

Douglas R. McGregor
Parker Hannifin Corporation

Appendix: Notches on Your Stock: Nine Measures of Dynamism

WORK PERCEPTIONS PROFILE
(R. Wayne Pace and Gordon E. Mills)

The Work Perceptions Profile describes perceptions that employees have about aspects of their work. Four key variables have been distilled from theory and research on work motivation and represent the focal points of the Work Perceptions Profile: expectations met, opportunity, performance and fulfillment. The Work Perceptions Profile approaches these issues from a variety of perspectives and generates new and powerful information upon which work revitalization and organizational renewal plans may be based.

Directions:

1. Using a lead pencil, begin by filling in the circles that represent your social security number on the answer form. Do not put your name any place on the answer form.
2. Do not think too long about the questions.
3. Read the directions for each part carefully.
4. Read each question carefully and mark your answer on the answer sheet.
5. Work through each part until you have answered all the questions. Do not leave any blanks.

Part A

When employees are hired, they make assumptions about how they will be treated, advanced, challenged in work assignments, recognized, consulted, respected, and developed during their tenure as employees in an organization. Listed below are 12 areas where assumptions are typically made. Record your observations below on how well these assumptions have been met for you today in your organization.

Today in this organization I am ———:

1.	treated fairly	rarely	1	2	3	4	5	almost always
2.	given regular advancements	rarely	1	2	3	4	5	almost always
3.	given challenging work assignments	rarely	1	2	3	4	5	almost always
4.	influential in affecting decisions	rarely	1	2	3	4	5	almost always
5.	recognized for my contribution	rarely	1	2	3	4	5	almost always
6.	highly respected by my superiors	rarely	1	2	3	4	5	almost always
7.	improving my work skills	rarely	1	2	3	4	5	almost always
8.	optimistic about the future	rarely	1	2	3	4	5	almost always
9.	able to do some things in original, creative ways	rarely	1	2	3	4	5	almost always
10.	able to take some risks	rarely	1	2	3	4	5	almost always
11.	able to depend on the support of others	rarely	1	2	3	4	5	almost always
12.	able to do some good things and achieve much	rarely	1	2	3	4	5	almost always

Part B

13. The work which I do _____ be done in unique and clever ways.

cannot 1 2 3 4 5 can

14. I _____ have the ability to do my work in unique and clever ways.

do not 1 2 3 4 5 do

15. I _____ trying to do my job in unique, clever, different, and original ways.

dislike 1 2 3 4 5 like

16. I would _____ to do my work in unique, different, original, and clever ways.

not like 1 2 3 4 5 very much like

17. This organization _____ my work in unique and clever ways.

discourages me from doing 1 2 3 4 5 encourages me to do

18. This organization _____ reward employees for doing their work in unique and clever ways.

does not 1 2 3 4 5 does

19. I am _____ with the support I receive from other employees when I try to do my work in unique and clever ways.

                   very displeased   1   2   3   4   5   very pleased

20. I am _____ by the challenges provided by the work I do.

                   discouraged   1   2   3   4   5   encouraged

21. I am _____ with the originality and uniqueness with which I do my work.

               very discontented   1   2   3   4   5   contented

22. I am _____ by the work I do in this organization.

               very unfulfilled   1   2   3   4   5   very fulfilled

Part C

23. I believe that I am _____ than well enough known throughout the organization to be appointed to a special task force.

                   less   1   2   3   4   5   more

24. I believe that I have _____ than sufficient status in the organization to be consulted about important company problems.

                   less   1   2   3   4   5   more

25. I believe that my leader is a _____ advocate in helping me receive regular advancements in this organization.

                   very weak   1   2   3   4   5   very strong

26. I believe that _____ of my colleagues would support me for advancement within the next few years.

                   few   1   2   3   4   5   many

27. I believe that it is _____ that I shall be advanced in this organization.

                   unlikely   1   2   3   4   5   encourages me to do

28. My leader feels that I have _____ potential to be advanced or recognized in my functional area in this organization.

                   little   1   2   3   4   5   great

29. My leader feels that I _____ perform my assigned duties well enough to receive special recognition this year.

                   never   1   2   3   4   5   always

30. My leader feels that my personality or style of interacting with others may be _____ to me in getting regular advancements in this organization.

                   detrimental   1   2   3   4   5   beneficial

31. My leader feels that the quality of my relationshiops with others is _____ to receive special support this year.

                   inadequate   1   2   3   4   5   adequate

32. My leader feels that I initiate _____ than enough new ideas to receive special recognition from the organization this year.

                   less   1   2   3   4   5   more

Part D

33. My leader feels that I _____ motivate other employees to do their very best.

    rarely   1   2   3   4   5   almost always

34. My leader feels that I _____ suggest ways to improve our organizational efficiency.

    rarely   1   2   3   4   5   almost always

35. My leader feels that I _____ work very well on my own.

    rarely   1   2   3   4   5   almost always

36. My leader feels that I _____ do quality work on time.

    rarely   1   2   3   4   5   almost always

37. My leader feels that I _____ offer to help others complete work assignments.

    rarely   1   2   3   4   5   almost always

38. My leader feels that I _____ manage time effectively.

    rarely   1   2   3   4   5   almost always

39. My leader feels that I _____ make effective contributions when assigned to work in a group.

    rarely   1   2   3   4   5   almost always

40. My leader feels that I _____ resolve conflict I have with other employees on my own.

    rarely   1   2   3   4   5   almost always

41. My leader feels that I _____ use the resources given to me in a prudent manner.

    rarely   1   2   3   4   5   almost always

42. My leader feels that I _____ handle the work skills and technical aspects of my job very well.

    rarely   1   2   3   4   5   almost always

Scoring and Analysis

The Work Perceptions Profile describes perceptions that employees have about aspects of their work. Four key variables have been distilled from theory, research, and experience on what releases the energy of employees so that they feel drawn to contribute their very best to their work and the organization, which are referred to here as vitality. At least five scores provide indications of levels of employee vitality.

Composite Perceptions Scores

Individual Composite Perceptions Index (ICPI): To calculate the Individual Composite Perceptions Index, sum responses to all 42 items for each individual completing the Profile and divide by 42. This general average gives you a Composite Perceptions Index for each person who completes the Profile. This is the single best indicator of the level of vitality for each individual.

Organization Composite Perceptions Index (OCPI): To calculate the Organization Composite Perceptions Index, sum all of the ICPI's and divide by the number of individuals who completed the Profile. This is the single best indicator of the level of vitality of all employees in the organization.

Norms for Interpreting Composite Indexes: Across the several thousand employees who have completed the Work Perceptions Profile, the composite indexes reveal that employees with high vitality score between 4.31 and 5.00. Those with moderate vitality score between 3.31 and 4.30. Those with low vitality score between 1.00 and 3.30. The composite mean score is approximately 3.50. Individuals have composite scores ranging from 1.10 to 4.8.

High vitality	4.31–5.00
Moderate vitality	3.31–4.30
Low vitality	1.00–3.30
Composite Index or Mean Score	3.45
Composite Range	1.10–4.80

POFE Perceptions Scores

Individual Scores on Each Perception: To calculate the Individual Perceptions scores, sum responses to the A, B, C, and D parts of the Work Perceptions Profile.

Part A represents Expectations Perceptions and has 12 items. Sum the responses to the 12 items and divide by 12 to get the individual Expectations mean score.

Part B represents Fulfillment Perceptions and has 10 items. Sum the responses to the 10 items and divide by 10 to get the individual Fulfillment mean score.

Part C represents Opportunity Perceptions and has 10 items. Sum the responses to the 10 items and divide by 10 to get the individual Opportunity mean score.

Part D represents Performance Perceptions and has 10 items. Sum the responses to the 10 items and divide by 10 to get the Individual Performance mean score.

Organization POFE Perceptions Scores: To calculate the Organization's POFE Perceptions Scores, sum the scores for each Part of the Profile (A, B, C, and D) and divide by the number of individuals who completed the Profile. These are the organization's scores on each of the Perceptions.

Norms for interpreting POFE Perceptions Scores: Across the several thousand employees who have completed the Work Perceptions Profile, the mean scores indicate that employees have the following *mean scores* on each of the POFE Perceptions:

Performance (Part D): 3.89

Opportunity (Part C): 3.12

Fulfillment (Part B): 3.49

Expectations (Part A): 3.32

In rank order, performance scores are typically the highest, fulfillment scores are next, expectations scores are third, and opportunity scores are usually the lowest. Thus, only performance scores above 3.90 are considered above average. On the other hand, opportunity scores above 3.20 are considered above average. Expectations scores above 3.5 are considered above average. However, only scores that exceed 4.30 are considered high or exceptional, although opportunity scores of 3.8 are high in comparison.

WORK SYSTEMS PROFILE
(R. Wayne Pace and Eric G. Stephan)

The purpose of this Profile is to help people understand the systems in which they work and how the systems affect their work lives. The Profile does not make judgments about individual employees. Thus, your honest answers can help make this organization more effective and your work more valued.

The items included in the Profile are intended to allow organization members to describe how they feel about different aspects of their work life. The items have been distilled from theory, research, and practices that characterize how organizations and those who work in them function.

We ask that you provide the most accurate answer you can to each item, because each item contributes to the description of the total workplace and is important in understanding the organization and its members preferences.

Directions for completing the survey most accurately:

1. Do NOT put your name on the Profile or the answer form.

2. Fill in the circles on the answer form that represent your social security number so that we may get back in touch with you if necessary. This hardly ever happens and no one will see your specific responses.

3. Read the directions carefully and mark your answer on the answer sheet.

4. Do not think too long about what the questions mean. Just give what seems to you at the time to be the most accurate answer.

Please answer all of the questions. Do not leave any blanks.

For statistical purposes, a demographic section is often attached. After you have completed the survey itself, if a demographic section is attached, please complete it. Demographics simply allow statistics to group data according to categories of people. Individual responses are obscured.

Instructions: On the answer sheet, fill in the bubble or circle the number that corresponds with the way that you feel about the organization in which you work.

1. To what extent do the actions of your manager positively affect your productivity?

    Not at all 1 2 3 4 5 Very much

2. To what extent do the actions of your manager help you to find opportunities where you work?

    Not at all 1 2 3 4 5 Very much

3. To what extent do the actions of your manager help you to do your work in unique, personal, and fulfilling ways?

    Not at all 1 2 3 4 5 Very much

4. To what extent do the actions of your manager help you to achieve your highest aspirations in the company?

    Not at all 1 2 3 4 5 Very much

5. To what extent does the way in which you are required to do your work positively affect your productivity?

    Not at all   1   2   3   4   5   Very much

6. To what extent does the way in which you are required to do your work help you find opportunities where you are employed?

    Not at all   1   2   3   4   5   Very much

7. To what extent do the actions of your manager help you to do your work in unique, personal, and fulfilling ways?

    Not at all   1   2   3   4   5   Very much

8. To what extent does the way in which you are required to do your work help you achieve your highest aspirations in the company?

    Not at all   1   2   3   4   5   Very much

9. To what extent do the company's policies, rules, and regulations positively affect your productivity?

    Not at all   1   2   3   4   5   Very much

10. To what extent do the company's policies, rules, and regulations help you to find opportunities where you work?

    Not at all   1   2   3   4   5   Very much

11. To what extent do the company's policies, rules, and regulations help you to do your work in unique, personal, and fulfilling ways?

    Not at all   1   2   3   4   5   Very much

12. To what extent do the company's policies, rules, and regulations help you to achieve your highest aspirations in the company?

    Not at all   1   2   3   4   5   Very much

13. To what extent does your organizational structure (teams, lines of authority) positively affect your productivity?

    Not at all   1   2   3   4   5   Very much

14. To what extent does your organizational structure (teams, lines of authority) help you find opportunities where you work?

    Not at all   1   2   3   4   5   Very much

15. To what extent does your organizational structure (teams, lines of authority) help you to do your work in unique, personal, and fulfilling ways?

    Not at all   1   2   3   4   5   Very much

16. To what extent does your organizational structure (teams, lines of authority) help you to achieve your highest aspirations in the company?

    Not at all   1   2   3   4   5   Very much

17. To what extent do you feel that you are able to do your work better each year in this company?

    Not at all   1   2   3   4   5   Very much

18. To what extent do you feel that you are able to grow and develop, improve your status, and move ahead in this company?

    Not at all   1   2   3   4   5   Very much

19. To what extent do you feel that you are able to do your work in unique, personal, and fulfilling ways in this company?

   Not at all   1   2   3   4   5   Very much

20. To what extent do you feel that you are able to achieve your highest aspirations in this company?

   Not at all   1   2   3   4   5   Very much

21. To what extent do you feel energized and enthusiastic as you work each day in this company?

   Not at all   1   2   3   4   5   Very much

Scoring and Interpretation

The Work Systems Profile measures the perceptions of organization members about how well several elements of a work system contribute to the well-being of organization members and promote a vitalized and energized workforce.

The Work Systems Profile uses a seven-point scale for responses, which means that the average scores must be slightly higher than instruments that use a five-point scale. The scores may be interpreted in the following manner:

4.51–7.00   High
3.76–4.50   Moderate
1.00–3.75   Low

Four elements of the work system and individual worker perceptions of the workplace are the focus of the Work Systems Profile. These are referred to in an abbreviated fashion as

MP or management practices

WI or the work itself

OG or organization guidelines

OS or organizational structure

IW or individual worker

MP Index is calculated by summing scores on items **1, 2, 3,** and **4**
and dividing by four to arrive at a Management Practices Index (MPI)   MPI _____

WI Index is calculated by summing scores on items **5, 6, 7,** and **8**
and dividing by four to arrive at a Work Itself Index (WII)   WII _____

OG Index is calculated by summing scores on items **9, 10, 11,** and **12**
and dividing by four to arrive at an Organization Guidelines Index (OGI)   OGI _____

OS Index is calculated by summing scores on items **13, 14, 15,** and **16**
and dividing by four to arrive at an Organizational Structure Index (ODI)   OSI _____

IW Index is calculated by summing scores on items **17, 18, 19, 20,** and **21**
and dividing by five to arrive at an Individual Worker Index (IWI)   IWI _____

A Composite WSI or work system index is calculated by **summing all of the Indexes** and dividing by five to arrive at a Work System Index (WSI)   WSI _____

Work Systems indexes assist you in identifying the source of potential weaknesses and strengths in the organization. Since the focus of the WSP is on how well the system encourages and supports a vitalized workforce, look first at which of the indexes has the lowest scores or are below a score of 4.5. This allows you to pursue critical elements and probe further into why those particular elements are having a negative effect. The IW Index provides information about how vitalized individual workers are. By summing the IWI scores for all employees who complete the Profile, you should get a quick overview of the level of vitality of individual workers across the organization.

Vitality is the positive use of energy to achieve both organizational and personal goals. Employees are often more vitalized when they can pursue personal goals. However, most employees bring a positive mindset to their initial employment, but they have experiences in the work system that undermine the positive perceptions and trigger negative perceptions. For example, organizational guidelines (policies, rules, regulations) may be viewed as being highly restrictive and detrimental to working at an employee's highest potential. Each time employees attempt to do more and achieve higher goals, they may feel that the system comes down on them.

Because employees' actions are monitored by elements of the work system, their perceptions of what they are able to achieve, prefer to have, seek to acquire, and believe about themselves is substantially affected by the work system. The work system has a powerful impact on employees because, as human beings, they have a natural tendency to value the expenditure of energy to achieve human goals—to build, to advance, to grow, to contribute, to acquire. On the other hand, the achievement of natural, human goals energizes individuals. The more often people are able to achieve natural goals, the greater is the likelihood that they will feel energized, enthusiastic, and excited by what they are doing.

One key to understanding vitality is to get measures of the so-called "causes" of or factors that deter and cultivate sustained positive feelings in specific contexts. In the work environment, perceptions of elements of the work system provide the strongest indicators of what is encouraging or offending individual vitality.

NATURAL WORK GOALS PROFILE
(R. Wayne Pace and Eric G. Stephan)

The goals depicted below represent the intentions and desires that are associated with human beings in general. Your responses simply indicate the extent to which you feel the organization in which you work provides the circumstances that allow these goals to be achieved. Please respond as honestly and accurately as you possibly can. All responses will be summarized so that no one can be identified with any particular reaction.

Instructions: Circle the number on the scale at the end of each statement to show how much you agree or disagree with each of the statements. Use the following descriptions to decide which number to circle.

1 SD Strongly Disagree
2 D Disagree
3 SID Slightly Disagree
4 SIA Slightly Agree
5 A Agree
6 SA Strongly Agree

1.	This organization enables me to work to my highest potential in a specific area of expertise.	1 SD	2 D	3 SID	4 SIA	5 A	6 SA	
2.	This organization enables me to develop excellence in several areas of knowledge and skill.	1 SD	2 D	3 SID	4 SIA	5 A	6 SA	
3.	This organization enables me to discover new ways of doing things.	1 SD	2 D	3 SID	4 SIA	5 A	6 SA	
4.	This organization enables me to discover new opportunities in my work.	1 SD	2 D	3 SID	4 SIA	5 A	6 SA	
5.	This organization enables me to initiate new ideas to improve my work.	1 SD	2 D	3 SID	4 SIA	5 A	6 SA	
6.	This organization enables me to influence others in order to improve my work.	1 SD	2 D	3 SID	4 SIA	5 A	6 SA	
7.	This organization enables me to contribute to the well-being of others.	1 SD	2 D	3 SID	4 SIA	5 A	6 SA	
8.	This organization enables me to do work that is meaningful.	1 SD	2 D	3 SID	4 SIA	5 A	6 SA	
9.	This organization enables me to do work that is significant.	1 SD	2 D	3 SID	4 SIA	5 A	6 SA	
10.	This organization enables me to do things in my own unique way.	1 SD	2 D	3 SID	4 SIA	5 A	6 SA	
11.	This organization enables me to do things in my own personal way.	1 SD	2 D	3 SID	4 SIA	5 A	6 SA	
12.	This organization enables me to have high aspirations about today's work.	1 SD	2 D	3 SID	4 SIA	5 A	6 SA	
13.	This organization enables me to do more than what seems possible.	1 SD	2 D	3 SID	4 SIA	5 A	6 SA	
14.	This organization enables me to feel optimistic.	1 SD	2 D	3 SID	4 SIA	5 A	6 SA	
15.	This organization enables me to feel proud of what others accomplish.	1 SD	2 D	3 SID	4 SIA	5 A	6 SA	
16.	This organization enables me to anticipate greater accomplishments in the future.	1 SD	2 D	3 SID	4 SIA	5 A	6 SA	

Scoring and Interpretation

Scoring: The NWGP is scored by summing the total number of points. A perfect score would be 96 points. To get the Profile Composite Index, divide the score by 6.

1. ____ 2. ____ 3. ____ 4. ____ 5. ____ 6. ____ 7. ____ 8. ____

9. ____ 10. ____ 11. ____ 12. ____ 13. ____ 14. ____ 15. ____ 16. ____ Total ____

Composite Index ____

The NWGP is divided into three factors consisting of the following items.

Enable/Constrain   1, 2, 3, 4, 5, 6 for a total of 36 points.

Add points for items 1–6 and divide by 6:   E/C Score ____

Apathy/Enthusiasm   7, 8, 9, 10, 11, 12, 13, 16 for a total of 48 points.
    Add points for items 7–13 and 16 and divide by 6:   A/E Score _____
Individuality   14, 15 for a total of 12 points.
    Add points for items 14, 15 and divide by 6:   I Score _____

The Composite Index and Scores may be interpreted in the following manner:

1.00–1.99	Very Low	Weary, Torpid, Impassive
2.00–2.99	Low	Lethargic, Sluggish, Spiritless
3.00–3.79	Moderate	animated, Enlivened, Invigorated
3.80–4.89	High	Excited, Energetic, Vigorous
4.90–6.00	Very High	Enthusiastic, Passionate, Fervent

THINKING MODE PROFILE
(R. Wayne Pace, Gordon E. Mills, and Eric G. Stephan)

The thinking Mode Profile is a unique instrument constructed for purposes of discovering the extent to which an individual leans toward optimistic versus pessimistic thinking. To complete the Profile, you are asked to imagine that you have experienced an unhappy event in your life and to write out a brief reason why the unhappy event occurred. After stating the reason why the unhappy event occurred, you are asked to analyze the reason you gave by providing an account of what happened. Then, the account is analyzed by marking on a seven-point scale the extent to which the reason you gave had to do with you as a person, was something that would cause unhappy events to occur in the future, and would cause unhappy events in other aspects of your life.

Instructions:

On the following pages is a brief description of an unhappy event. Imagine that the event actually happened to you.

Below the unhappy event is a statement you must complete. Write the reason why the unhappy event occurred. Write your answer on the lines provided.

For Example: Unhappy Event——You are late to an important party. You are devastated. Reason——I was late for the party because I am always late; it runs in my family. I just can't help being late.

Note: The reason should be one that represents how yc   illy feel. Just explain what you feel is an accurate reason.

Then, respond to the three questions listed below the re   .. These questions are about the reason you wrote. Fill in the circle on the answer sheet or circle the number (from 1 to 7) that represents the most accurate analysis of the reason.

For example, the above reason "I am always late; it runs in my family" might be scored a 2 for the first question because it has to do with you as a person, and it might be a 2 or 3 for the second question because it may cause you to miss future parties, and it might also be a 2 or 3 for the third question because it may also cause you to be late at school, at work, and for family gatherings.

Think about the reason you give for each incident and answer the three questions for each of them using your best judgment about why you chose that reason.

STATEMENT I: You miss an important party/social gathering. You are devastated.

Reason: I missed the party/social gathering because . . .

1. To what extent did the reason for missing the party/social gathering have to do with you as a person, your usual way of doing things, versus something different than you as a person, such as other people, circumstances, or luck?

| The reason had to do entirely with *me* as a person. | 1 2 3 4 5 6 7 | The reason had to do with something *other than* me as a person. |

2. To what extent was the reason something that caused you to miss only this party/social gathering versus causing you to miss parties/socials in the future?

| The reason will cause me to miss future parties/socials. | 1 2 3 4 5 6 7 | The reason caused me to miss only this party/social. |

3. To what extent was the reason something that caused you to miss only this party/social gathering versus causing other unhappy events in your life?

| The reason causes other unhappy events in my life. | 1 2 3 4 5 6 7 | The reason caused only this unhappy event in my life. |

STATEMENT II: You are contradicted by a respected friend when you express an opinion. You are humiliated.

Reason: I was contradicted by my friend because . . .

4. To what extent did the reason for being contradicted have to do with you as a person, your usual way of doing things, versus something different than you as a person, such as other people, circumstances, or luck?

| The reason had to do entirely with *me* as a person. | 1 2 3 4 5 6 7 | The reason had to do with something *other than* me as a person. |

5. To what extent was the reason something that caused you to be contradicted at this particular time versus causing you to be contradicted in the future?

| The reason will cause me to be contradicted in the future. | 1 2 3 4 5 6 7 | The reason caused me to be contradicted only this time. |

6. To what extent was the reason something that caused you to be contradicted at this particular time versus causing other unhappy events in your life?

| The reason causes other unhappy events in my life. | 1 2 3 4 5 6 7 | The reason caused only this unhappy event in my life. |

STATEMENT III: You complete a project that contains errors. You are disappointed.

Reason: I completed the project with several errors because . . .

7. To what extent did the reason for completing the project with several errors have to do with you as person, your usual way of doing things, versus something different than you as a person such as other prople, circumstances, or luck?

The reason had to do entirely   1   2   3   4   5   6   7   The reason had to do with
with *me* as a person.   something *other than* me as a
                                               person.

8. To what extent was the reason something that caused you to complete the project with errors at this particular time versus causing you to complete projects with errors in the future?

The reason will cause me to   1   2   3   4   5   6   7   The reason caused me to com-
complete a project with errors   plete a project with errors
in the future.   only this time.

9. To what extent was the reason something that caused you to complete the project with errors at this particular time versus causing other unhappy events in your life?

The reason causes other   1   2   3   4   5   6   7   The reason caused only this
unhappy events in my life.   unhappy event in my life.

STATEMENT IV: You make a ridiculous suggestion to an important person in your life. You are upset.

Reason: I made the ridiculous suggestion to the important person because . . .

10. To what extent did the reason for making the ridiculous suggestion have to do with you as a person, your usual way of doing things, versus something different than you as a person, such as other people, circumstances, or luck?

The reason had to do entirely   1   2   3   4   5   6   7   The reason had to do with
with *me* as a person.   something *other than* me as a
                                               person.

11. To what extent was the reason something that caused you to make the ridiculous suggestion at this particular time versus causing you to make other ridiculous suggestion at this particular time versus causing you to make other ridiculous suggestions in the future?

The reason will cause me   1   2   3   4   5   6   7   The reason caused me to
to make a ridiculous   make the ridiculous sugges-
suggestion in the future.   tion only this time.

12. To what extent was the reason something that caused you to make the ridiculous suggestion at this particular time versus causing other unhappy events in your life?

The reason causes other   1   2   3   4   5   6   7   The reason caused this un-
unhappy events in my life.   happy event in my life.

STATEMENT V: You knock over a glass full of grape juice during dinner. You are mortified.

Reason: I knocked over the glass of juice because . . .

13. To what extent did the reason for knocking over the glass of juice have to do with you as a person, your usual way of doing things, versus something different than you as a person, such as other people, circumstances, or luck?

The reason had to do entirely   1   2   3   4   5   6   7   The reason had to do with
with *me* as a person.   something *other than* me as a
                                               person.

14. To what extent was the reason something that caused you to knock over the glass of juice at this particular time versus causing you to knock over other glasses of juice in the future?

| The reason will cause me to knock over other glasses of juice in the future. | 1 2 3 4 5 6 7 | The reason caused me to knock over the glass of juice only this time. |

15. To what extent was the reason something that caused you to knock over the glass of juice at this particular time versus causing other unhappy events in your life?

| The reason causes other unhappy events in my life. | 1 2 3 4 5 6 7 | The reason caused only this unhappy event in my life. |

STATEMENT VI: You are unprepared to make an important presentation to a group of which you are a member. You are embarrassed.

Reason: I was unprepared to make the presentation because . . .

16. To what extent did the reason for being unprepared to make the presentation have to do with you as a person, your usual way of doing things, versus something different than you as a person such as other people, circumstances, or luck?

| The reason had to do entirely with *me* as a person. | 1 2 3 4 6 7 | The reason had to do with something *other than* me as a person. |

17. To what extent was the reason something that caused you to be unprepared to make the presentation at this particular time versus causing you to be unprepared to make presentations in the future?

| The reason will cause me to be unprepared in the future. | 1 2 3 4 5 6 7 | The reason caused me to be unprepared only this time. |

18. To what extent was the reason something that caused you to be unprepared to make the presentaiton at this particular time versus causing other unhappy events in your life?

| The reason causes other unhappy events in my life. | 1 2 3 4 5 6 7 | The reason caused only this unhappy event in my life. |

Scoring and Interpreting

Scoring: Scores on the Thinking Mode Profile are derived by summing the items reflecting each of the primary variables of Source, Time, and Space as indicated in the Scoring Key. Derive the average score for each variable across all six incidents by summing the scores and dividing by six. Sum the averages for each of the three primary variables and divide by three to determine the TM Index Score. The Index Score should be expressed as a figure ranging from 1.0 to 7.0.

	Source	Time	Space
Incident I. Missed Social Gathering			
	1.__ 2.__	3.__	I Total ____
Incident II. Contradicted by Friend			
	4.__ 5.__	6.__	II Total ____
Incident III. Project with Errors			
	7.__ 8.__	9.__	III Total ____
Incident IV. Ridiculous Suggestion			
	10.__ 11.__	12.__	IV Total ____
Incident V. Knocked over Glass of Grape Juice			
	13.__ 14.__	15.__	V Total ____

	Source	Time	Space
Incident VI. Unprepared to Make Presentation			
	16.__ 17.__	18.__	VI Total ____

I'm the cause of unhappy things	I'm the cause of all future unhappy events	I'm the cause of unhappy events in my entire life	I'm a pessimistic person

Source	Time	Space	Index
Total ____	+ Total ____	+ Total ____ ÷ 3 =	Score ____

Interpretation of Scores: Your TM Index score may be interpreted in the following way:

If your index score is 5.51 or higher, you have a very positive way of reacting to unhappy events in your life.

If your index score is between 4.01 and 5.50, you tend to react to unhappy events in your life slightly positively or slightly negatively, depending on your mood for the day.

If your index score is 4.0 or lower, you have a somewhat negative way of reacting to unhappy events in your life.

Those who react negatively to unhappy events feel that they are the cause of unhappiness in their lives, and that unhappiness is with them all the time and everywhere. Persistent negative reactions or pessimism leads to feelings of hopelessness and helplessness in coping with life.

Those who react positively to unhappy events feel that the cause of unhappiness in their lives is something other than them personally, and that unhappiness occurs only occasionally and in limited situations. An optimistic view of life comes from reacting to negative events in a positive way.

OPERATING STYLES PROFILE
(R. Wayne Pace, Gordon E. Mills, and Eric G. Stephan)

Instructions: Choose one term from each set of four that most clearly represents an accurate analogy or comparison of the way in which you interact or work with other people.

For example, Mohammed Ali described his boxing style with the phrase "I float like a butterfly and sting like a bee." Do you, for example, interact like a trumpet or a violin?

Select the one term in each group that characterizes in metaphorical form the way in which you interact or work with others.

1. a. Tiger
   b. Fox
   c. Tortoise
   d. Bluebird

2. a. Fighter Jet
   b. Corporate Plane
   c. Cargo Plane
   d. Frisbee

3. a. Parade
   b. Vocal Quartet
   c. Instrument Case
   d. Harp

4. a. Sand Blaster
   b. Brillo Pad
   c. Bucket
   d. Facial Tissue

5. a. Tornado
   b. Whirlwind
   c. Cold Front
   d. Breeze

6. a. Freeway
   b. Interchange
   c. Storage Unit
   d. Rest Area

7. a. Football Player
   b. Card Player
   c. Chess Player
   d. Croquet Player

8. a. Steel Cable
   b. Rope
   c. Scaffold
   d. Slipper

9. a. Office
   b. Den
   c. Shed
   d. Bedroom

10. a. Chainsaw
    b. Shears
    c. Box
    d. Carpet

11. a. Stomp
    b. Dance
    c. Stroll
    d. Tiptoe

12. a. Mack Truck
    b. Mercedes
    c. Boxcar
    d. Volkswagen Bug

13. a. Printing Press
    b. Computer Mouse
    c. Filing Cabinet
    d. Letter

14. a. Boxing Glove
    b. Polo Pony
    c. Dugout
    d. Badminton Birdie

15. a. Bat
    b. Pitcher
    c. Mitt
    d. Base

Scoring and Interpretation

Scores on the Operating Style Profile are derived by summing the number of times each of the "a," "b," "c," and "d" items is selected. A indicates Mover, B indicates Dealer, C indicates Holder, and D indicates Giver. The highest number of a, b, c, or d items selected indicates the primary operating style.

Because these results constitute a continuum, it is possible for a subject to fall near the center or at the extreme ends of a particular style and still be classified as having that style. An eleven Dealer may in fact be quite different from a one Dealer. To account for this peculiarity in the data, in cooperation with a mathematics faculty member, a formula for calculating a Styles Intensity Index was created.

Once the type of operating style is identified, the next step is to calculate the relative intensity of the style. This is achieved by taking into account the number of items selected in each of the style areas. The intensity index indicates the extent to which a person's primary style is ameliorated or diminished by the tendencies represented by the other styles, some of which are complementary and some of which are contradictory. Thus, a person may have a Dealer style, but diminished by other factors so that it is low in intensity.

The formula for calculating intensity scores is:

$$D - H = + \text{ if Dealer, } - \text{ if Holder}$$
$$M - G = + \text{ if Mover, } - \text{ if Giver} \quad < \text{ Higher of these two numbers is the style.}$$

The square root of the sum of both numbers squared equals the intensity index score:

$$\sqrt{a^2 + b^2} = \text{Intensity score}$$

An intensity score for a distribution of selected metaphors might be:

$$D = 3 \quad M = 2 \quad G = 3 \quad H = 7 \quad 3D - 7H = -4H \quad 2M - 3G = -1\,G$$
$$4H = \text{Holder Style}$$
$$\sqrt{4^2 + 1^2} = \sqrt{17} = 4.12 \ (\text{intensity score})$$

The primary style of this subject is Holder. The intensity score is 4.12. The closer to zero, the lower the intensity of the particular style.

INDIVIDUAL VITALITY INVENTORY
(R. Wayne Pace and Douglas R. McGregor)

The Individual Vitality Inventory (IVI) is an instrument that gives a measure of your spirit, vigor, and dynamism in the organization of which you are a member. The focus of this inventory is on you as a member of this organization. As you respond to each item in the inventory, think of yourself in the organization as defined for purposes of this survey.

Instructions: Please respond to all questions as honestly and frankly as you possibly can. In no way will your identity be associated with your responses nor will your responses be used in a manner that jeopardizes you or your job.

Unless the wording of a particular item specifically indicates otherwise, describe yourself in terms of the entire organization in which you work as defined for purposes of this survey.

Indicate your response to each item by selecting just one of the five numbers in the right-hand column. Please do not omit any item! Use the following code to interpret the meaning of the numbers:

5 Select this number if, in your honest judgment, the item is an accurate description of how you feel.

4 Select this number if the item is more accurate than inaccurate as a description of how you feel.

3 Select this number if the item is about half accurate and half inaccurate as a description of how you feel.

2 Select this number if the item is more inaccurate than accurate as a description of how you feel.

1 Select this number if the item is an inaccurate description of how you feel.

Please do not attempt an intensive "word analysis" of the items. And, of course, your responses should reflect your own judgments, not those of other organization members. There are not right or wrong answers.

Answer all questions in terms of your impressions of how you feel as a member of the organization as defined for purposes of this survey.

Instructions: On the answer sheet, fill in the bubble (circle) that corresponds with the way that you feel about yourself and the organization in which you are currently working. Do not try to analyze the questions, but think about how you feel at this time. Many of these statements refer to a general feeling of well-being, but we would like to focus your response on the specific feeling mentioned.

Read each question, but answer as quickly as you can.

1. How *happy* are you in this organization? — Very unhappy 1 2 3 4 5 Very happy

2. How *excited* do you feel about working in this organization? — Very unexcited 1 2 3 4 5 Very excited

3. How *successful* are you in this organization? — Very unsuccessful 1 2 3 4 5 Very successful

4. How *energetic* are you in your work over the course of a day in this organization? — Very unenergetic 1 2 3 4 5 Very energetic

5. How *innovative* are you in your work in this organization? — Very uninnovative 1 2 3 4 5 Very innovative

6. How *enjoyable*, overall, is your work in this organization? — Very unenjoyable 1 2 3 4 5 Very enjoyable

7. How *significant* do you feel your work is in this organization? — Very insignificant 1 2 3 4 5 Very significant

8. How *vigorously* do you approach your work in this organization? — Very unvigorously 1 2 3 4 5 Very vigorously

9. How *exuberant* are you in your work in this organization? — Very unexuberant 1 2 3 4 5 Very exuberant

10. How *dynamic* are you in your work in this organization? — Very undynamic 1 2 3 4 5 Very dynamic

11. How much *joy* do you get from your work in this organization? — Very little joy 1 2 3 4 5 Great deal of joy

12. How *alive* do you feel as you work each day in this organization? — Very unalive 1 2 3 4 5 Very alive

Scoring and Interpretation

The Individual Vitality Inventory (IVI) is an instrument that gives a measure of your spirit, vigor, and dynamism in the organization of which you are a member.

Scoring. The Individual Vitality Inventory is a single-factor instrument in which the overall score is the best measure of feelings of vitality. Simply sum the scores on each item and divide the total by 12. The result is a score between 1.0 and 5.0. Interpret the index in terms of the categories listed below.

Nevertheless, the Individual Vitality Inventory has two dimensions that can be scored. The first represents positive and pleasant feelings—a pleasantness scale; the second represents feelings of greater intensity—an animated scale.

The Pleasantness Scale consists of items, 1, 3, 5, 6, 7 and 11.   Sum these scores and divide by six; interpret the index in terms of the categories listed below.

The Animated Scale consists of items 2, 4, 8, 9, 10, and 12.   Sum these scores and divide by six; interpret the index in terms of the categories listed below.

Interpretation. Vitality is revealed more clearly when the Animated Scale (excited, energetic, vigorously, exuberant, dynamic, alive) is higher than the Pleasantness Scale (happy, successful, innovative, enjoyable, significant, joy).

Scores may be interpreted as follows: 4.21–5.00 High Vitality

                                         3.21–4.20 Moderate Vitality

                                       1.00–3.20 Low Vitality

TEAM VITALITY INVENTORY
(R. Wayne Pace and Douglas R. McGregor)

The Team Vitality Inventory (TVI) provides a measure of the strength of the four critical perceptions as well as the overall feeling of vitality of team members. The TVI indicates how team members perceive the team in terms of its effect on P, O, F, E, and V. Thus, think of your team as a whole as you complete the TVI.

Instructions:

1. Please respond to all questions as honestly and frankly as you possibly can. In no way will your identity be associated with your responses nor will your responses be used to jeopardize or compromise your position on the team.

2. Unless the wording of a particular item specifically indicates otherwise, mark your answers in terms of the team in which you work.

3. Indicate your response to each item by filling in the appropriate space on the answer sheet. Please do not omit any items.

4. Please do not attempt an intensive word analysis of the statements. Your responses should reflect your own judgments, not those of anyone else. There are no right or wrong answers.

1. This team is recognized by all team members as being vital.

    Disagree   1 2 3 4 5   Agree

2. This team creates products and/or services that are of great value.

    Disagree   1 2 3 4 5   Agree

3. This team provides all members with opportunities to excel.

    Disagree   1 2 3 4 5   Agree

4. This team anticipates that its members will achieve their goals and aspirations.

    Disagree   1 2 3 4 5   Agree

5. This team encourages its members to do their work in unique and clever ways.

    Disagree   1 2 3 4 5   Agree

6. This team expects to surpass its former goals and accomplishments.

    Disagree   1 2 3 4 5   Agree

7. This team encourages all members to do their work at the highest levels of technical skill they are capable of.

    Disagree   1 2 3 4 5   Agree

8. This team anticipates meeting the individual needs of its members

    Disagree   1 2 3 4 5   Agree

9. Members of this team have committed themselves to pursuing its goals with vigor.

    Disagree   1 2 3 4 5   Agree

10. This team expects to find answers and challenge the status quo.

    Disagree   1 2 3 4 5   Agree

11. This team learns, grow, and develops from the work it does.

    Disagree   1 2 3 4 5   Agree

12. This team encourages its members to engage in various functional activities to achieve its goals.

    Disagree   1 2 3 4 5   Agree

13. This team supports important values, has a great future vision, and mobilizes energy to solve problems.

    Disagree   1 2 3 4 5   Agree

14. This team encourages individual team members to improve their skills.

    Disagree   1 2 3 4 5   Agree

15. This team values individual and unique contributions from each member.

    Disagree   1 2 3 4 5   Agree

16. This team enjoys working together.

Disagree   1 2 3 4 5   Agree

17. This team works so that its members will be successful and rewarded for what they do.

Disagree   1 2 3 4 5   Agree

18. This team gives responsibility to all members and allows them to share in supervising themselves.

Disagree   1 2 3 4 5   Agree

19. This team believes in constantly fighting team decay and lost vitality.

Disagree   1 2 3 4 5   Agree

20. This team prizes highly skilled team members.

Disagree   1 2 3 4 5   Agree

Scoring Procedures

The Team Vitality Inventory may be scored in two ways:
Calculate the mean score by summing the values across all scales and dividing by 20. The mean score will be a value between 1.00 and 5.00.
Values or mean scores may be interpreted in the following manner:

Mean scores between 4.21 and 5.00 are considered high.

Means scores between 3.21 and 4.20 are considered average.

Mean scores between 1.00 and 3.20 are considered low.

Calculate the means scores for each of the subfactors (POFE and V) measured by the TVI. Again, the mean scores will be values between 1.00 and 5.00, with scores between

4.21 and 5.00 considered high,

3.21 and 4.20 considered average, and

1.00 and 3.20 considered low.

P or performance perceptions are revealed by calculating the sum of the values for items 2, 7, 12, and 20 and dividing by four.

O or opportunity perceptions are revealed by calculating the sum of the values for items 3, 11, 14, and 17 and dividing by four.

F or fulfillment perceptions are revealed by calculating the sum of the values for items 5, 15, 16, and 18 and dividing by four.

E or expectations perceptions are revealed by calculating the sum of the values for items 4, 6, 8, and 10 and dividing by four.

V or overall vitality perceptions are revealed by calculating the sum of the values for items 1, 9, 13, and 19 and dividing by four.

Scoring Form

Vitality		Performance	
1		2	
9		7	
13		12	
19		20	
Total		Total	
Divide by Four		Divide by Four	
Mean		Mean	
Opportunity		Fulfillment	
3		5	
11		15	
14		16	
17		18	
Total		Total	
Divide by Four		Divide by Four	
Mean		Mean	
Expectation		Composite of V, P, O, F, E	
4		V	
6		P	
8		O	
10		F	
		E	
Total		Total	
Divide by Four		Divide by Five	
Mean		Mean	

ORGANIZATIONAL VITALITY INVENTORY
(R. Wayne Pace and Douglas R. McGregor)

The Organizational Vitality Inventory (OVI) is an instrument that gives a measure of the spirit, vigor, and dynamism of the overall organization. The focus of this inventory is on the organization as a whole and reflects the views of organization members regarding how vital it is. As you respond to each item in the inventory, think of the organization as a whole as defined for purposes of this survey.

Instructions: On the answer sheet, fill in the bubble (circle) that corresponds with the way you feel about the organization in which you are currently working. Do not try to analyze the statements, but think about how you feel at this time. Read each statement, but answer as quickly as you can.

1. This organization is recognized by all employees as being vital.   1 2 3 4 5

2. This organization creates products and/or services that are of great value.   1 2 3 4 5

3. This organization provides all employees with opportunities to excel.   1 2 3 4 5

4. This organization anticipates its members will achieve their goals and aspirations.   1 2 3 4 5

5. This organization encourages its members to do their work in unique and clever ways.   1 2 3 4 5

6. This organization expects to surpass its former goals and accomplishments.   1 2 3 4 5

7. This organization cncourages all members to do their work at the highest levels of technical skill they are capable.   1 2 3 4 5

8. This organization anticipates meeting the individual needs of its members.   1 2 3 4 5

9. Members of this organization have committed themselves to pursuing its goals with vigor.   1 2 3 4 5

10. This organization expects to find new answers and challenge the status quo.   1 2 3 4 5

11. This organization places a high priority on learning from its work.   1 2 3 4 5

12. This organization encourages its members to cross organizational lines, functions, and positions.   1 2 3 4 5

13. This organization supports important values, has a great future vision, and mobilizes enrgy to solve problems.   1 2 3 4 5

14. This organization encourges individual team members to improve their skills.   1 2 3 4 5

15. This organization values individual and unique contributions from each member.   1 2 3 4 5

16. This organization's employees enjoy working together.   1 2 3 4 5

17. This organization's employees work so that they will be successful and rewarded for what they do.   1 2 3 4 5

18. This organization gives responsibility to all memers and allows them to share in supervising themselves.   1 2 3 4 5

19. This organization believes in constantly fighting negative perceptions and lost vitality.   1 2 3 4 5

20. This organization prizes a highly skilled workforce.   1 2 3 4 5

Scoring and Interpretation

Scoring. The Organizational Vitality Inventory is an instrument that provides a quick measure of overall perceived vitality of members of an organization. Five variables or themes emerge from the results: (1) direct perceptions of the vitality of the organization and its members, (2) employee perceptions of their performance, (3) employee perceptions of their opportunities, (4) employee perceptions of their fulfillment, and (5) employee perceptions of their aspirations and expectations.

The OVI is scored by summing the items for each theme and deriving an average or mean score by dividing the score for each theme by four. This yields an index for each of the themes.

A vitality composite score is calculated by summing the index or mean scores for each of the themes by dividing by five. The overall composite score is an indication of the level of vitality in the organization.

Vitality Score	Performance Score	Opportunity Score
13____	2 ____	3 ____
16____	7 ____	12____
19____	10____	14____
20____	11____	18____
_____	_____	_____
Total	Total	Total
[Divide total by 4]	[Divide total by 4]	[Divide by 4]
Mean_____	Mean_____	Mean_____
Fulfillment Score	Expectations Score	Composite Score
5 ____	1 ____	V score: ____
6 ____	4 ____	P score: ____
15____	8 ____	O score: ____
17____	9 ____	F score: ____
		E score: ____
_____	_____	_____
Total ____	Total ____	Total ____
[Divide total by 4]	[Divide total by 4]	[Divide by 5]
Mean ____	Mean ____	Mean ____

Interpretation. The OVI index or mean scores may be interpreted according to the following categories:

High Vitality	4.21–5.00
Moderate Vitality	3.21–4.20
Low Vitality	1.00–3.20

Low overall vitality scores mean that employees feel that they are unable to cope, are frustrated, feel overworked, disappointed, and confused. They feel unable to maintain their energy, enthusiasm, creativity, and innovativeness. When others notice a decline in a person's vitality, they sense that the other person lacks personal commitment, confidence, and dedication to work. They also lose a sense of vision for the future. They begin to talk about themselves as peaked, burned-out, stomped on and passed over, and plateaued.

Low or average scores on performance perceptions indicate that organization members lack self-confidence in their ability to achieve their goals. They have doubts about their abilities to accomplish their goals. When these perceptions develop, employees are likely to avoid doing what is necessary to be successful.

Low or average scores on opportunity perceptions indicate that organization members feel that they are unable to move ahead in the organization. Lack of opportunity is central to losses of self-esteem, lowered aspirations, reductions in levels of commitment, an increase in negative comments about the organization, and increases in grumbling, and some indications arise that organization members delight in seeing the organization in trouble.

Low or average scores on fulfillment perceptions indicate that organization members feel that they are unable to move ahead in the organization. Lack of opportunity is central to losses of self-esteem, lowered aspirations, reductions in levels of commitment, an increase in negative comments about the organization, and increases in grumbling, and some indications arise that organization members delight in seeing the organization in trouble.

Low or average scores on fulfillment perceptions indicate that organization members feel that the organization is restricting the amount of freedom and autonomy they have in the organization. They also feel that their efforts have not added up to something meaningful. They feel that work is without dignity and that they are working in a prison.

Low or average scores on expectations perceptions indicate the organization members feel that real or imagined promises on which they were counting have not been met as they would like. Low scores are an indication of bitterness and anger.

COMMUNICATION CLIMATE INVENTORY
(R. Wayne Pace and Brent D. Peterson)

Please respond to *all questions* as honestly and frankly as you possible can.

In *no way* will your identity be associated with your responses nor will your responses be used in such a manner as to jeopardize you or your job.

Unless the wording of a particular item specifically indicates otherwise, respond in terms of your own impressions of the entire organization in which you work.

Indicate your response to each item by circling just one of the five numbers in the right-hand column. Please do not omit any item! Use the following code to interpret the meaning of the numerical symbols:

5 Circle this number if, in your honest judgment, the item is a true description of conditions in the organization.

4 Circle if the item is more true than false as a description of conditions in the organization.

3 Circle if the item is about half true and half false as a description of conditions in the organization.

2 Circle if the item is more false than true as a description of conditions in the organization.

1 Circle if the item is a false description of conditions in the organization.

Please, do not attempt an intensive "word analysis" of the questions. And, of course, your responses should reflect your own judgments, not those of other people. There are no right or wrong answers.

Answer all questions in terms of your impressions concerning your own organization!

1. Personnel at all levels in the organization demonstrate a commitment to high-performance goals (high productivity, high quality, low cost).   5 4 3 2 1   (1)

2. Superiors seem to have a great deal of confidence and trust in their subordinates.   5 4 3 2 1   (2)

3. Personnel at all levels in the organization are communicated to and consulted with concerning organizational policy relevant to their positions.   5 4 3 2 1   (3)

4. Subordinates seem to have a great deal of confidence and trust in their superiors.   5 4 3 2 1   (4)

5. Information received from subordinates is perceived by superiors as important enough to be acted upon until demonstrated otherwise.   5 4 3 2 1   (5)

6. All personnel receive information that enhances their abilities to coordinate their work with that of other personnel or departments, and that deals broadly with the company, its organization, leaders, and plans.   5 4 3 2 1   (6)

7. A general atmosphere of candor and frankness seems to pervade relationships between personnel through all levels of the organization.   5 4 3 2 1   (7)

8. There are avenues of communication available for all personnel to consult with management levels above their own in decision-making and goal-setting processes.   5 4 3 2 1   (8)

9. All personnel are able to say "what's on their minds" regardless of whether they are talking to subordinates or superiors.   5 4 3 2 1   (9)

10. Except for necessary security information, all personnel have relatively easy access to information that relates directly to their immediate jobs.   5 4 3 2 1   (10)

11. A high concern for the well-being of all personnel is as important to management as high performance goals.   5 4 3 2 1   (11)

12. Superiors at all levels in the organization listen continuously and with open minds to suggestions or reports of problems made by personnel at all subordinate levels in the organization.   5 4 3 2 1   (12)

Definition of Variables

Our research indicates that there are at least six major factors that affect an organization's communication climate. A short discussion of each of the six follows:

1. Trust—Personnel at all levels should make every effort to develop and maintain relationships where trust, confidence, and credibility are sustained by statement and act.

2. Participative Decision Making—Employees at all levels in the organization should be communicated to and consulted with on all issues in all areas of organization policy relevant to their positions. Employees at all levels should be provided with avenues of communication and consultation with management levels above theirs for the purpose of participating in decision-making and goal-setting processes.

3. Supportiveness—A general atmosphere of candor and frankness should pervade relationships in the organization, with employees being able to say "what's on their minds" regardless of whether they are talking to peers, subordinates, or superiors.

4. Openness in Downward Communication—Except for necessary security information, members of the organization should have relatively easy access to information that relates directly to their immediate jobs, that affects their abilities to coordinate their work with that of other people or departments, and that deals broadly with the company, its organization, leaders, and plans.

5. Listening in Upward Communication—Personnel at each level in the organization should listen continuously and with open minds to suggestions or reports of problems made by personnel at each subordinate level in the organization. Information from subordinates should be viewed as important enough to be acted upon until demonstrated otherwise.

6. Concern for High Performance Goals—Personnel at all levels in the organization should demonstrate a commitment to high performance goals—high productivity, high quality low cost—as well as a high concern for other members of the organization.

The Communication Climate Inventory attempts to measure attitudes toward each of these factors of climate. The Inventory can also be used to obtain a composite climate score. This is the average of all six factors.

Procedures for Using the Inventory

1. Distribute copies to all personnel in the organization. It is best to distribute copies as close to the same time as possible.

2. Read through the instructions on the cover page as the respondents read silently with you. Ask if there are any questions. Instruct the respondents to turn the page and complete the Inventory.

3. Collect and score all copies in the Inventory.

Scoring and Analysis

1. Composite Climate Score—To get the Individual Composite Climate Score (ICCS) sum the individual's responses to all twelve items and divide by twelve. This general average gives you a Composite Climate Score (CCS) for each respondent. For the Organization Composite Climate Score (OCCS) sum all the ICC's and divide by the number of total respondents.

2. Trust Climate Score—To get the Trust Climate Score sum number two and number four on each inventory and divide by two. This is an individual score. To get a composite trust score sum all the inventories and divide b the total number of respondents.

3. Participative Decision Making Score—To get the Participative Decision Making Score sum number three and number eight on each Inventory and divide by two. This is an individual score. To get a composite participative decision making score sum all the inventories and divide by the total number of respondents.

4. Supportiveness Climate Score—To get the Supportiveness Climate Score sum number seven and number nine on each Inventory and divide by two. This is an individual score. To get a composite supportiveness score sum all the Inventories and divide by the total number of respondents.

5. Openness in Downward Communication Score—To get the Openness in Downward Communication Score sum number six and number ten on each Inventory and divide by two. This is an individual score. To get a composite openness in downward communication score sum all the Inventories and divide by the total number of respondents.

6. Listening in Upward Communication Score—To get the Listening in Upward Communication score sum number five and number twelve on each Inventory and divide by two. This is an individual score. To get a composite listening in upward communication score sum all the Inventories and divide by the total number of respondents.

7. Concern for High Performance Goals Score—To get the Concern for High Performance Goals Score sum number one and number eleven on each Inventory and divide by two. This is an individual score. To get a composite concern for high performance goals score sum all the Inventories and divide by the total number of respondents.

Selected Bibliography

Bandura, A. 1977. Self-Efficacy: Toward a Unifying Theory of Behavioral Change. *Psychological Review*, 84, pp. 191–215

Bennis, Warren. 1966. Organizational Revitalization. *California Management Review*, Fall, pp. 51–60.

Burns, David D. 1980. *Feeling Good: The New Mood Therapy*. New York: Signet Books.

Dixon, Nancy. 1994. *The Organizational Learning Cycle*. London: McGraw-Hill Book Company.

Druckman, D. and Bjork, R.A. (Eds.). 1994. *Learning, Remembering, Believing: Enhancing Human Performance*. Washington, DC: National Academy of Sciences.

Hackman, J. Richard and Oldham, Greg H. 1980. *Work Redesign*. Reading, MA: Addison-Wesley Publishing Company.

Harmon, Frederick G. and Jacobs, Garry. 1985. *The Vital Difference*. New York: AMACOM.

Harrison R. 1987. Harnessing Personal Energy: How Companies Can Inspire Employees. *Organizational Dynamics*, Fall, pp. 5–20.

Hellriegel, Don, Slocum, John W., and Woodman, Richard W. 1986. *Organizational Behavior*, Fourth Edition. St. Paul, MN: West Publishing Company.

Herzberg, F., Mausner, B., and Snyderman, B. 1959. *The Motivation to Work*. New York: John Wiley & Sons.

Hornstein, Harvey A. 1986. *Managerial Courage: Revitalizing Your Company without Sacrificing Your Job*. New York: John Wiley & Sons.

Huber, George P. 1991. Organizational Learning: The Contributing Processes and the Literature. *Organizational Science*, 2 (1), pp. 88–115.

Limerick, David and Cunnington, Bert. 1993. *Managing the New Organization: A Blueprint for Networks and Strategic Alliances.* Chatswood, NSW: Business & Professional Publishing.

Locke, Edwin A. and Latham, Gary P. 1990. *A Theory of Goal Setting and Task Performance.* Englewood Cliffs, NJ: Prentice-Hall.

Marquardt, Michael J. 1999. *Action Learning: Transforming Problems and People for World-Class Organizational Learning.* Palo Alto, CA: Davies-Black Publishing.

Miller, Donald B. 1977. *Personal Vitality.* Reading, MA: Addison-Wesley Publishing Company.

Naisbitt, John and Aburdene, Patricia. 1985. *Re-inventing the Corporation.* New York: Warner Books.

Peterson, C., Semmel, A., Von Baeyer, C., Abramson, L.Y., Metalsky, G.I., and Seligman, M.E.P. 1982. The Attributional Style Questionnaire. *Cognitive Therapy and Research*, 6, pp. 287–299.

Pfeffer, Jeffrey. 1994. *Competitive Advantage through People.* Boston: Harvard Business School Press.

Pollard, C. William. 1996. *The Soul of the Firm.* New York: HarperBusiness.

Scott, William G. and Hart, David K. 1989. *Organizational Values in America.* New Brunswick, NJ: Transaction Publishers.

Seligman, Martin E.P. and Schulman, Peter. 1986. Explanatory Style as a Predictor of Productivity and Quitting among Life Insurance Sales Agents. *Journal of Personality and Social Psychology*, 50, pp. 832–838.

Snider, J.G. 1968. Studies of All-Inclusive Conceptualization. *General Semantics Bulletin*, pp. 51–54.

Spreitzer, Gretchen. 1995. Psychological Empowerment in the Workplace: Dimensions, Measurement, and Validation. *Academy of Management Journal* 38 (5), pp. 1442–1465.

Townley, Barbara. 1994. *Reframing Human Resource Management: Power, Ethics and the Subject at Work.* London: Sage Publications.

Watkins, Karen E. and Marsick, Victoria. 1993. *Sculpting the Learning Organization.* San Francisco: Jossey-Bass Publishers.

Index

About the Author

R. WAYNE PACE is Professor Emeritus of Organizational Leadership, Marriott School of Management, Brigham Young University, and an independent consultant and management development specialist. Among his research and teaching specialties are organizational communication, behavior, and change, socio-technical systems design, and human resource development. He is author of numerous books and articles and is a past president of the International Communication Association, the Western States Communication Association, and the Academy of Human Resource Development.